‖‖‖‖‖‖‖‖‖‖‖‖‖‖‖‖‖‖ KT-521-691

Please return/renew this item by the last date shown. Books may also be renewed by phone or internet.

🖥 www.rbwm.gov.uk/home/leisure-and-culture/libraries

☎ 01628 796969 (library hours)

☎ 0303 123 0035 (24 hours)

www.rbwm.gov.uk

Royal Borough
of Windsor &
Maidenhead

William Collins' dream of knowledge for all began with the publication of his first book in 1819.

A self-educated mill worker, he not only enriched millions of lives, but also founded a flourishing publishing house. Today, staying true to this spirit, Collins books are packed with inspiration, innovation and practical expertise. They place you at the centre of a world of possibility and give you exactly what you need to explore it.

Collins. Freedom to teach.

Published by Collins

An imprint of HarperCollins*Publishers*

The News Building, 1 London Bridge Street, London, SE1 9GF, UK
1st Floor, Watermarque Building, Ringsend Road, Dublin 4, Ireland

Browse the complete Collins catalogue at
www.collins.co.uk

ISBN 978-0-00-841292-0

British Library Cataloguing-in-Publication Data

A catalogue record for this publication is available from the British Library.

Dedication: For Isobel and Alice

Authors: Sarah Cant and Jennifer Hardes
Publisher: Katie Sergeant
Product manager: Catherine Martin
Development editor and copyeditor: Sonya Newland
Proofreader: Catherine Dakin
Permissions researcher: Rachel Thorne
Cover designer: Ken Vail Graphic Design
Cover image: Andrew Makedonski/Shutterstock
Internal design and illustration: Ken Vail Graphic Design
Production controller: Katharine Willard
Printed and bound by CPI Group (UK) Ltd

This book is produced from independently certified FSC™ paper to ensure responsible forest management.

For more information visit: www.harpercollins.co.uk/green

Acknowledgements
Thank you to Peter Watts for conversations about parables and Trabants.
We would like to thank the following teachers for reviewing chapters of the book in development:
Balkar Gill, Joseph Chamberlain Sixth Form College, Birmingham; Simon Henderson, Teeside School and Sixth Form, Barnard Castle; Fran Nantongwe, Reepham High School and College, Norwich; Wilhelmenia Etogo Ngono, Brighton and Hove Sixth Form College, Brighton; Annalisea Whyte, London

MIX
Paper from
responsible sources
FSC™ C007454

This book is produced from independently certified FSC™ paper to ensure responsible forest management.

For more information visit: **www.harpercollins.co.uk/green**

CONTENTS

INTRODUCTION: WHY BE A SOCIOLOGIST?

There has never been a more important time to study sociology and to become a sociologist. Understanding what makes societies work, how people can live amicably together, and how we navigate rapid social change has never been more pressing. Our world is home to over 7.5 billion people, and we have never been more connected – through the internet, global media channels, migration and shared work. Yet across the globe, people's lives are characterised by differences, diversity and division. Some live comfortably, while others struggle to survive and feed their families. Some have had the good fortune to have lived for generations in peace and security, while others fear for their safety every day.

Despite the hope that societal progress would bring collective rewards, enduring **poverty** and entrenched economic inequalities, even within wealthy societies, continue to define people's life chances. More than this, divisions between and across social classes, genders, ethnicities, sexualities, body types, generations, nations, faiths, and **ideologies** require our attention and our understanding.

The ecological crisis is, in large part, the unintended consequence of mass production and mass consumption – the need to produce, sell, and buy more and more things. There seems to be an unstoppable imperative to extract still more from our planet in order to afford ourselves fulfilling and well-lived lives. This ecological crisis is juxtaposed with the rise of the **gig economy** and reduced job opportunities. Many people today live with the spectre of unemployment, competition and uncertainty. Perhaps, then, it is not surprising that experiences of mental distress are rising steeply, suggesting that societal change has a real and negative impact on our inner selves. In the face of these challenges, we need sociology to help us consider how we can responsibly and collectively secure our future.

Described by Auguste Comte (1853/2009) as the 'queen' of the social sciences, sociology is unique in its orientation. Sociology studies human society through examining both the large-scale social forces that shape our personal experiences and the small-scale social interactions that give our lives meaning. It seeks to understand our everyday lives in the context of our histories, our cultural values, our social relationships, our economic foundations and aspirations, and our political ideologies.

From this holistic perspective, sociology challenges apparent 'truths', to shine a light on inequality, injustice and **power** imbalances. At the same time, it identifies what makes a good society, what enables communities to cohere, and recognises factors that foster belonging and **conviviality**. Sociology, then, is a discipline that asks difficult questions, but also offers hope.

Despite its important insights, sociology has been subject to critique. First, since sociology often asks probing questions, and because some of its suggested solutions demand social and economic changes, the discipline is sometimes regarded as radical: politically rather than scientifically driven. Second, because sociology studies the social world that non-sociologists inhabit, it has been described it as 'soft' or 'easy' – an 'ology' that anyone can master (Cant et al., 2020). Neither critique has foundation. It is true that sociology is impactful, and that it may advocate for change, but its solutions and suggestions are grounded in evidence derived from rigorous and ethical study. Moreover, sociology is far from easy. Sociologists must demonstrate: engagement with complex concepts and theories; mastery of a range of research methods with statistical competency, and the knowledge of when best to use them; critical and analytical capacities that interrogate not just the social world but the very evidence and methods that sociologists produce and use. Sociologists are always mindful of the limitations of their work, and assess what questions remain unanswered. For these reasons, sociology is a social science, bound by rules and **ethics**, that aims to produce objective, lucid and careful enquiry. There is one further critique of sociology that does have foundation. While the subject matter is undoubtedly engaging, some areas of the school sociology curriculum have been criticised for being both dated and **Eurocentric**. In this book, we draw on contemporary research and recognise the important work that scholars are undertaking to **decolonise the curriculum** in sociology.

How to be a Sociologist is designed for those new to sociology in school, college or university, or those who want to know more about the discipline and its promise. It is intended as an introduction to the subject, to ignite your interest and to indicate the breadth of sociological work. We hope that you will find it interesting and relevant, and that you will want to revisit the ideas here as you progress on your sociological journey.

In this book, we outline the sociological project and identify the six key dispositions that characterise the discipline. Sociologists must be: 1) imaginative; 2) conceptual; 3) rigorous; 4) knowledgeable; 5) reflexive; 6) transformative. We also outline what you need to do to 'be' a sociologist – the sociological 'how-tos'. We hope that this approach will enable you to see the importance and value of sociology, and encourage you to become a sociologist yourself!

Chapter 1 introduces the importance of being *imaginative* – a disposition that enables sociologists to challenge assumptions about the social world. An imaginative disposition allows you to see the deeper connections between the individual and the society in which they reside, and in turn to ask where that society sits in a broader historical and global context. Once you develop a sociological imagination, you can apply it to everything that human beings do. This capacity makes sociology endlessly fascinating. However, it can also be unsettling: the sociological imagination can shine a light on aspects of the social world that we may otherwise have taken for granted, but it can also call into question personal truths and the stories we tell ourselves about our own and others' experiences of the world.

But there is much more to being a sociologist than simply developing an imagination to think in different ways. Chapter 2 explores what it means to be *conceptual*. Sociologists need theories, made up of concepts, to enable them to develop questions, test ideas and explain what they see. Each theory and its concepts provide a different pair of glasses through which sociologists view the social world. There are so many different theories within sociology that it would be impossible to cover them all here, or even to provide a comprehensive overview of the ones that *are* mentioned, so you should see this book purely as a starting point.

Despite the theoretical diversity that characterises sociology, all sociological theories focus on answering the following questions:

- What is the proper subject matter of sociology?
- How are societies possible?
- What is the relationship between self and society? How do individual actions shape the social world and, in turn, how are individual actions constrained by social structures and social norms?
- How and why do societies change over time?

Each theoretical perspective has a different response to these questions, and a different understanding of what the focus of sociology should be. This means that sociologists gather **data** about the world in different ways, using different techniques. Chapter 3 explores the variety of research methods that make up the sociological toolkit and shows the importance of being *rigorous*. Together, these conceptual and methodological tools help sociologists generate careful and considered knowledge about the social world.

Being *knowledgeable* is central to sociology. Chapter 4 explores the importance of this disposition by focusing on three key sociological questions and by drawing on contemporary research studies to help answer them:

- How and why society is divided? We explore this through the sociologies of class, gender and ethnicity in relation to education and health.
- What gives society order, and why do some people break the rules? We examine this through the sociology of **crime**.
- How do cultural norms and values influence our thinking, what we do and who we think we are? In response to this question, we explore the sociologies of the family and religion.

Sociology asks important questions and provides different lenses through which to see the world. However, the complexity of the social world means that sociology will not always provide definitive answers, so sociologists must also learn to be *reflexive*. This involves being self-critical – turning the sociological imagination onto the practice of sociology itself. Because sociologists see the world from different perspectives, this can prevent them from asking all the important questions. Being reflexive also demands that work is careful and ethical, and ensures that the people being studied are protected. Chapter 5 introduces the importance of seeing the world from different points of view, of being aware of your own social location and bias, and of making sure that your work is ethical.

Being imaginative, conceptual, rigorous, knowledgeable and reflexive all help sociologists strive to improve the human condition. This is a contested but significant feature of sociology. It suggests that the discipline can and should have an impact on the societies and people that are studied – that sociologists should aim to be *transformative*. This capacity is what Burawoy (2005) called 'public sociology' and what Plummer (2013) defined as 'humane sociology'. Indeed, as Plummer so eloquently and importantly wrote:

> *The challenge for sociology is to grasp this complex, ever changing humanly produced, lived and everyday social world: to sense that we both miraculously and terrifyingly make and remake this world ourselves; and that the challenge is for us to make it a little better, if we can, in our short lifetimes.* (2013:491)

Chapter 6 describes some of the important sociological work that has made a lasting difference to the society it has sought to understand. Warde (2020) describes it this way:

> *Sociologists apply their knowledge in the hope of minimising social damage, learning from the comparison of collective arrangements what might produce least suffering and maximum happiness and justice.*

This final disposition underscores why sociological study, and becoming a sociologist, remains so very important. Chapter 6 also looks at the ways in which sociology can be personally transformative. Studying sociology prepares you for many jobs, it can change your outlook, and it can mobilise you to make a difference too.

We hope to show you that sociology has the potential to transform not only society but also those who take on board its skills and teachings. By becoming a sociologist, you will learn to be careful, considered and creative, analytical and rigorous, reflexive and ethical. These dispositions will prepare you for education, work and life.

In drawing the book to a close, we outline a sociology of hope and detail reasons to be optimistic about our social futures, living together.

CHAPTER 1
BE IMAGINATIVE: MAKING CONNECTIONS BETWEEN THE PERSONAL AND THE PUBLIC

On 25 May 2020, Black American **citizen** George Floyd was murdered in public view. The police had been called after a shopkeeper accused Floyd of using a counterfeit 20-dollar bill. In the course of his arrest, a White police officer, Derek Chauvin, knelt on Floyd's neck for 9 minutes and 29 seconds, during which Floyd uttered the words 'I can't breathe' repeatedly before he died.

At the time of Floyd's death, hundreds of thousands of people were also struggling to breathe, as coronavirus (COVID-19) cases surged around the world. There were accusations between nation states over the origin of the virus. For example, did it come from China's wet markets or did it leak from a viral biotechnology laboratory? Thus, as the pandemic became viral in biological form, engulfing human bodies, it also went viral in another way, spreading through social and news media and into the popular consciousness.

Ought we to see the death of George Floyd and the COVID-19 pandemic as separate events, connected only by the coincidence of their timing? Or can sociology help us see some deeper links?

Floyd's death served to reveal patterns of overt **institutional racism** within some police forces in the USA. **Racism** also characterised many of the narratives about COVID-19. For instance, some news outlets in the USA and the UK drew on what could be described as **culturally racist** narratives in their negative depictions of Chinese wet markets as unhygienic. More than this, COVID-19 statistics showed the embedded nature of institutional racism and **structural racism**. A disproportionate number of people from Black and minority ethnic communities died from COVID-19. This statistical pattern has been linked to several factors that help explain why people from deprived areas were also disproportionately affected by the virus. For example, these groups were more likely to be employed in the public sector, in care work and in low-paid jobs, where it was not possible to simply stop working, and where social distancing was difficult, making these groups more vulnerable to contracting COVID-19.

There were also stark differences in how countries were able to respond to the pandemic. For example, although there was initial anxiety in the UK about the lack of ventilators, the number available – 12,000 for a population of 67 million when the pandemic first took hold – stood in stark contrast to the lack of medical equipment in other countries. Anderson (2020) reported that across 41 African states that replied to a World Health Organization (WHO) survey, only 2,000 ventilators were available. Nigeria alone had only 100 ventilators for a population of 201 million; Somalia's 16 million inhabitants had none.

It is not only issues of **race**, **ethnicity**, nationhood and **social class** that intersect in these examples. As racism and COVID-19 (even as they overlap) took the living breath of Floyd and of millions of others around the world, in some ways and in some places the consequences of the virus made breathing easier. Air pollution may have worsened the symptoms of COVID-19, highlighting inequalities between places with greater or lesser degrees of pollutants, between cities and rural areas, and between manufacturing centres in southern global states and cleaner-air business centres in northern parts of the world. However, one positive consequence of the pandemic was a rapid reduction in air pollution caused by the sudden drop in the use of personal vehicles and public transport (Wu et al, 2020). National lockdowns vividly showed how the stalling of human activity can have a considerable impact on our 'natural', physical world.

The social and economic impact of COVID-19 extended into private homes and social relationships. Beyond the social isolation felt by those who had to fully 'shield' from others, and the tragedy for those unable to say goodbye to their dying relatives, COVID-19 reinforced existing social inequalities. While wealthier people benefited from larger homes and private gardens, others endured the pandemic in densely populated, overcrowded areas, where social distancing was challenging. Entrenched familial power relations worsened. For example, there was a rise in domestic violence during national lockdowns (ONS, 2020), a pattern repeated across the globe. In India, for example, various celebrities made videos and took to Instagram to highlight the rapid increase in domestic violence in the country during the pandemic (Vijayalakshmi, 2020). At the same time, record numbers of adults in the UK contacted the National Society for the Prevention of Cruelty to Children (NSPCC) with child welfare concerns. Job losses and the reliance on food banks also increased.

Examples like these, showing the real social consequences of COVID-19, are central to sociological study, which seeks to draw connections between what might be described as individual experiences and personal difficulties, and society's broader social, economic, cultural and political structures.

In the remainder of this chapter, we describe the focus and scope of sociology, and outline the first key disposition of a sociologist – the importance of being *imaginative*. While we all have close-up experiences of the social world by virtue of being human, the task of the sociologist is to be able to 'imagine' and to 'see' this social world differently.

What is sociology?

Sociology is the study of society and the ways in which social life is organised, structured and experienced. Humans live together in groups, communities and societies, but these vary across time and place. So, sociologists ask: What makes societies possible? How is social order maintained? What brings about social change? What is the relationship between the individual and society? How are people connected?

This means that sociology examines anything and everything that people do. Sociologists study **macro** (big) issues and social problems, such as those explored above relating to policing, health, work and family life. Macro issues also include poverty, homelessness, inequality, discrimination and crime. Sociologists are interested in the ways that society is organised, so they research institutions such as religion, education and healthcare. Sociology analyses people in terms of their socio-demographic characteristics, including their social class, gender, ethnicity, religion, generation and **sexuality**, and explores how these characteristics shape an individual's life chances and experiences. Sociology charts the differences in income, education and health that are features of all societies, and seeks to understand them.

While the focus on these big questions and the way that **social institutions** shape people's life experiences is central to the discipline, sociologists also investigate our interpersonal and everyday lives – our connections with one another, our **beliefs**, cultural values and **social norms**. This **micro** (close-up) focus leads to questions, such as: How do we get a sense of who we are? Who do we make friends with? Who do we fall in love with? How do we decide who to marry or, indeed, whether to marry at all? As such, sociologists look at all aspects of *being human* and all stages of *human life*. There are sociologists of pregnancy and childbirth, of death and dying, and even sociologists of sleep!

Sociological thinking

The scope of sociology is enormous – and endlessly fascinating. Studying sociology involves understanding how your own activities, relationships, beliefs and **identity** are shaped by the society in which you live, but also how, in turn, your actions produce and change the social world around you. Sociology seeks to understand the dynamic relationship between self and society, between individual and institution, and this sets it apart from other disciplines.

Indeed, sociological thinking is different from other kinds of thinking, such as psychological or biological interpretations of human life, because sociology focuses on:

- the structures and institutions in society
- cultural values, social norms and beliefs
- the processes of **socialisation**, our relationships, identity and **social roles**
- the ways in which society and the globe are unequally divided
- who or what holds power
- why there is conflict as well as order.

Most importantly, sociology explores the relationship between society and individuals, between self and community, between biography and history. But how exactly do sociologists do this? They need to have a particular and distinctive disposition – what Mills (1959/2000) called the **sociological imagination**.

Mills argued that at the heart of the sociological project is both the endeavour and the ability to reveal connections between what he called 'personal troubles' and 'public issues of social structure'. By **personal troubles**, he meant any experience that people have in their own lives. He was referring in part to difficulties, such as unemployment, divorce, poverty and racism, but he meant much more than 'troubles'. He was also referring to values and aspirations, marriage, parenthood, schooling, love… everything that humans experience. As such, we prefer to describe social life as being characterised by personal troubles, truths and triumphs – the 'personal Ts'.

Dying from police brutality, losing one's job during a pandemic or suffering violence at the hands of a partner are experienced at the level of the individual. So are falling in love, developing an Instagram account and deciding what to eat for dinner. Whether you vote for a left- or right-wing party, believe in a god or support feminism are also seen as individual choices. However, sociology contends that it is insufficient to understand these 'personal Ts' as difficulties, choices and beliefs. Rather, sociologists examine these deeply felt, lived experiences with reference to history, society, **culture**, politics and economics. This is what Mills called the 'public issues of social structure'. As the examples at the beginning of this chapter show, sociologists look beyond common sense, personal or politically driven explanations, and seek a holistic, societal view to show that 'neither the life of an individual nor the history of a society can be understood without understanding both'. (Mills, 1959:3).

The sociological imagination is, then, a 'quality of mind' that allows us to see what is 'going on in the world' (Mills, 1959), to ask different questions, to identify connections that might initially appear invisible, to find patterns and ask why they exist, and to use this capacity to understand society and our own place in it. The aim and the promise of the sociological imagination is to make considered, creative and critical connections.

The development of a sociological imagination is liberating, but it is not always straightforward or easy. Indeed, having a sociological imagination can be disturbing: once you see the world as a sociologist, it is hard to turn back, and you may find that some of your fondly held assumptions about the world are deeply unsettled. The example below illustrates this.

Charles is a 19-year-old White man. He achieved excellent examination results at school and is the captain of his football team. Charles worked hard both at school and at his sport. He studied every evening, took an unpaid internship over the summer, and earned a scholarship at a top university where he could also compete in football. At university, Charles is given the opportunity to take a module studying sociology. His professor talks to the class about **meritocracy** – the notion that achievements reflect individual talent and commitment. Charles initially believes this to be true, and feels he earned his place at university because he worked hard. The professor then asks the students to examine what privileges they may have had that enabled their 'individual' successes. What factors might Charles consider as he unpacks what sociologists call his **positionality**? Who *is* Charles? What social and economic advantages might he have had?

Think for a moment about who you are as a person. What is your family background? How is your family structured? What is your ethnic origin? What is your gender? Are you able-bodied? Could any of these factors help you up the social ladder – or hold you back? Might any of them help explain any personal troubles, truths or triumphs in relation to your educational achievements? These are the types of questions that sociologists pose.

When reflecting on the challenges posed by his professor, Charles realises that his successes cannot simply be read as individual triumphs; they must also be considered alongside the structural opportunities afforded to him by his social position. He was able to take an unpaid internship because his parents were middle class and could support him financially. Charles's ethnicity and his gender also allowed him to take educational opportunities without encountering prejudice. Charles acknowledges that his triumphs, while not personally insignificant, were supported by a system in which he received privileges that others did not have. This was unsettling for Charles, but also deeply moving.

Mills acknowledges that the sociological imagination is 'both terrible and magnificent', commenting that while it allows us to 'grasp what is going on in the world' and enlivens our 'capacity for astonishment', it can be personally challenging (1959:7-8). For Charles, it was challenging because his fundamental beliefs about his own life and his own identity – successful, hard-working, and even deserving – were exposed. Yet, this personal challenge is necessary as a sociologist: one must 'move beyond one's own nose' and see the world in a more considered way.

Applying the sociological imagination

The scope of sociology can be illustrated with another everyday example – that of clothing. Think for a moment about the clothes you are wearing. Why did you choose this outfit today? Sociology teaches us that our experiences are socially shaped, so we cannot understand the 'choices' we make in life as simply individual ones. We must always explore the intimate connection between personal circumstances and choices and the wider social context in which we find ourselves. You might have grabbed the clothes you are wearing because they were clean or because they were heaped on the floor nearby. You might just like these trousers or this dress. However, our choices are framed by many factors – so much so that the idea of free choice is actually quite problematic for sociologists. How is this different to other approaches to studying clothing choices?

A student of biology may look to explain clothing choices in relation to human nature, so they might draw upon evolutionary theories to explain why humans developed clothing. Or they may ask how clothing choices are a matter of instinct, driven by biological necessity to attract a mate, for example. Biologists explain that people act in certain ways because they are born to do so, but sociologists often find such explanations worrying because they may reinforce dangerous stereotypes about people. (This is not to say that there is no usefulness or importance in sociology engaging in discussions with biology, as we discuss in Chapter 5.)

A student of economics or psychology might look at the strategies that clothes companies use to encourage people to buy an item of clothing. Or they might consider the negative effects that clothing choice can have on a person's self-esteem.

Sociologists ask different questions. They are critical of the idea that human behaviour is driven purely by instinct, or that it can be explained through individual choice alone. In fact, sociologists often regard these positions as **reductionist** and **deterministic**. Instead, sociologists explore the social context of clothing choice. For example, you might start unpacking the social context of clothing by noting that clothing choices are shaped by what is actually available to buy. As fashion is a billion-pound industry, clothing companies all need to compete with one another and make a **profit**. In turn, this increases the production and supply of clothing.

The influence of global history

Consider desire versus necessity. How many pairs of shoes do you have? How many do you need? We obviously need to wear shoes, but do we need several different pairs? The more we buy, the more profit a company will make. And these profits are often made possible by historically founded and exploitative working relations. A demand for cheap clothes in one country requires someone else making them cheaply, often in a different country. Indeed, the United Nations Children's Fund website (unicef.org, 2020) highlights the issue of child labour in the fashion supply chain. Sociology teaches us that clothing choice is underpinned by a global system of exploitation, both economic and cultural. Some design prints, such as Paisley, were imported from colonised countries and have been **culturally appropriated** as part of a commercialised fashion industry.

Clothing fabrics such as cotton were key to enabling Britain to become prosperous in the Industrial Revolution. Cotton fabric was made in Britain, copying Indian weaving techniques, but the raw product was grown in the British colonies and harvested by enslaved peoples (Bhambra, 2010). Cotton mill workers (**proletariat**) in the UK were also exploited by factory owners (**bourgeoisie**), working long hours for low wages, often in dangerous working conditions. The mass production of clothes in the 19th century made many entrepreneurs rich, but at huge cost for workers across the globe. Sociology therefore shows us that our present lives are very much part of our history.

Today, clothes continue to be made in former colonies and sold so cheaply that the wages paid to workers are perilously low (Zafar et al, 2016).

Cotton was grown and harvested on plantations in the American South and in British-ruled India by slave labour.

Cotton factories in Manchester employed women and children who spun and wove the imported cotton from slave plantations, in dangerous working conditions.

Gender expectations

Clothes choices are also shaped by expectations linked to **gender**. 'Baby blue' and 'baby pink' still strongly shape how we dress newborns (Lindsey, 2016). A visit to a clothes shop will reveal the extent to which these colours continue to influence clothing designs and the choices available. However, according to Paoletti (2012), the association of boys with blue and girls with pink is a 20th-century phenomenon. Before that, blue was considered a feminine colour (linked to the Virgin Mary) and pink was considered a masculine colour because of its close association to red.

Sociologists have found that once children are dressed differently, they are treated differently: children are socialised into gender roles through the way that parents choose to dress them. Shakin et al (1985) suggest that clothing colour plays a significant role in **labelling** infants as boys or girls, which in turn affects how people behave towards those infants. Therefore, sociologists differentiate between **nurture** and **nature** to show that much human behaviour is learned, rather than predetermined.

> What do you think about the way we colour-code gender? What other examples of social gendering can you think of?

Feminists are particularly interested in how gender is represented through clothing choices. Early feminists fought for the right to wear non-restrictive clothing and were critical of items such as corsets, which were designed to shape women in a way that was pleasing to men – as well as being extremely uncomfortable for the wearer.

However, today women often wear high heels, which some feminists may view as oppressive. Interestingly, high heels were originally invented for men, when Persian soldiers used them to secure their feet in stirrups. The style was later co-opted by male designers to lift a woman's bottom and contort her calves, making her more attractive to men, without any consideration of her comfort and ability to walk. High heels, therefore, can be viewed as part of **patriarchy**, where dominant **heterosexual masculinity** is reinforced, and where male interests are served (see Chapters 2 and 4 for more about these ideas). One relevant case study here is that of Nicola Thorp. In 2016, Thorp, a receptionist at PricewaterhouseCoopers in London, was sent home from work because she was not wearing heels of 2 to 4 inches (5 to 10 centimetres), which she was told was company policy. This was widely seen as discriminatory, and it led to a government inquiry into workplace dress codes. The case highlighted the pervasiveness of gender norms, but also showed that they can be contested.

Consider also the example of flight attendants. It was only in March 2019 that Virgin Airlines relaxed its dress code for female workers and allowed them to wear trousers. Gender sociologist Lisa Wade noted that flight attendants were originally men (in fact, women were banned by many airlines) but later, when women came to dominate the profession, they were expected to act as 'cheerful domestic workers and sex pots' to entertain the largely male clientele (Wade, 2017).

Many feminists believe that the fashion sector is highly sexist, pointing to the historical use of Size 2 models and the reproduction of norms about how women should look. Feminist sociologists of crime, such as Carol Smart (1995), have shown how sexist views about clothing can have dangerous consequences. Smart described how judgments about a woman's dress (for example, whether clothing is regarded as 'provocative') may undermine allegations of rape in a court of law – a finding confirmed by other studies, including Osborn et al (2018).

Feminists such as Sarah Baker, however, suggest that wearing heels and dressing in a 'feminine' way through 'glamorous' choices of clothing can be liberating as well as oppressive (Baker, 2017). Wearing heels to feel tall can be empowering, for example. This shows that feminism can take a variety of positions, so it is more accurate to talk of *feminisms*. Sociology embraces the notion that the social world is complex and is comfortable in having many contested views and positions.

Sexism implicit in gender choices is not restricted to women. How might gender influence men's clothing choices? In 18th-century Europe, men's fashion was more extravagant than women's, so why did it become more uniform over time? It is likely that, as men felt obliged to show they were focused on work, their clothes became more understated. They may also have chosen to display their wealth through the way that their wives were dressed.

It is possible to argue that men are still more constrained than women in their clothing choices, yet gender boundaries in clothing are not so clearly defined any more. Most shops are still divided into men's and women's sections, but choices are not so tightly bound by these categories. In 1998, England footballer David Beckham famously attracted attention when he wore a sarong. He described this as his 'worst menswear mistake', but he argues that today no one would think twice about it. This tells us much about the possibility of **social change**. However, gender differences in clothing remain pervasive, as evidenced by the controversy – both criticism and praise – that singer Harry Styles created when he wore a dress on the front cover of *Vogue* in 2020.

> Changing gender norms have an impact on clothing choice. What other social changes have affected clothing choices? For example, how might fast-fashion, transgenderism and environmentalism shape someone's wardrobe?

Social class and social control

Fashion is something we all engage in, whether we like it or not. Even choosing not to bother about fashion makes a fashion statement! But fashion reflects and reinforces wider social differences and hierarchies. Clothing choices are determined by the amount of money someone has and so are linked to social class. Bourdieu (1984) points to the ways that clothing produces lines of **distinction** between groups of people, and Jones (2016) highlights the visibility of class in clothing. The way that clothing choice can be used as a class marker can be seen in the example of Burberry. Traditionally this brand was associated with the upper classes, but it was appropriated by the working classes, who were labelled and stigmatised as 'Chavs' by the upper and middle classes (see page 77).

This photograph shows boys in London in 1937. The clothing of the upper-class boys on the left is visibly different to the three boys in the right.

> Do you think the upper middle classes continue to dress differently today? If so, how?

King and Smith (2018) note that the Jack Wills brand, associated with the Henley regatta, signifies belonging to the upper and middle classes.

A person's choice of clothes can make a statement about their tastes and their friends, which sociologists refer to as **cultural capital** and **social capital**. Clothes can help you belong to a group, or help you disassociate yourself from others. Sociologists use the term **subculture** to capture the way that people are grouped by shared cultural ideas and identities. Often, subcultures use clothing as a marker of distinction. A classic sociological example of subcultures is Stanley Cohen's study (1972/2002) of mods and rockers.

Members of these two groups were strongly distinguished by their clothing and music tastes (see photographs below).

Mods rode scooters and wore large parker coats over their suits or other clean-cut outfits.

Rockers rode motorbikes and wore leather jackets and jeans.

Can you think of other subcultures that differentiate themselves through fashion and clothing? Consider, for example, goths or hipsters.

Religious and political influences

Clothing choices may also be shaped by someone's political values. For example, you might be committed to reducing climate change and so will only buy second-hand clothes from charity shops. Differences in religion or ethnicity can affect clothing choices, too. Muslim women may wear head or full body coverings, including the hijab, burqa or niqab. In Judaism, clothing signifies religious affiliation; for instance, Jewish men may wear the kippot, tallit, or shtreimel. Many Orthodox Hasidic men will wear black suits intended to replicate the clothing of 18th-century Polish nobility, illustrating how clothing can reflect and reinforce history, identity, ethnicity, religion and class.

Fashion is also a space where cultural differences can become sites of political contestation. Clothing can be used to *assimilate* (used to fit in) with a different culture or it can be *appropriated* (taken) from different cultures. Clothing, then, can act as a mechanism of both belonging and exclusion. For example, feminists interpret the wearing of head coverings differently. In some countries such as France the veil is banned, and some feminists (e.g. Lazreg, 2009) support this, viewing the veil as restrictive and oppressive for women. However, some **decolonial feminists** argue that such a view dismisses the agency of women who choose to wear the veil. Moreover, as Saeed (2016) suggests, wearing the veil can be regarded as liberating in its protection of women from the 'male gaze' and the tyranny of 'Western' beauty myths.

From the example of clothing explored in this chapter, you should start to see the scope of sociology. It sets the choosing of clothes in its social, cultural, political, economic and historical context. Sociologists ask a range of questions and can disagree about what they see, but in all cases the sociological imagination is both careful and critical, focused on drawing out the connections between the personal and the public.

Sociological how-tos

Since this book is called *How to be a Sociologist*, we finish here with some 'how-tos' from this chapter. To be a sociologist you must learn how to:

- think differently
- distinguish sociological thinking from other forms of thinking (such as biological and psychological)
- challenge assumptions about the social world
- make connections between personal troubles, truths and triumphs, and broader **social structures**.

CHAPTER 2
BE CONCEPTUAL: PUTTING ON SOCIOLOGICAL GLASSES

Many people like to think that they are sociologists – they engage in conversations about the social world, after all. People chat in cafés, parks, at dinner parties, in school canteens, at sports events and on social media about the sorts of issues explored in Chapter 1. You may overhear people talking about feminist issues, exploitation in the workplace, differences in educational attainment, racism and other forms of discrimination, or matters concerning disability rights, for instance. Many people are interested in crime, climate change, the replacement of people by robots, the encroachment of technology into personal life, the rise in poverty and the reliance on food banks. They may even use sociological terms to describe these issues.

Consider the following dialogue:

> Alice: In my workplace there's only one senior manager who is a woman – the rest are all men.

> Nisha: Ugh, I know. Same at mine – the patriarchy continues…

> Alice: I don't expect a promotion either. The only thing my boss wants me to do all day is make him cups of tea.

Alice and Nisha are engaging in a conversation about women's lower status in the workplace, and Nisha even uses the concept of patriarchy. But does that make them – or anyone else who has this type of conversation – sociologists? Is sociology a unique discipline or is it simply common sense? How much can we rely on sociology's sources of knowledge compared to other forms of knowledge? How do we separate everyday knowledge from sociological expertise?

Sociology is not just about setting the world to rights with your friends or arguing over social matters with your foes. Sociology is much more than this: it has the considered, creative and critical ability to make sense of the complexities of the social world and to secure this understanding with evidence. In Chapter 1 we introduced you to the *sociological imagination*. Now we explore some of the many concepts and theories that sociologists employ, each of which reveals something different about the social world. But first, let's unpack a little more the difference between common-sense knowledge, or what we might call 'lay' knowledge, and sociological knowledge.

The trouble with 'knowledge'

It is more difficult in sociology to separate specialist knowledge from lay knowledge than it is in other disciplines. Research from the hard sciences, such as physics and chemistry, does not normally make its way into everyday discussion. The quantum physics that underpins scientific work on the Higgs boson, for instance, is not typical dinner-party conversation! By contrast, sociologists study the kind of topics that lay people experience for themselves, as Alice and Nisha's dialogue demonstrates. Moreover, sociologists do not test their ideas in laboratories, or use specialist equipment that allows them to see the world in ways that ordinary people cannot. As Bauman and May (2019) point out, in sociology there are no equivalents of giant accelerators or radio telescopes.

However, this does not mean that sociological knowledge is nothing more than common sense. On the contrary, there are clear differences between these two sets of knowledge. Specifically, sociological knowledge and common-sense understanding differ in three distinct ways:

- Common-sense knowledge tends to be 1) value-laden, 2) subjective and biased, and 3) judgment-based.
- Sociological knowledge aims to be 1) value-free (or at least value-reflexive), 2) as objective and impartial as possible, and 3) evidence-based.

Giddens (2015) argued that most of the time, common sense really explains very little. Sociologists must instead attempt to provide value-free rather than value-laden statements about the social world. This means they try to remove their biases and must not simply rely on their own judgments and experiences to make sense of the world. This does not mean that lay experiences are not useful – they may, for example, alert us to a social problem or a puzzling question – but it is not sociological simply to use one's own experiences as evidence. In this respect, the discipline of sociology aims to be impartial and objective.

What does it mean to be conceptual?

All academic disciplines have concepts and theories. In science, these are as wide-ranging as cell theory, Darwin's theory of evolution, the Big Bang theory, the theory of relativity and germ theory, among many others! Each theory guides what a scientist will study, their mode of enquiry and the methods that they should use.

Sociology is no different: it draws on theories to explain the social world – what Comte (1853/2009) described as 'social physics'. To be conceptual is to develop explanations of the social world that cannot necessarily be seen, fully proven or completely known. Our theories and concepts also direct us toward deciding what evidence we need to gather in order to know about the social world. However, because the social world is so complex, multiple theoretical positions (what we describe here in terms of different 'pairs of glasses') have developed to make sense of it.

To understand why sociologists have multiple pairs of glasses, consider the Sufi parable of the elephant.

A group of blindfolded men come across an elephant. They have never seen one before, and because they are blindfolded, they can only make sense of what the elephant is like by touching it. Each man touches a different part of the elephant's body, describing what he feels and comprehends.

'An elephant is a big snake,' one man exclaims as he touches the elephant's trunk.

'No, you are wrong, this is a breathing mountain,' says the man climbing a ladder set against the elephant's side.

Another, grabbing hold of the elephant's leg claims, 'Actually, it is a tree stump!'

'What are you saying?' shrieks another, stroking the elephant's ear. 'It's a sheath of leather.'

'You're all wrong!' claims the final man, tickling the end of the elephant's tail. 'It's like a little furry mouse.

There are two important points to draw from this parable. The first is illustrated by the fact that no single man could understand the whole elephant on his own: each had his own insight, but each insight was partial. This shows that different perspectives are needed for something as big as an elephant to make sense to a blindfolded man – or something as complex as society to a sociologist. The second point is that ideas, concepts and theories can and should be contested. To be properly conceptual, you need to recognise that while theories can be illuminating, they also have limitations and may blinker you to other viewpoints.

It is also important to remember that while social theories evolve as society changes, they are also a *product* of their social context. They do not evolve impartially to make sense of the social world; rather, all theories are formulated by particular people in particular social contexts, so they are *shaped by* the point in time in which they are generated. And while theories aim to be objective and useful, they must also adapt to make sense of a changing world. As such, theories may become redundant or even controversially outdated. For example, early sociologists did not give much attention to the question of gender divisions. This was because such sociological theories developed at a time when women did not have the same educational rights and opportunities as men, and male sociologists did not question this reality: their own sociological imagination was blinkered to some features of the social world. This does not make their insights worthless but, as in the elephant parable, it means they only shone a light on *some* important issues – not all.

Sociological concepts and theories arise and change as more of the social world comes into view. Of course, this means that in the future today's concepts and theories may turn out to be inadequate, or blinkered to certain realities. That is why being a sociologist requires us to be both conceptual and reflexive (a capacity that we explore in Chapter 5). This is also why our next section is entitled a 'history' of concepts, theories and ideas: we use scare quotes to show that the history of sociological theory is a contested one, and it is important for us to always be mindful of other versions of this history, and the social conditions that enabled some theories to gain more credibility than others.

With these important points in mind, the next section of the chapter explores how different sociological theories can help interrogate some important questions, including:

- What is the proper subject matter of sociology?
- What is the relationship between the individual and society?
- How do we explain social change?

> Before we lead you through the history of these sociological theories, reflect on these questions yourself. For instance, do you think we are individuals making free choices about how to lead our lives, or do you think we are simply 'puppets' that follow social norms unquestioningly?

A 'history' of sociological concepts and theories

Sociologists often make a distinction, albeit crudely, between classical and contemporary theory. Classical refers to those theories associated with the birth of sociology in the latter part of the 19th century, which developed to make sense of the dramatic social, political, economic and cultural changes that occurred during the period of what is termed **colonial modernity**, beginning in the late 17th century and escalating through the 18th and into the 19th centuries. You will often see this period referred to as **modernity** but it is important to recognise that these social changes were rooted in **colonialism**. Contemporary theories refer to those that have developed since the end of the Second World War in 1945.

In terms of classical sociological theories, three changes were particularly significant. First, humans were increasingly successful in crossing the globe, in discovering new lands, materials, peoples and ideas. However, the opportunities that these explorations afforded to White men from the **Global North** in particular, were made possible by oppression and enslavement of people who lived in countries that were colonised.

Second, this period was also characterised by technological developments, changing the way agriculture was organised and goods were produced. There was an increasingly accelerated move from **feudal** to industrial societies. In turn, these changes shaped how people worked, where they lived, how they communicated, what they believed and who they trusted. Such changes affected class, gender and ethnic relations, how people were born, aged and died, who they married and what kind of life chances they were afforded. All this impacted every facet of the social world and people's social lives.

Look at the two images here. What sort of social, economic and cultural changes do you think occurred in the shift from feudalism to industrialisation?

Third, existing theological and philosophical ideas could not adequately capture these new social complexities and, in an increasingly **secular society**, were not always fit for purpose. As a result, there arose a new emphasis on scientific and rational thought.

A new discipline – sociology – was required to make sense of the socio-economic, cultural, political and intellectual changes that were taking place. Many textbooks describe three 'founding fathers' of the new discipline: Marx, Durkheim and Weber. It is true that the work of these three theorists was ground-breaking and contributed significantly to the sociological theoretical canon. But they were not the only people thinking and writing about societal changes at the time, and there are other important founders of sociological thinking to consider. Among these are early feminists, such as Mary Wollstonecraft, Harriet Martineau, Ida Wells-Barnett, Anna Julia Cooper and Charlotte Perkins Gilman, who documented the consequences of social and economic change for women, and Black sociologists such as Sojourner Truth, W.E.B. Du Bois, Charles Spurgeon Johnson, C.L.R James, among others, who drew attention to race relations and discrimination on the basis of colour and assumed differences between 'races'. Moreover, while much teaching emphasises the sociological thinking coming out of north-western Europe and North America, there were many important sociological thinkers in the **Global South** who shaped the ideas of European scholars – often without credit. There were also southern knowledges and social and economic histories that were overlooked, or simply erased (Meghji, 2021).

This is an important point. As Bhambra (2007) points out, the history of sociology as it is often told is **Eurocentric**. Accounts tend to focus on the uniqueness and superiority of scholars from the Global North and this minimises the important contributions of those from other regions. It can also blinker us to the fact that modernity was not confined to the Global North but, importantly, grew out of exploitation in the Global South. Therefore, sociology is best described as the study of colonial modernity, and indeed was itself shaped by colonialism (Meghji, 2021).

The vast body of work that comprises classic and contemporary theory refers to a hugely divergent set of ideas that cannot be adequately covered in a short introduction such as this. Later theorists developed the work of Marx, Durkheim and Weber. There are numerous feminisms to help make sense of all women's experiences, and **critical race theories** to make sense of racism and ethnic inequalities. There are theories of post-industrial, late, post and reflexive modernity; theories of globalisation; disability theories and theorists; theories to make sense of changing norms about sexuality, changing social structures and changing ways of living, loving and working.

There is no neat or universally accepted way of summarising the wonderful technicolour of sociological concepts and theories. Learning about them is a journey that takes time, but through the information that follows, we hope to give you a sense of the scope of sociological concepts and to show you how important they are.

Trying on different sociological glasses

In the remainder of this chapter, you will try on a few (but not all) pairs of sociological glasses. Each pair allows you to 'see' the world differently and, as a play on this idea, you will get to explore what it is they 'C' – which concepts each perspective develops and uses, and how they can be applied. Throughout this chapter, we use the example of mental illness to illustrate this.

The first thing to note is that sociologists choose to focus on different aspects of the social world: either the macro (big structures) or the micro (everyday life). Some sociologists prefer to look at the way social structures and forces shape individual lives (a top-down approach), while others examine how individuals shape and make the social world in which they live (a bottom-up approach); still others combine these insights.

Sociologists also vary in how pessimistic or optimistic they are about social change. Some focus on conflict between groups and the ways in which people's lives are controlled, while others focus on how order is built and maintained, and how societies are predominantly consensual and convivial.

Drawing on these divisions within sociological theory, the rest of the chapter explores the approaches taken by several key sociological figures, including:

- Karl Marx, the development of Marxist analyses, and the ways that social class and **economic capital** can be used to explain life chances, as well as ideas about how the concept of capital can be expanded.
- Émile Durkheim, the development of functionalist theory and the study of **social facts**.
- Max Weber, the developments of interactionist sociology, surveillance and rationalisation.
- W.E.B. Du Bois and the development of critical studies into race and racism.
- Mary Wollstonecraft and the various ways that feminisms have been developed to make sense of women's lives and those of men.
- Theories of modernity, and how sociology must continue to make sense of contemporary social change.

Many concepts and theories are covered in the remainder of this chapter. Remember that learning theory is like learning a language; it takes time and practice – and sometimes it will seem unintelligible and sometimes too difficult. Try to latch onto the 'C' concepts. The glossary at the end of the book will also be a helpful resource to enhance your familiarity with, and understanding of, some key sociological terms and ideas.

Karl Marx and beyond

C is for conflict, class and capital(ism)

Let us begin with the theorist who is, arguably, the most famous and the most influential beyond the field of sociology. Karl Marx (1818–83) was born into a wealthy Prussian family, but lived most of his adult life in Britain and witnessed first-hand the poverty and poor living conditions that accompanied industrialisation: the overcrowding, the lack of sanitation and the long hours toiling in hazardous factories that characterised the lives of the people in the cities he visited and described.

Marx developed what has become known as a **grand theory** of society. Put simply, he argued that changes to the economy (for example, the shift from feudalism to **capitalism**) could and should explain all other changes within the social world.

Karl Marx

Marx focused on the way that the economy (the material base of society) had changed and was now organised. Looking at the world through these glasses helped him see that some people were the winners, while others were losers as the result of a move to capitalism. Marx also considered the way that the economy shaped **social institutions** and ideas. He famously described religious ideas as the 'opium of the people', because he saw these ideas as validating poverty and inequality. He described how factory workers tolerated poor living conditions and many other real, lived personal problems because they believed they would be rewarded in the afterlife. As such, Marx focused on *structures* over individuals. For him, societal change did not emanate from new ideas and new **values**; rather, any changes to ideas, institutions and values reflected the ways that the economic structure was organised.

The move from a feudal society to a capitalist one was the result of developments in technology and changes to the way that goods were produced – the shift from **cottage industry** to the mass production of goods in factories. Marx referred to this as changes to the **means of production**. This in turn affected what he called the **relations of production** – people's social roles and relationships, their ways of working and living.

> How do you think that changes in the way that work was organised might have impacted family life?

Marx argued that all societies are class societies. In feudalism, the major class divide was between lords and serfs. Under capitalism, he described the emergence of two new and very distinct social classes – the bourgeoisie (the factory owners, for example) and the proletariat (those that had to sell their labour for a wage in order to live). For Marx, this class division was the most important factor in explaining life chances and how social life was organised (more important than gender or ethnicity, for example). With these 'glasses' on, political ideologies, religious beliefs, school policies, healthcare systems and family relationships are all shown to ultimately serve the bourgeoisie and oppress the proletariat.

Marx's intention was to reveal the historical and material structures that organised social life, and to uncover the real, but often hidden, economic mechanisms that determine social life. He examined the consequences of the inherent conflict between the bourgeoisie and the proletariat. For instance, he predicted that the working classes would become **alienated** from one another and from their work, but also **immiserated** – poorer over time while their employers enjoyed increasing wealth. (Rising rates of national and global inequality show that some of Marx's theoretical predictions have been realised – see Chapter 4.)

Marx's ideas have been subject to critique, not least because he predicted that the proletariat would eventually recognise the oppressive and exploitative reality of capitalism, unify (become a **class for themselves**), overthrow capitalism, and replace it with **communism**. However, capitalism has largely remained unquestioned in many parts of the world. The wealth and power of the ruling classes is generally regarded as *deserved* – a product of talent and hard work. Indeed, the belief in meritocracy has never been as strong as it is today (Mijs, 2019). It is also the case that the lived experience of the class system is much more complex than the binary division between two social groups that he described.

Case Study: Marxist glasses and mental illness

Many sociologists continue to use key Marxist concepts to make sense of modern phenomena such as mental illness. For example, in a study entitled 'Anxious? Depressed? You might be suffering from capitalism', Prins et al (2015) suggest that there is a new mental health epidemic that can be explained by social class relations. The authors show how alienation, job strain and lack of control at work have a strong impact on the psyche, which accounts for the increase in mental health difficulties.

Marx's work was developed in the 20th century, when French and German thinkers focused on the link between economic structures and ideas. This work helped to explain how and why capitalist class relations were not more strongly questioned. Antonio Gramsci (1971) explained how the bourgeoisie is supported by the state and how the ruling classes succeed in securing **hegemony** over all ideas and institutions, thus keeping the proletariat in their place. Hegemonic control captures how the dominant class retains political and ideological power by way of 'popular consensus' (opinion) in civil society, rather than through physical force. Power is thus achieved not by violence but through consent – the ruling class (the minority) dominates

Antonio Gramsci

by persuading the masses to adopt their own values and ideas. Ideologies produced by the ruling class become part of the masses' consciousness and seem natural and normal. Religion and meritocracy both illustrate this point. In relation to the latter, Mijs (2019) argued that a belief in, and increased support for, meritocracy, means that success or failure is seen as a consequence of one's personal efforts (as a personal triumph or trouble) rather than as an outcome of economic and societal inequality (public issue).

Louis Althusser (2006) was interested in how the bourgeoisie maintained control. He drew attention to how ideology works and the ways in which people submit to dominant ideas, without questioning their subjugation. His enormously influential concept of the **ideological state apparatus (ISA)** describes how institutions such as education, the Church, social and sports clubs, the family and the law all produce and circulate ideologies that reinforce the control and power of the ruling class. You can see here how Marxist scholars show that personal truths are underscored by economic inequalities.

Louis Althusser

Marx's ideas have been developed in other ways too – not just to explain why capitalism persists, but also to consider how his concepts can and should be used to make sense of enduring societal divisions. One such important sociologist is Pierre Bourdieu.

Bourdieu's (1984) writing draws on the work of all three 'founding fathers', but shows the particular influence of Marx. However, where Marx focuses on economic capital, with social class as the central division in society, Bourdieu elaborates a more nuanced understanding of capital. He agrees that an individual's life chances are shaped by their access to economic capital, but he does not relate capital simply to income and wealth. Rather, Bourdieu expands the sociological understanding of **capital** to include **social capital** (our social networks, our relationships, who we know), **cultural capital** (our knowledge, lifestyle choices, values, leisure activities), **symbolic capital** (our status and prestige) and **physical capital** (our bodily dispositions and

Pierre Bourdieu

shape). He shows how each of these forms of capital situate us in a societal hierarchy and shape our life chances and success in education and work. This is a good example of how the founding sociological concepts – in this case capital – remain relevant even when they need to be further elaborated. (This is explored in more detail in Chapter 4.)

Émile Durkheim and beyond

C is for consensus, co-operation and collective conscience

Émile Durkheim (1858–1917) was born in France. Like Marx, he developed a grand theory and emphasised the impact of wider social structures over individual human **agency** (our capacity to act freely), but his conceptual tools and theoretical lens were quite different. Durkheim recognised that northern European societies had undergone significant changes as they industrialised. However, he focused on how new social bonds and norms were formed and how people's lives were shaped by what he called **social facts**, which he considered to be the proper subject matter of sociology.

By 'social facts', Durkheim meant that our individual lives are shaped by external social forces, norms, customs and institutions that exist before we are born, persist after our death, and constrain all that we do. Social facts include language, family structures, marriage and laws, to name a few. For Durkheim, every act, however individual it might appear, can be explained by focusing on such social factors. Durkheim also argued that sociologists must study the social world as any scientist would – objectively. As such, he is described as a **positivist**. (There is more on this in Chapter 3.)

Émile Durkheim

His most famous illustration of social facts was that of suicide, which he argued was far from an individual and personal act. He showed that the different rates of suicide in different societies could be explained by the extent to which an individual is integrated into society (included in it) and the extent to which individual actions are subject to control (regulated by society). Based on these factors, some societies, he argued, are more prone to suicide than others. In particular, he described how **anomie** (an absence of shared norms or values), often a feature of modern societies, can be experienced as profoundly unsettling and account for higher suicide rates. In terms of the sociological imagination, therefore, Durkheim's work identifies the social causes of life's troubles and triumphs.

Just because social facts exist before and after our own lives, it does not mean that they do not change. Durkheim argued that pre-modern societies were characterised by their overwhelming uniformity: most people's lives were the same. Individuals existed in close connection with one another and had the same aspirations and expectations. Through this sameness came integration and solidarity (what Durkheim termed **mechanical solidarity**) – people were joined by a **collective conscience**, a set of shared values, beliefs and moral attitudes.

In contrast, in modern societies there are multiple specialist roles and jobs – what Durkheim called a sophisticated **division of labour** – where everyone is highly individual, but intimately dependent upon one another. For example, we do not build our own houses, we do not make our own clothes, and most of us do not grow our own food. Such specialisms result in solidarity and integration born of a profound need for one another (which he termed **organic solidarity**).

'The butcher, the baker, the candlestick-maker…' In a widely recited nursery rhyme, we recall that new and specialised jobs emerge as society develops. What are the consequences of having different people making bread, butchering meat and making candles?

In modern societies we are bound by interconnections rather than by shared values. However, the absence of shared values in modern social groups might foster greater degrees of difference and therefore anomie.

You might already have identified some parallels between Marx's concept of alienation and Durkheim's concept of anomie. Both are a negative consequence of modernity: alienation is produced by oppressive economic relations and impacts on individual and group cohesion; anomie is observed to be the result of a breakdown of shared moral codes that can result in a feeling of normlessness.

Durkheim's work was the inspiration for **functionalist theory**, exemplified in the work of Merton, Parsons, Davis and Moore, among others. These sociologists tend to focus on consensus: how dramatic social change produces order and harmony, and how this emerges from interdependency (our reliance on one another). Functionalists consider:

- the functions that each social role, social institution and social norm plays in maintaining society
- the relationships between all the various parts of society.

These ideas are often presented as an analogy with the human body, which cannot function unless all the separate parts – heart, lungs, etc. – are working properly in connection with each other. Society is viewed in a similar way. Put simply, in order to function society needs families, education systems, healthcare systems, legal systems and many other institutions, and each part is connected and interdependent.

In some ways, this is similar to Marxism – as you have seen, the capitalist economic system needs political, familial and educational systems to maintain it. But there are two critical differences. First, in functionalism no individual societal part is more important than others (whereas in Marxism the economy is fundamental). Second, there is no direct critique of the functional relationship between the various parts of society: attention to power and inequality is therefore not central to functionalist theory. In some ways, functionalism can be seen as a 'feel-good' theory that lacks a critical edge. It has thus been critiqued for taking functions at face value and for not explaining their deeper roots and consequences. It has also been criticised for making a teleological mistake – that is, explaining phenomena in terms of the purpose they serve rather than the cause from which they arise.

Functionalist theories have lost considerable sociological support and are often not part of the curriculum at university. However, this does not mean that the insights afforded by Durkheimian theory are simply dead legacies. Durkheim was particularly interested in what held society together – the glue of social life, if you like. Therefore, sociologists who are interested in shared values and culture still find his work important. This is evident in the sociology of consumption. Consider, for example, the role of Christmas. It is a religious festival, but it is also a consumerist ritual – the exchange of gifts and the coming together of families stand as an important shared or communal experience that reinforces solidarity – a moment of what Durkheim called **collective effervescence**. Gabriel et al (2020) suggest that these Durkheimian concepts are still relevant today, pointing to the human need to live in groups and experience social connections.

Case Study: Durkheimian glasses and mental illness

Many scholars have used Durkheimian-inspired concepts to explain mental illness. A classic study by Brown and Harris (1978/2012), *Social Origins of Depression*, identified the social facts that explain why more working-class women suffer from depression than women of the middle or upper classes, drawing attention to the impact of stressful life events such as unemployment, poverty and lack of social support. This work was ground-breaking in its attention to the social causes of mental illness. Greenfeld (2013) similarly made a link between modernity and 'madness'. She described how the unfettered freedoms to follow personal ambitions, to forge our own identities, to become self-made, that characterise the contemporary period, also induce anomie. Indeed, she posited that limitless self-fulfilment is making millions of people desperately ill.

Max Weber and beyond

C is for contingency, complexity and construction of meaning

Max Weber (1864–1920), like Marx, was of Prussian descent, but his work is very different to both Marx and Durkheim. Indeed, much of his writing was produced as a reaction to Marx's ideas. Marx and Durkheim developed grand theories, with Marx focused on **conflict** between social classes and Durkheim on **consensus** and solidarity within society. Weber's work might be more accurately described as focusing on *contingency* and what he called **meaningful social action**. His approach was also more pessimistic and modest.

Max Weber

Weber believed that rather than looking at how societies shape individuals, sociologists should consider how individuals shape society. He shifted the focus to how individuals act and create social meanings (norms and values), which become shared and in turn, shape individual choices and actions. He is thus described as a micro sociologist. To study the social world, he argued that sociologists must develop an empathetic, **interpretivist** understanding of people in their social settings, using a technique he called **verstehen**. It is important to note that this does not mean Weber did not aspire to study the world objectively. On the contrary, he argued that sociologists have the capacity to step outside of social meanings and study them in a value-free way, without personal bias. He was interested in how meanings are constructed.

Weber also wanted to explain the change from feudal to modern society. His focus, however, was not on the changing structural economic conditions (Marx) or new forms of social organisation (Durkheim). Instead, he turned to the way that meaningful **social action** underpinned social change, and to do this he studied the association between the development of capitalism and religious ideas. Specifically, he argued that Calvinist Protestantism, a particular form of Christianity, emphasised a new ethic: the importance of hard work during mortal life that would lead to gains in the afterlife. Protestants were not capitalists themselves – in fact, they were not motivated by personal wealth, and invested any profits back into work. Capitalism, therefore, was an unintended consequence of this religious ethic.

The important point here is that Weber was less **deterministic** than Marx, who saw individual actions as the product of economic structures, and Durkheim, who regarded social meanings as objective social facts. Rather, Weber described change as the complex coming together of several factors – for example, he did not suggest that it was the Protestant ethic alone that caused the social and economic changes that resulted in capitalism. Therefore, Weber looked for complex relationships and focused on the way that individuals meaningfully go about their social lives. As such, he advocated a modest sociology that could produce models (**ideal types**) rather than a grand theory of what society looks like, that would enable sociologists to capture the complexity of social life. For example, when thinking about social class, he wanted to go beyond economic divisions (rich and poor) to also look at how social and political power produced more complex class divisions. Some parallels can be drawn here with Bourdieu's work, described above.

Weber was also more pessimistic than his fellow founders. Of course, Marx described capitalist society in negative terms, with alienation as an inevitable by-product, but he saw light at the end of the tunnel when capitalism would be overthrown. Likewise, Durkheim acknowledged that anomie existed in modern societies, but he also emphasised the consensual features of modernity, as societies were characterised by interdependence and organic solidarity. Weber, in contrast, did not regard the move to modernity as entirely positive, and he was not particularly optimistic about the future. He was concerned about the increased rules, policies and regulations that he saw as an inevitable and necessary consequence of modernity, describing an enveloping **iron cage of bureaucracy** that stifled and controlled human living. For Weber, bureaucracies and rationality became the dominant ways of organising social life which were inevitable but also disenchanting.

By disenchantment he meant that social life had lost its mystery and magic, and was increasingly impersonal and controlled. (See Chapter 4.)

One consequence of **bureaucracy** is that there is more paperwork to complete. What might be the advantages and disadvantages of having to engage in this sort of work?

Weber's ideas have been taken up in myriad ways. Here, we concentrate on three directions:

1   interpretive/social action sociology (and within this, **symbolic interactionism** and **ethnomethodology**)

2   **discursive power** and **surveillance**

3   **McDonaldization**.

1 Interpretive/social action sociology

Weber's work spawned many schools of thought within interpretive sociology. Two of these are symbolic interactionism and ethnomethodology.

Symbolic interactionism

Symbolic interactionism shifts our focus to the ways that individual actors make sense of their world, and how their own sense of self is produced by interacting with others and by working out how they are perceived by others. The word 'symbol' deliberately draws attention to the fact that humans interact with one another using both verbal and non-verbal forms of communication. Symbols are used to develop shared meaning. A facial expression can act as a symbol – for example, a frown may stand for, and be interpreted as, disapproval depending on how we have been socialised into the meaning and collective use of this symbol. We use both language and symbols to communicate and maintain interactions with others.

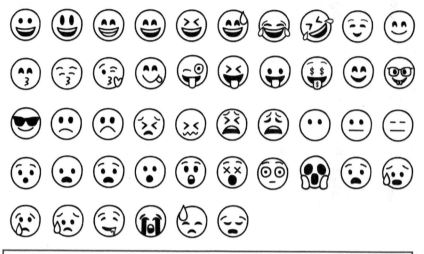

What emojis do you frequently use and what do these symbols attempt to convey?

Symbolic interactionists focus on how our understanding of self and others, and our characteristic ways of thinking, feeling and acting, are the products of socialisation. Socialisation is a lifelong process whereby we learn the shared customs, norms, values and rules of human interaction. Social interactionists therefore argue that social order is made and remade through everyday human interaction.

Putting on symbolic interactionist glasses shifts our focus to considering how our sense of self (who we 'are') is produced through our interactions with others. Who we think we are is based on how we believe other people perceive us. This theory saw the development of important concepts such as labelling, in the work of Becker (1973), for example. Labelling shows the power that other people's views can have on us. If we are labelled negatively, we often develop a negative view of ourselves; in this way, labels become a **self-fulfilling prophecy**. (In Chapter 4, you will see how the self-fulfilling prophecy operates within school settings.)

Erving Goffman, perhaps the most famous symbolic interactionist, also focused on everyday interactions and how these shape our sense of self (1959). He showed how human interaction is essentially a performance, and he used the term **dramaturgical** to capture this account of society. Drawing an analogy with the theatre, he said that in social life we have both backstage and front-stage personhoods.

The front stage is where we act out expected roles and manage how we appear to others. Backstage is where we are more relaxed. For example, think about the way you act at school, college or the workplace compared to when you are at home. At school or work you may dress smartly, speak more politely to others and present yourself more formally, while at home you may wear your pyjamas, speak in a more relaxed manner and generally act in ways that you may not if you were in the company of others – breaking wind, for instance! Goffman did not think that our 'selves' were shaped by our economic situation or other social structures, but instead said that the self was a social phenomenon that was *accomplished* through different social interactions.

This does not mean you can be whoever you want to be, though. While we put on different performances, they are shaped by humanly produced social rules that govern our interactions. This explains why we act in a different way on the front stage: social rules are more deeply felt when we are in the company of others.

Goffman also showed how the audience – the people around us – responds to the ways that we present ourselves. Sometimes the audience will endorse our performance, and sometimes they will be **stigmatising**, especially if our performance is deemed to be somehow different or even deviant. This can lead to what he called a **spoiled identity**. Goffman gave a number of examples of the ways that identities could be spoiled. For example, he spoke of how one's body shape or blemishes such as scarring can shape other people's interactions with us and in turn impact on our sense of self.

Ethnomethodology

Harold Garfinkel (1967) also focused on the ways that individuals interact with one another to create the social world. He coined the term 'ethnomethodology' to describe the study of how people (ethno) make (through the methods they use) social life.

Garfinkel deliberately unsettled social life through **breaching experiments** to reveal the methods that people use to create social order and shape interactions. For example, he asked his students to act as if they were a lodger in their own home, by being polite and offering to help. What he found was that students' family members were immediately perplexed by their actions, which went against their norms of family life. Family members then tried to make sense of the changed interaction, by asking the student if they were ill or upset, for example. Garfinkel's work revealed how we constantly make the world meaningful, but do not usually notice how much work we do to produce and reproduce social life.

Case Study: Weberian glasses and mental illness

Scholars who see the social world through a symbolic interactionist lens (influenced by Weber), examine where social meanings of normality and mental illness come from. They teach us that ideas of mental illness are socially defined and vary by historical and cultural context. For example, it used to be a sign of mental illness if a woman had a baby out of wedlock, and homosexuality was once diagnosed as a mental illness. These glasses require us to interrogate the social meanings behind our understanding of normality and **deviance** and, in this case, medical diagnoses.

There are several famous studies that explore these ideas. Rosenhan (1973) examined the real consequences of labelling when he sent his mentally well students to a medical facility, complaining of hearing voices. Once admitted to hospital, some of their 'normal' and 'rational' behaviours were interpreted as signs of mental illness by the hospital staff. One student said they wanted to leave and explained that they were there studying how mental hospitals were organised. They were diagnosed by the medical staff as delusional! Another student, making notes to record their experience, was diagnosed as suffering from 'writing behaviours'. Rosenhan showed how behaviour was made sense of in the context of the medical establishment and the labels of mental illness stuck. Goffman's study *Asylums* (1961) also illustrated the impact of being admitted to mental hospitals and being treated as a mental patient, arguing that patients undergo a 'mortification of the self'. Treated as children, they became like children.

2 Discursive power and surveillance

There are also some similarities between the work of Weber and that of the French theorist Michel Foucault, which are especially useful to those new to sociology. It is not accurate to say that Foucault was *inspired* by Weber, but he and Weber were both influenced by the French philosopher Friedrich Nietzsche, so it is worth briefly exploring Foucault's ideas here. (There is more on Foucault's work in Chapters 4 and 5.)

Foucault is often described as a historian of ideas, and while he did not consider himself a sociologist, his work has been hugely influential for sociology. He explained how society changes over time, and how the norms and assumptions that help us make sense of our world are humanly constructed.

Michel Foucault

Foucault was particularly interested in social order and control. Importantly, he argued that power was not something held only by the government or state, but that it was diffused, from the bottom up, through all social relationships. Thus, rather than locating power in institutions headed up by powerful elites, Foucault said that power operated through dominant forms of knowledges produced in society, which he called **discourses**. When a discourse or a way of knowing becomes dominant it is said to be powerful, as it governs people's conduct. This dominant discourse cannot be traced back to a particular group that holds power over it. Instead, discourses become dominant but can be adopted or contested by all people. Psychiatric knowledge is an example of a dominant discourse that explains the causes and consequences of mental illness. In particular, psychiatry emphasises bio-chemical causes of mental illness. However, there are other competing discourses that explain mental illness using very different ideas. For example, sociological knowledge would look to explain the social causes of mental illness.

Discursive power emerged in what Foucault called **disciplinary societies** during the 18th century in the Global North. His work *Discipline and Punish* (1975) outlines how these new disciplinary societies governed social life differently. No longer was it entirely necessary (or possible) to wield power over people to get them to conform to the social order. Instead, people would increasingly internalise social norms and subject themselves to their own surveillance practices.

Foucault's work on surveillance was influenced by philosopher Jeremy Bentham's diagram of the **panopticon** – a metaphor for how society is governed.

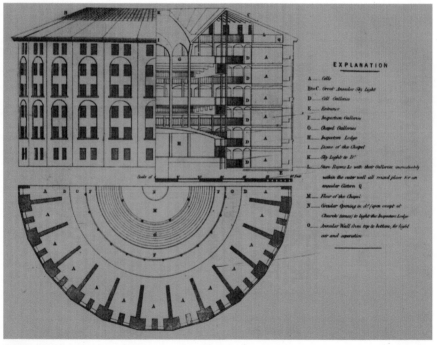

Jeremy Bentham's panopticon

The panopticon was a circular prison with a central observation tower and cells around the outside that faced inwards. From the tower shone a bright light, so that if you were standing in the tower you could see into each prisoner's cell. The prisoners, by contrast, knew they were on display but could not see into the tower because of the bright light. They never knew if they were being watched or not, as they could not see whether a guard was present. The idea was that prisoners would modify their behaviour because they believed they may always be under surveillance – creating a form of **self-surveillance**. This is where links to Weber can be seen. Where Weber described the creeping advance of bureaucracy, Foucault described the endless ways in which contemporary citizens are surveilled and increasingly engage in self-surveillance.

3 McDonaldization

George Ritzer's (2013) work on the McDonaldization of society also revealed the continued relevance of Weber's work, particularly his concepts of bureaucracy and rationality.

Ritzer argued that the principles of fast-food chains like McDonalds, characterised by efficiency, calculation, predictability and control, dominate the globe. Consider how specialised they are – you can go to McDonalds or Burger King for your burgers, to Dominoes for your pizza, to KFC for chicken. Ingredients are pre-prepared, and meals are produced on an assembly line. Fast food is a useful metaphor for explaining how many elements of society have become rationalised, developed for efficiency and profit, with high levels of rules and regulations at the expense of degrees of freedom and creativity.

What other examples can you think of that illustrate McDonaldization, other than food? For instance, Ritzer (2002) suggested that the university system is McDonaldized in four ways:

- It must be efficient by successfully ensuring students pass through it seamlessly.
- It must be predictable by becoming increasingly standardised in terms of modules and credit offerings.
- It must be calculable by introducing performance measures that can evaluate its success compared to other universities.
- It must be controlling by ensuring its staff go through appraisals and meet new training standards and regulations.

W.E.B Du Bois and beyond

C is for colour, colonialism and raCism

William Edward Burghardt Du Bois (1868–1963), a contemporary of Marx, Durkheim and Weber, should be given his rightful place as a founding father of sociology, and credited with drawing attention to the pervasive reality of racial inequality, segregation and discrimination. Du Bois argued that the 'most significant problem of the 20th century is the colour line' (1903/1968:1) and as such, this was the proper subject matter for sociology.

William Edward Burghardt Du Bois

In *The Philadelphia Negro* (1899), Du Bois described an in-depth study of the lives of African Americans based on census data and over 2,500 in-person interviews. At this point in time, although slavery had been officially abolished in 1865, American society remained highly segregated. A number of laws were passed in the 1890s that established separate drinking fountains, bathrooms, restaurants, hotels, trains, beaches, parks and theatres along the colour line. Du Bois drew attention to continued structural racism and focused on revealing the racial inequalities produced through capitalism, showing how racism served the interests of the (White) capitalist class. Racism permitted both extreme exploitation and prevented radical social change, he argued. He called for African Americans to develop a **double consciousness** – to see themselves as ordinary people, members of families and communities, but also to be aware of the way that they were seen through the eyes of White people, who viewed them as inferior.

A segregated water-cooler in Oklahoma, USA, 1939

Du Bois campaigned against racism and **cultural assimilation**, demanding equal rights and championing the cultural achievements of people of African descent. It is therefore astonishing that his work has taken so long to be considered central to the sociological canon.

This speaks to the enduring legacy of racism, even within sociology as a discipline, and underscores a need for the decolonisation of the curriculum (see Chapters 5 and 6).

Du Bois' work needs to be read alongside the work of many other Black scholars. For instance, in his famous work *The Black Jacobins* (1938), C.L.R. James (1901–89) documented the slave revolution in Haiti (1791–1804), showing that this was as important as the 1789 French and 1776 American revolutions for understanding the rise of modernity. It would be very easy to infer from history books that the Global North was responsible for the rise of liberty and equality. However, these writers reveal the silencing of non-European and non-Anglo American histories and knowledges. Indeed, as Bhambra (2007) states, the Haitian revolution was more radical in bringing about equality and rights than either the French or the American revolution, both of which continued to disenfranchise large swathes of the population.

Frantz Fanon (1925–61) extended the concept of double consciousness in *The Wretched of the Earth* (1961/2007), showing how Black people in White-dominated societies have to 'perform whiteness' to be able to live in the world, which prevents the possibility of ever knowing oneself. He thus showed the importance of reworking sociological concepts so that they could speak to the experiences of all people. For instance, as Meghji (2021) outlines, he argued that while the Marxist concept of alienation could provide insights into the impact of capitalism on the working classes in the Global North, it did not capture the experience of alienation that emanates from colonialism and the oppression of Black peoples.

Frantz Fanon

Fanon was referring to the ways in which Black people internalise knowing themselves as 'other', as a 'sub-species' existing in a 'zone of non-being', distinct from White people. The internalisation of these self-definitions, Fanon argued, alienated Black people from themselves. The feelings of stigmatisation and judgment by White standards mean never being able to know or feel oneself except in terms of the imposed categories of selfhood that derive from colonialism and define Black people as subordinate and 'other'.

Understanding the causes and consequences of racial and ethnic differences remains central to the sociological project. Sociologists show how 'race' remains a powerful construct for organising social relations. Importantly, it also establishes that race is not a fixed biological category but a **social construct**. The idea that we can be neatly divided into distinct human 'races' is a product of social processes of categorisation, rather than a reflection of natural and biological differences between people. (In Chapter 4, you will see that there is no scientific evidence for significant biological differences across 'races'.) However, the idea of biological and racial difference has a long and dangerous history: it supported the racism that permitted enslavement and the Holocaust, for example, and continues to explain contemporary examples of differential and oppressive treatment.

This way of thinking has been developed by several important writers. We cannot do justice to their work in this introduction, but one illustration is Edward Said's (1978) work, *Orientalism*. This describes how the telling of history reflects colonial interests, producing a binary between the East and the West, between the Orient and the Occident. The East, Said argued, is exoticised, and is depicted in derogatory terms that exaggerate differences, while the West is depicted as culturally superior. Said's work highlights the importance of interrogating history and the way it is told. This is a lesson that needs to be applied to sociological theory, too.

Edward Said

Importantly, sociological work in this area has explored three key areas. Firstly, it has interrogated the concept of race to show that it is a socially constructed idea. In this way, sociological studies have helped develop a more widespread use of the concept of ethnicity to understand social diversity, while also alerting us to its own inherent dangers (see Chapter 4 for more on this).

Secondly, sociological work has shown how racism comes in many forms but, importantly, endures. Sociology teaches us that racism is not simply a set of ideas held by individuals, but is located within and generated by societies. From the late-17th century through to the Second World War, there were dishonourable attempts to establish biological differences between races. This form of scientific racism has been discredited now, but racism did not disappear with it. The latter part of the 20th century saw the rise of cultural racism, in which some cultural practices and beliefs are judged and stigmatised. Some sociological **cultural deprivation** theories have been criticised for reproducing this type of thinking. For example, these deprivation theories tend to blame doing less well at school or having poorer health on the values and lifestyles of some groups. Sociology has also named and documented institutional racism – a form of racism that is much harder to see, but which occurs in the practices, rules and decisions made within organisations such as schools, the police, banks and health services. All these different forms of racism reinforce the more visible and lived everyday racism that minority groups continue to experience.

Thirdly, sociological studies have explored how race and ethnicity intersect with gender and class. This idea is explored in more detail in the next section and in Chapter 4.

Case Study: Critical race glasses and mental illness

Sociology demands that we document, understand and question the ways that racism shapes people's lives. Important sociological work, for instance, charts the link between racism and mental illness (Littlewood and Lipsedge, 1997 and Fernando, 2010). This has a long history. For example, enslaved people who attempted to escape from their 'owners' were diagnosed with a mental illness called drapetomania – their desire to flee was explained by their individual mental fragility rather than the terrible conditions in which they were held. Nazroo et al (2020) showed how structural, institutional and interpersonal racism continue to explain why more minority ethnic people are diagnosed with mental illness than the White majority in the UK today. They draw on evidence to show that minority ethnic groups are economically disadvantaged, subject to interpersonal racism in their everyday lives, and experience prejudice in the health service, leading to over-representation in the mental health system and the potential over-diagnosis of mental illness by psychiatrists. These particular glasses focus on the multiple ways that racism underscores the experience of mental illness.

Mary Wollstonecraft and beyond

C is for cages, constraint and patriarChy

In this section, we begin with the work of Mary Wollstonecraft (1759–97), a writer regarded as one of the first feminists. Within the broad church of feminism there are, however, many iterations, and it is better to talk of *feminisms*. What joins most of the work is a concern to understand gender divisions within society, and the powerful and enduring differences that characterise men's and women's lives. Feminists are especially interested in how the social structure of patriarchy shapes social experiences and this is deemed to be the proper subject matter of sociology.

Mary Wollstonecraft

Feminist writers make an important distinction between **sex** and gender and this continues to be useful. Sex refers to the biological traits that society associates with being male or female, while gender refers to the *learned ways* of being male or female. Historically, feminists have tended to focus on the concept of gender rather than sex. More recently, however, the simplicity of this binary has been questioned, and towards the end of this section we look at some of the contemporary ways that sex has also been viewed as a social category, and how transgender has been conceptualised and studied. Finally, because feminism mainly concentrates on the experiences of women, we close this section with a short focus on men's studies and masculinity.

It is sometimes helpful to think about various feminist theories according to when they were written. You may read about 'waves' of feminism (first, second, third and now fourth), but it is important to remember that there are still differences within each wave.

Mary Wollstonecraft is an example of a writer and scholar in the first wave of feminism (**liberal feminism**). In her book *A Vindication of the Rights of Women* (1792), she described the impact of the Industrial Revolution on the lives of middle-class women in the Global North, including herself, where she detailed her passive social role. While she oversaw the running of the household and her servants she, like many of her peers, felt under-stimulated. Wollstonecraft described herself as a 'caged bird' (hence the 'c' concept, 'cages'). She championed the importance of education for women, at least so that they could be more interesting company for their husbands! She wrote from a liberal tradition, focused on securing *equal rights* to education.

These liberal ideas were developed later by Harriet Taylor (1807–58) and John Stuart Mill (1806–73) who, together and separately (they were married), championed the idea of equal opportunities and rights, extending beyond education to include paid work, voting rights and economic independence – the right to remain husbandless, for instance. It is worth remembering that at the time they were writing, women did not have many rights: they were effectively owned by their father or husband, and had few property or familial rights (they did not even have legal rights over their own children).

It is here that we begin to see a critique of the role of marriage for women, which was often associated with powerlessness. Marianne Weber (Max Weber's wife, who certainly contributed to some of the work published in her husband's name) described the restrictive ways in which married women's lives were shaped. Most feminist writers at this time described the confinement that women experienced, and called for economic and political change that would liberate them. However, these writers were middle class and the experiences of their working-class contemporaries were quite different – often working long hours in factories – and their stories remained largely unwritten.

British first wave feminists were also White, and did not concern themselves with the way that 'race' intersected with gender. In fact, many feminists of this period held racist ideas. Charlotte Perkins Gilman (1860–1935) critiqued the traps that held White women, but she did not see a problem with making the 'black race' undertake forced labour. And Marie Stopes (1880–58), often celebrated for her contribution to the development of contraception – a liberating intervention for many women – was also involved in the **eugenics** movement, encouraging the deliberate restriction of reproduction among certain classes and races of women.

In America, the way that race and gender interacted was more carefully explored. Sojourner Truth (1851/2020) campaigned against enslavement and championed women's rights. Her famous speech 'Ain't I a woman?' demanded equal human rights for all women as well as for all Black people. Ann Julia Cooper (1858–1964) is another early Black feminist. In her treatise *A Voice from the South* (1892/1988), she called for the right to education and challenged the representations of African American people in many popular texts.

Sojourner Truth

If first wave feminism demanded equal rights, second wave feminism developed these ideas and demanded a more radical rethinking of gender differences. This next iteration of feminisms emerged from the 1960s. Some writers continued to focus their demands within the liberal tradition, campaigning for equal pay, equality in the law, maternity pay, etc. For example, Betty Friedan (1963) blamed unfulfilled lives for the high numbers of women with mental health problems, and called for men to share the burden of domestic and parenting responsibilities.

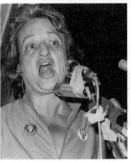

Betty Friedan

> Why do you think Betty Friedan described housework as 'unfulfilling'?

While Friedan's work described the domestic experiences of women, **radical feminists** and **Marxist feminists** began to ask *why* women's lives remained so constrained. They found their answer in the often-hidden structure of patriarchy – a universal system whereby men dominate women and where male interests trump those of women, and which, for Marxist feminists such as Heidi Hartmann (1979), supports capitalism. Here, the focus was on the combined influence of patriarchy and capitalism. Hartmann explains that women's domestic labour does a huge amount to support the workforce but is regarded as less significant than paid labour. Moreover, strong patriarchal ideologies meant that women in employment were also paid less than men, as their contribution was deemed to be less important.

There were so many women writing during this second wave of feminism that we cannot do justice to the breadth and depth of their enquiries. Collectively, they have drawn attention to the many ways – both overt and hidden – that patriarchy works in areas such as education (women are historically less likely to go onto higher education), work (women are paid less and more likely to work part time), in the home (including taking on not only the burden of housework, but also the brunt of domestic violence), through motherhood, pregnancy, and cultural ideas of femininity that socialise women into being more submissive and less questioning. As a starting point for finding out more, it is worth exploring the works of Simone de Beauvoir, Kate Millett, Mary Daly, Andrea Dworkin, Sylvia Walby and Germaine Greer.

Case Study: Second wave feminist glasses and mental illness

More women are diagnosed with mental health issues than men. Ground-breaking work was written in this area by feminist Jane Ussher. In her book *Women's Madness: Misogyny or Mental illness?* (1991), she argued that women are more likely to be labelled as 'mad'. Elaine Showalter's feminist glasses (1985) also brought into focus the role that patriarchy plays in explaining differential rates of mental illness by gender. She described how cultural ideas about 'proper' feminine behaviour have resulted in more women being defined as mentally ill, especially if they challenge these norms. Joan Busfield (1988) documented not only how women's lives are inherently stressful because of the demands of female gender roles and their unequal social status, but also how women are more likely to be labelled as mentally ill by a patriarchal psychiatric profession.

This rich body of work has undoubtedly brought unparalleled insights and has instigated much progressive change. However, second wave feminism was, like the first wave, predominantly written by White middle-class women, and this perspective only enabled them to see part of the 'elephant'.

Third and fourth wave feminisms have, in various forms, attempted to respond to some of these limitations. While there are numerous feminist schools in these waves, here we explore two examples: **intersectionality** and **transgenderism**.

Intersectionality

Black feminism sought a more nuanced understanding of the way that gender intersects with other axes of discrimination. The concept of intersectionality comes from the work of a feminist called Kimberlé Crenshaw (1991), who recognised a theoretical gap in feminism that could not specifically account for Black women's and Black men's experiences.

Kimberlé Crenshaw

Feminism needed to acknowledge how women's lives were also shaped by racism and classism, and how these structural positions of disadvantage deepen and reinforce inequality. Crenshaw, amongst others, showed how many feminists had not appreciated how racism compounded some women's experiences. For example, second wave feminism had campaigned for sexual liberation and the right to abortion and contraception, but this did not speak to the experiences of Black women who were forced to take long-term contraception. Racist stereotypes have been shown to be entrenched in medical decision-making. Black Caribbean women, in particular, were assumed to be unable to be trusted to take contraception and so were disproportionately prescribed the contraception Depro-Provera (Lambert, 2019). The work of feminists including bell hooks, Patricia Hill Collins and Angela Davis showcased the importance of moving beyond a simple male–female divide, towards recognising differences between women, rather than assuming sameness.

Transgenderism

Feminism has also considered how to respond to other forms of experience, such as the experiences of trans women. Just as we speak of various feminisms, it is important to recognise that trans experiences are not homogeneous.

The ways in which sex and gender are discussed depends on the perspective sociologists take – the 'glasses' they put on. For example, second wave feminists distinguished between sex and gender, and focused on the way that gender was socially constructed. Likewise, in her work *Gender Trouble: Feminism and the Subversion of Identity* (1990), Butler argued that gender is not predetermined but that it is performed. This means that gender is something that is learned and is acted out according to dominant cultural norms. She thus argued that woman is made (not born) out of a female body. Other feminists turned their attention to the question of biological sex, claiming that it, too, was socially constructed. Anne Fausto Sterling, for example, says that humans' bodies are too complex to clearly differentiate between sexes:

> The more we look for a simple physical basis for 'sex', the more it becomes clear that 'sex' is not a pure physical category. What bodily signals and functions we define as male or female come already entangled in our ideas about gender. (2000:4)

Transgender unsettles the connection between sex and gender again. Transgender means different things to different people. For some people it means that one has been born into the wrong body. This position holds that gender is innate and that one's gender identity, expression or behaviour may not conform to the gender that is typically associated with one's assigned sex at birth. From this perspective, being 'male' or 'female' is not a product of socialisation but is an essential identity. For others, transgendering is about having a fluid relationship with one's gender and choosing to move between pre-existing gender categories, and for others still, it is about radically challenging and moving beyond the pre-existing gender categories themselves (Ekins and King, 1999).

There is a group of feminists coming from the radical feminist tradition who have questioned the identification of trans women as women. They have sometimes been called TERFs (trans-exclusionary radical feminists). They regard biological sex as defining men and women, and have raised concerns about transwomen stepping into female-only spaces such as women's sport or refuges (e.g. Greer, 1994). Other feminists actively challenge this position, arguing that it not only reinforces a biologically essentialist assumption that sex is innate, but that it also does not respect the equality and dignity of trans people (Hines, 2019). As always, sociology aims to develop a careful and considered analysis.

There are many contrasting positions, but each reveals different dimensions of the lived experience of 'being a woman'. What it means to 'be a woman' is contingent upon how we define both sex and gender, and who is doing the defining. This is why there is a whole range of feminisms. Sociologists do not yet know all the possible social meanings of gender or sex, so new 'glasses' may be required to make sense of these concepts.

Recent sociological work has investigated transgender people's experiences. For example, Sumerau (2020) shows how **cisnormativity** – the assumption that all humans have a gender that matches the biological sex they were born with – is another form of discrimination: it excludes people who believe their gender to be different to that of their sex. Sociology is also involved in developing concepts and theories that speak to the experiences of people who classify as **non-binary** (not falling into one gender category or another).

Just as some forms of feminism argue that gender is socially constructed, **queer theory** examines how sexual identities are also socially, culturally and historically defined. Drawing on the work of Judith Butler, for instance, queer theorists question the ways in which our sexual lives are restricted by normative assumptions and attitudes. This theoretical frame focuses on being inclusive of bisexual, lesbian, gay, trans, pan and asexual people, those that cross-dress and those who are **intersex**. Queer theory examines identity, experience, power and discrimination. As Adam Green explains:

> Sociologists have been challenged to sharpen their analytical lenses, to grow sensitized to the discursive production of sexual identities, and to be mindful of the insidious force of **heteronormativity** as a fundamental organizing principle throughout the social order. (2002:521)

What about men?

Feminism's focus on women has also created the space for sociologists to critically engage with questions of male gender and the ways in which men's lives are also constrained. A key writer in this tradition is Raewyn Connell (2005), who described the cultural dominance of **hegemonic masculinity**. While she recognised that men generally dominate women, she argued that such a reading is too simplistic. Connell described the multiple ways that masculinity can be expressed and is hierarchically judged. She drew attention to a **gender order** that has an impact on both men and women. For instance, men that do not fulfil the expectations of hegemonic masculinity – authority, aggression, strength, heterosexuality – also find themselves stigmatised, **marginalised** and subordinated. Likewise, Connell described the way that women conform to prescribed ideals of **exaggerated (emphasised)**

femininity – emotional, passive, fragile and heterosexual – and find themselves in positions of subordination to those men fulfilling hegemonic masculine expectations.

A scantily clad boxing ring girl holds a board with the round number during a WBO Intercontinental Cruiserweight Title fight. The male boxer has passed out behind her.

The photograph here provides one example of hegemonic masculinity and emphasised femininity as expressed through sport. What other examples can you think of where society reproduces hegemonic masculine and exaggerated feminine ideals?

Modernity and beyond: post, late and liquid modernity, and the rise of individualisation and neoliberalism

One issue that we have not tackled yet in this chapter is recent societal change. If sociology was born to make sense of the changes from feudal to industrial society, what happens when further significant social changes occur? Sociology is a fundamentally adaptive discipline – it must keep pace as society evolves. Sociologists have argued that 'modernity' is no longer a relevant concept for describing the type of society we live in today, and have given this new 'era' a new set of descriptors. In this chapter, we introduce you to *some* of these theories and ideas. We will cover 'postmodernity', 'late or reflexive modernity', 'liquid modernity', 'individualisation and neoliberalism'.

Postmodernity

Theorists of postmodernity suggest that we have moved beyond modernity and are living in an entirely different social world. Postmodernity is defined by three key characteristics:

- a critique of **metanarratives** – particularly of science, technology and religion

- technological changes that bring about different versions of 'reality'
- new and changing personal identities.

First, Jean-François Lyotard (1984) defines postmodernism as the 'incredulity towards metanarratives'. By this he means that people are losing faith in grand stories about society that claim to be universal and enduring truths. The religious truth that characterised pre-modernity was replaced by scientific and technological truths in modernity. However, in postmodernity, people's once-unshakeable faith in scientific and technological truths that promised new and better worlds has been shaken. The world has witnessed the hazards created by science – its negative impact on the environment, and the use of technology to enact wars on other humans and the planet.

Second, postmodern theorists show that one reason people are exposed to many more competing truths and ways of living is because technology has developed and expanded across the globe. Television, satellite, the internet and now social media, have all made it possible for people to be connected to one another across time and space.

Jean Baudrillard (1983) argued that people are bombarded with media images that produce a **hyperreality** – a state in which individuals find it hard to differentiate between what is real and what is imaginary. Baudrillard uses the term 'simulacrum' to describe the way that simulations (different representations) of reality emerge, after which our worlds become distorted. He identified the effect that television has on individuals (we might now extend this to the internet and social media), pointing out, for example, that people are likely to know more about a doctor in a fictional medical drama on television than they know about their own doctor.

Reality is presented in so many ways and through so many different channels that it is hard to determine which representations are real and which are not. The concept of 'fake news' highlights this very point – so many different versions of news stories are put into the public domain by so many different people, with so many varying perspectives, that when exposed to them all, it is hard to know what is real and what is not. People may conclude that there is no 'truth', only *depictions* of truth from different perspectives.

Third, the diverse images and truths we are bombarded with also impact on our identities. Where modern identity was something relatively fixed by social position – class, gender, age or ethnicity – postmodern identity is described as far more fluid. Postmodernists argue that individuals have greater capacity to create their own identities, and indeed to have multiple (sometimes even contradictory) versions of themselves.

What different identities do you have? Consider how you present yourself online in different ways. Do you have a different 'gaming' identity if you play online video games to your identity at home, for example? Do you present yourself differently on different social media platforms?

Late (or reflexive) modernity

Anthony Giddens (1992/2013a; 1992/2013b) states that in fact we have not entered into a new era, but rather that we are living in an exaggerated state of modernity, where the true consequences of modernity have been realised. He outlines four key features of late (reflexive) modernity:

- **globalisation**
- surveillance
- risk
- **ontological insecurity** and **reflexivity**.

Giddens' work is supported by Ulrich Beck (1992), who used a different term – **risk society**.

Anthony Giddens

Globalisation

Globalisation is often spoken of as a feature of recent times. It has a long history, but while humans have always travelled, the world is more connected today than ever before and, as a consequence, people are increasingly interdependent. Giddens describes globalisation rather grandly as 'time-space distanciation', to capture the idea that our social lives are no longer constrained by living in different places and time zones (think how easy it is to chat to a friend or relative on the other side of the planet). The world is a smaller place.

We live in a global economy and marketplace, connected through a global financial system. Huge multinational organisations such as Google, Facebook, Coca Cola and McDonalds cross national borders. Some describe this as a process of 'westernisation' rather than globalisation. It may even be considered a form of **consumer colonialism**. We are connected by the internet, international news media, by social media and our mobile phone networks. Indeed, Castells (2011) describes the contemporary era as a 'network society'. The digitisation of our social networks has transformed social relations. Today nearly two-thirds of the world's population have a mobile phone.

As Giddens points out, though, this does not mean that all people have the same experiences and benefit from global exchange, as you saw from the example of the fashion industry in Chapter 1, where fast fashion in the West relies on low-paid (often child) labour in other parts of the world.

Surveillance

The concept of surveillance is central to Foucault's work (see page 37). Giddens also draws attention to the fact that surveillance has rapidly increased and has penetrated all aspects of people's lives in **late modernity**. For example, the British Security Industry Authority (BSIA, 2017) estimated that there are 5.9 million surveillance cameras in the UK. That is one camera for every 11 people.

Another example is mobile phones. These enable you to surveil others, but also subject you to endless surveillance. When you 'check in' to different locations, anyone in your network can see where you are (and also where you are not). Granting apps such as Facebook or Instagram access to your phone allows intelligence agencies to collect your data. When you grant an app access to your camera and microphone, it may access the front and back camera and can record you when the app is in the foreground.

> How else are we watched? In what other ways do we watch each other? Has surveillance become normalised? For example, consider how reality television shows such as *Big Brother*, *Love Island* and *Gogglebox* put everyday lives on display for others to see.

Risk

The concept of risk is also central to theories of late modernity. Of course, human beings have always had to respond to risks – the risk of flooding or drought or plagues, for instance. These risks have always had a disproportionate impact on poorer populations, which cannot afford to insure themselves against the potential damage such risks might cause.

But for Giddens and Beck, risk takes on a new form as modernity progresses. Rather than being in a stronger position to identify, predict and protect ourselves against risks, our modern ways of living actually generate new risks. For example, we trust science to protect us from the risks of disease and hunger, but the very solutions that science generates (e.g. drugs and mass food production) produce new, unintended risks, such as the side-effects of drugs, pollution, global warming, overproduction and waste. Now risks are human-made and far-reaching, and it is much more difficult to protect ourselves from them. In turn, people increasingly question science and trust scientists less. There is a connection here with what Lyotard called the 'collapse of the metanarrative'. However, for Giddens and others, the response cannot be a rejection of science, because this is all we've got. People must continue to put their faith in experts.

This leaves us living in a contradictory age, one where science is often the source of new social problems, but still remains the solution. For example, we now know the risks to our environment of burning fossil fuels. Therefore, we look to science to offer an alternative – fracking or wind turbines or solar farms, perhaps. But each of these alternatives brings its own risks and consequences, which we need to address.

Ontological insecurity and reflexivity

According to Giddens, another key feature of late modernity is the diverse opportunities open to us – far more than in previous generations. We are no longer required to follow a 'script' for our life assigned to us based on gender or family ties, for example. With the decline in religious belief, the change in traditional family structures and new gender roles we can see that individuals have far more freedom to choose who they want to be and what they want to do in life. Elliott (2013) regarded this as a promise of reinvention: we can endlessly reconstruct and reinvent ourselves. Cosmetic surgery, fashion choices, therapeutic sessions, diets and dating, even new digital enhancements to the self are possible!

Reinvention requires deep self-examination – what Giddens calls 'reflexivity'. On the one hand, reflexivity enables us to make choices, but on the other hand, it can be deeply unsettling. When presented with so many options in all areas of life, from what we study at school, to what career we choose, to who we date, we may start to question the choices we make and the ways that our lives turn out. Should I go to university? Should I take a gap year? Should I stay with this partner or try someone else? Would there be something better around the corner if I made a different choice? This endless questioning situates us in a state of what Giddens calls 'ontological insecurity' (see Chapter 4 for more on this).

Liquid modernity

Bauman's (2013) discussion of **liquid modernity** is similar to Giddens' idea that modernity provides us with multiple choices that grant us many opportunities as well as challenges. He deliberately uses the term 'liquid' to emphasise the lack of solid foundations in life. In the early stages of modernity, people believed in such solid foundations (human rationality, the predictability of life, scientific progress), but they have now been shown to be imaginary. Bauman describes how people are now not so strongly confined by social norms, but instead have far more choices available to them. He refers to this as a state

Zygmunt Bauman

of enhanced **individualisation**. There is greater fluidity and complexity to life, but also incredible uncertainty.

Bauman illustrates individualisation by examining the way that interpersonal/romantic relationships change. He demonstrates that we now expect to achieve two, sometimes conflicting, outcomes from our relationships:

- We have individual desires and a need for freedom, so we want our relationships to be 'loose' so that we can have space from our partner if and when we desire; in this respect we want to still be able to express ourselves as an individual who is separate from our partner.
- We also seek security in relationships in an uncertain and changing world.

Therefore, Bauman describes new relationship formations as inherently unstable. He describes 'liquid modern' relationships as 'semi-detached' and 'top pocket'. By this, he means that we engage with our partner when it suits us, and we want to be able to break away from the relationship whenever we choose. He compares attitudes to relationships to the blackcurrant squash Ribena, which is undrinkable in a concentrated form and is only palatable when diluted. In simple terms, his argument is that relationships are much more expendable and not as deep as they were in the past.

Individualisation and neoliberalism

While Bauman introduces the idea of individualisation and its consequences for relationships, the implications are much wider-reaching. Sociologists have explored the way that individualisation is part of a wider ideology of **neoliberalism.**

Neoliberalism is generally acknowledged to have emerged in the 1980s under the political administrations of Margaret Thatcher in the UK and Ronald Reagan in the USA. This is a political position that puts responsibility onto the individual and rolls back state support, emphasising competition, free trade and the private sector. The neoliberal ideology requires that individuals become competitive, self-interested consumers, who act independently from one another.

In this regard, neoliberalism requires and cultivates individualisation: we are encouraged to become individual subjects who are responsible for ourselves and who do not obligate or burden others or the state. It also requires us to believe that we are acting freely as individuals. However, because neoliberalism is an ideology, individualisation can never be seen as a choice.

Case Study: Neoliberal individualisation, the gig economy and mental illness

Late modernity is characterised by rapid social change, technological development, increased risk, less job security and ontological insecurity. These social conditions are fostered by the political ideology of neoliberalism, which requires us to be individual economic actors. The neoliberal economy aims to reduce public spending. In doing so, it encourages people to take responsibility for themselves and their own wellbeing and welfare. This ideology can be seen operating in the field of employment.

One result of neoliberal capitalism is the emergence of the gig economy, characterised by temporary and freelance jobs, where working hours are never guaranteed. While some types of work have always had these characteristics – musicians, for instance, often only get paid when they get a 'gig' – it has, since the 1990s, come to define the reality of many workers' employment. Uber, Deliveroo and Amazon delivery services are all part of the gig economy. There has been an explosion in gig economy jobs, with the UK government's Department for Business, Energy and Industrial Strategy (2018) estimating that 4.4% of the population (about 2.8 million people) undertake this type of work, and that numbers are growing.

MacDonald and Giazitzoglu (2019) note that the gig economy follows on from earlier forms of entrepreneurial work. People find such work attractive because, on the face of it, they can work on their own terms and for as many hours as they like. However, in reality, the gig economy often exploits the most economically vulnerable members of society.

(The 2019 film *Sorry We Missed You*, directed by Ken Loach, vividly depicts a character caught up in this economy.) People turn to the gig economy to gain financial independence but instead often find themselves struggling to make money on zero-hours contracts or over-working to make ends meet.

The gig economy has three defining impacts:

- It isolates workers from one another by placing them in direct competition.
- People constantly strive to beat their peers to get more work, causing the job to creep into all areas of personal life – the phone is always on in case more work becomes available.
- It alienates people from their work, so they eventually find that it lacks meaning.

These examples show how people's lives in the gig economy become more precarious, and how it can have a significant impact on mental health and wellbeing. There are no pensions or employment benefits in the gig economy, which contributes to a sense of insecurity. Insecurity can result in a feeling of meaninglessness as well as a permanent state of risk and anxiety about getting work and securing an income.

Gregory (2020) undertook interviews with 25 couriers working in the gig economy, and revealed how uncertainty characterised their work and home lives. One of the couriers stated: 'This is not worth it. My life is more valuable than this.' (2020:7) The interviewee continues by talking about how she would deliver to customers on her bike in strong winds, which she regards as dangerous work. However, she also noted: 'My safety is my responsibility; I cannot put that on Deliveroo. I make a choice whether I go out or not. I don't get paid for it if I don't go and it can be very tempting to choose to go when it's really not safe.' This demonstrates an internalised neoliberal mentality – the idea that we are each supposed to be responsible for our own physical and mental health, and shows that the gig economy actively instils this in people by making those working in precarious positions take even greater health risks out of financial necessity. Indeed, research at the London School of Economics (Mousteri et al, 2020) suggests a marked rise in mental illness as a result of the rise of the gig economy.

Summary

This is an enormous chapter, in which we have only scratched the surface of sociological theory. Nonetheless, we hope that you can see the value of having multiple 'pairs of glasses' through which to view the world and the different questions and explanations each affords. We expect that you will want to keep revisiting this chapter as you become more confident, and as you become steadily more fluent. We, too, still revisit theories that we know well, as you can always see new ways of using and applying the concepts.

Sociological how-tos

To be a sociologist you must:

- try on lots of pairs of sociological glasses
- learn the conceptual definitions
- practise using the concepts
- be aware that all theories are inevitably partial and are socially produced
- be aware of the insights and limitations of the theories that you use.

CHAPTER 3
BE RIGOROUS: EXPLORING THE SOCIOLOGICAL TOOLKIT

Sociology students typically start to nod off at the mention of research methods. Methods are often regarded as dry and tedious – the part you want to get out of the way so you can move on to the more interesting stuff. In this chapter, we aim to prove not only that a good understanding of research methods is essential to becoming a successful sociologist, but also that studying these methods can be exciting.

Methods provide an evidence base for the discipline: they separate a sociologist from a layperson, a journalist, a politician, a painter, a novelist or a poet. Sociologists are not the only people interested in social life, but they study it differently.

Sociology is an applied and **empirical** discipline. Research methods are the sociologist's toolkit, enabling them to go out into the social world to study it and gather information. Sociologists study humans by observing, assessing, questioning and interrogating the very things that non-sociologists take for granted. To do this, sociologists carefully choose which research methods to use to generate knowledge about social phenomena – in this respect they are *rigorous*.

As you discovered in Chapter 2, sociologists have a wide range of theoretical 'glasses' at their disposal, each of which reveals a different dimension of the social world and requires that different questions are asked and explored. As such, sociologists often need different research tools. At a very basic level, it is possible to identify four approaches to sociological research: **positivism**, interpretivism, **realism** and **constructionism**.

Sociologists that follow Durkheim are interested in studying social facts, and are committed to positivism. These sociologists want to study the social world as objectively as possible. They are interested in observing statistical patterns – who does well at school, who is most likely to suffer a heart attack, etc. – and they seek to explain these patterns by looking for **causation** or **correlation**. Such sociologists tend to use **quantitative research** methods – methods such as surveys that produce numerical data about the social world. They aspire to be detached and value-free, and tend to start with a **hypothesis**, which they test through their research. This is known as a deductive research approach, or **deductivism**.

Sociologists that follow Weber's insights also want to engage in objective and rigorous study, but they focus instead on how people make sense of the world. They seek an empathetic understanding (verstehen) and tend to use **qualitative methods**, such as interviews and observations. This approach is known as interpretivism. Researchers in this tradition aim to be objective by looking for groups of meanings and patterns emerging from their research – an inductive research approach (or **inductivism**).

Sociologists that draw on Marxist, critical race or feminist theories are interested in revealing the hidden structures or discourses (e.g. capitalism, racism, patriarchy) that shape and define people's lives. They use methods that show how these structures and discourses operate. Researchers working in these traditions often use a mixture of qualitative and quantitative methods. Some sociologists in this camp can be described as realists, focused on revealing the hidden truths and causes behind social phenomena – for example, Marx was interested in showing how the economy shaped all other aspects of social life. Other sociologists can be described as constructionists, focusing on the way that concepts like race and gender are socially constructed. These sociologists aim to reveal how constructs are created in social contexts, and they often use **discourse analysis** methods (for example, media analysis, policy analysis) to explore how this occurs.

You can see from these four approaches that sociologists do not always agree about the questions that need asking, which methods to use and the types of knowledge they consider important. However, this disagreement is a positive thing: studying phenomena from a range of perspectives and using a range of different tools results in a more fulsome understanding. It reveals all aspects of social life, and enables us to be self-critical.

Gathering evidence like a sociological detective

To generate a body of evidence, sociologists need to gather data. Data refers to empirical material (observable 'bits' of evidence) that are generated about the social world. Gathering data is a form of sociological detective work – sociologists work with data like detectives work with pieces of evidence, to develop a rigorous, big-picture view of the issue under investigation.

First, sociologists must establish what the social problem is. This is usually clear for a detective: they are presented with a crime about which they must discern the facts through investigative methods.

Sociologists get a much wider scope: they can choose to investigate anything at all that happens in the social world. While some sociologists choose to investigate crime as a topic, there are many other areas of research to explore – religion, the family, health, education… the list is endless. Because of this vast choice, it is important for sociologists to narrow their scope. But how do they decide what to study out of all these possibilities?

Selecting a topic and asking good research questions

Several factors may influence your choice of research topic. You might be driven by personal interest and values, or by current events such as globalisation, climate change or immigration. Perhaps there is some puzzle you want to solve. A particular theoretical 'lens' can also affect your choice of research – or the subject matter may be decided simply by what you can access.

Once you have decided on your topic, you need to frame your research questions clearly. This is a key part of the detective's investigation and is also central to sociological investigations. A detective examining a crime scene does not approach every single person in the vicinity and ask if they 'did it'; they narrow it down first to establish some ideas about who might have committed the crime and what their motives could have been. Similarly, as a sociologist, you need to narrow your focus to a specific aspect of the social problem you want to examine.

However, sociological questions are different to criminological questions (and others). Sociological questions seek to understand the connections between personal troubles, truths and triumphs and public issues of social structure. You must frame your questions carefully to ensure that they remain sociological. For example, if you were exploring the field of education, you would not ask a research question about an individual student ('Why is this student failing?'), as this would suggest that educational failure was simply a personal trouble of the individual. Instead, you need to frame the question in such a way that will allow you to examine this 'failure' in relation to wider issues of social structure.

As a sociologist, you may begin your project by looking at broader social issues in order to identify something more specific to investigate. For instance, you might be interested in a news report claiming that young people from more deprived social backgrounds perform worse in A Levels than their peers, or that girls outperform boys at GCSE level. To be an effective sociologist, you would take these 'claims' and examine the evidence surrounding them. So, you might ask:

- Do girls perform better than boys in GCSEs? If so, what social and cultural factors might explain why girls outperform boys at GCSE?
- Are there differences between working-class and middle-class children's educational attainment? If so, why is this the case?

> A newspaper headline reads 'Britain failing its white working-class boys in education'. What sociological questions might you want to ask about this headline?

You must then gather data to help answer these questions. And it is important to remember that, as with a criminal investigation, not everything counts equally as evidence. Relying only on newspaper reports or hearsay is not substantial enough to 'prove' your case.

The question on which you have chosen to base your research will inform the approach you take to the investigation. Just as detectives do not rely on the same techniques for every crime (for example, one may require a blood spatter report, the next an examination of digital evidence), so sociological research relies on a variety of tools – these are your research methods. In the remainder of this chapter, we explore the key research methods sociologists use, illustrating each one with the example of sex work drawn from contemporary research studies.

Quantitative and qualitative data

Sociologists typically distinguish between two types of data used or gathered in research: data that comes in the form of numbers (quantitative data) and data that comes in written form (qualitative data). Both types can be accessed in two ways: by drawing on data that already exists (**secondary data**), or by gathering your own (**primary data**).

Secondary data

Secondary data sets come from official statistics, historical records, newspapers, films, autobiographies and diaries.

Official statistics

Official statistics are commonly used by sociologists. Research questions sometimes emerge out of official statistics that have made their way into media headlines and become a focal 'social problem' that needs to be examined more carefully. For example, a news headline might announce 'Girls outperform boys in another year of GCSE results' or 'Those from deprived backgrounds fare worse in A Levels'. Researchers may then delve into the official statistics reported by the journalist (they would not rely on the media report itself as a source of evidence).

At other times sociologists use secondary data, because it is ready-made and often available in exceptionally large data sets. This is more cost-effective for sociologists than having to develop their own survey. Often these large-scale surveys are produced by governments and gather data on a larger scale than a sociologist can – examples that sociologists have found useful include the British Social Attitudes Survey, the Census and the Labour Force Survey, among others.

Case Study: Sex work: secondary data

Henriksen (2020) examined the relationship between social background and prostitution by utilising the Register Data from Denmark. She was able to use data collected on 1,128 female sex workers to reveal that female sex sellers typically come from socially vulnerable backgrounds and have been marginalised in both childhood and adulthood.

Using secondary data can be helpful. It is already there, so you do not have to devise your instrument (the questionnaire, for example), identify your sample or gather the data. Such data, however, is limited by the choices of the original researchers who developed the instrument and generated this data set. The way that questions were asked, the way that concepts were **operationalised** (how the abstract concepts were turned into something measurable), and the choice of people who comprised the sample are already set in stone. Sociologists using this secondary data cannot change any of it. Some sociologists are also critical of the accuracy of the data itself, recognising that official statistics are socially constructed and socially produced. (See Chapter 4 for more detail on this in relation to crime statistics.)

Document and media analysis – content and discourse approaches

Humans are very good at documenting their lives, whether privately or in official documents – think about the huge number of government documents and newspaper reports that are available. Sociologists can make use of this swathe of secondary data and subject it to rigorous documentary analysis.

This analysis comes in various forms, and we will look at two of these briefly. Content analysis is the most straightforward. This usually involves quantitative analysis of documents, whereby the researcher counts the number of times certain words appear in texts. For example, Mijs and Savage (2019) used Google Ngram to look at how many times the terms 'plutocracy' and 'meritocracy' appeared in English language books between 1950 and 2000. Their research showed the disappearance of the former in comparison to the widespread use of the latter.

Discourse analysis, in contrast, analyses texts using a more detailed thematic review. Here, the sociologist is looking at the meaning of the language used in documents. They are not counting how many times a word appears, but instead are interested in exposing the hidden meanings and cultural assumptions behind the use of words and images. For instance, a sociologist might look at the way that pictures of psychiatric drugs in medical journals are displayed alongside images of women, and pick up on the hidden suggestion behind these images that women are more mentally fragile than men.

Both content and discourse analysis are used by sociologists when they examine all forms of media, including newsprint, television, film and social media.

Case Study: Sex work: content and discourse analysis

Putnis and Burr (2019) examined the representation of female sex workers in mainstream documents published by the National Health Service (NHS) in England. They analysed all publications from 2010–16 and looked at every reference to sex work using both content and discourse (thematic) analysis. They argued that prostitutes are depicted as 'others', in both medical and criminal ways – vulnerable and deviant – 'mad' and 'bad' and a 'victim'.

Primary data

Social surveys and questionnaires

Many sociologists still prefer to gather their own data and to generate primary data. Even though social survey research can be cumbersome and time-consuming

(Townsend's famous study *Poverty in the United Kingdom*, in 1979, took over ten years to complete), many sociologists still choose to develop it themselves. This is usually because existing data sets in the form of official statistics do not provide the type of data that the researcher needs. The scale of social surveys produced by sociologists ranges from fewer than one hundred people to surveys of thousands.

Surveys gather data through questionnaires – sets of written questions. There are two key types of questions used in questionnaires: closed questions, which give discrete categories for the respondent to choose from, and open questions, which allow participants to provide answers in their own words and give space for them to elaborate.

Closed questions are most easily turned into numerical data, so these are associated with producing quantitative research. Open questions allow sociologists to delve into the lived experience of those they are researching, and to gain rich insight into their lives and the phenomena they are studying. Typically, questionnaires are uniform: everyone is asked the same (mainly closed) questions, in the same order. The questions aim to be unambiguous, so that everyone interprets them in the same way.

Sociological research needs to be both valid and reliable – that is, sociologists must ensure that they measure what they intend to measure (**validity**), and that the survey is repeatable such that if different researchers applied the same method, they would achieve the same results (**reliability**). Quantitative questionnaires are very reliable research instruments. However, the extent to which they are valid is more complicated because the questions must be framed in a way that is completely unambiguous, and this is not always easy to achieve. For example, when measuring social class, sociologists must operationalise the concept by using a **proxy** (substitute) **measure** such as 'occupation'. However, people may not consider that their occupation defines their social class, so sociologists might question whether this is a valid measure.

Sociologists who use surveys are trying to build a big picture, or macro view, about something socially important. For example, sociologists have used survey research to find out the extent to which people live in poverty and what factors (**variables**) might affect the chances of this. Others have tried to discover why there are higher rates of police surveillance practices such as stop and search targeted at minority ethnic communities. Once sociologists have a large number of responses to surveys like this, they can confidently describe what is going on (descriptive statistics). They can also sometimes make inferences, or predictions (inferential statistics), to explain why things are happening as they are.

To produce a meaningful (valid and reliable) set of data, sociologists need to ensure that the participants completing the questionnaire are the people they want to target.

Selecting people to take part in sociological research (and in this case specifically who should complete a questionnaire) occurs through a process called 'sampling'.

Sampling

In most cases it would be impossible to survey every single person who falls into a population research category, so a sample is a *section* of the wider population that the sociologist wants to research. Imagine a sociologist wants to study pensioners' social interactions and loneliness, for example. It would be too difficult to send out a questionnaire to every pensioner in the UK, so instead the sociologist selects a sample of this population. But how do they decide on this sample – which pensioners get the questionnaire?

The key consideration is that the sample should be *representative*, which means that the people chosen for the sample must share the same characteristics as the wider population. For example, the sample must not only include people of an earlier pensionable age, only female pensioners, or just those living in private accommodation; it must include a range of people – some older pensioners, men and those in nursing facilities too. If a sociologist is confident that their sample is representative, they can also feel confident that their results will be valid.

Samples can be chosen in various ways. First, if the researcher knows all the people in the population from which they can draw their sample (i.e. if they have a **sampling frame**), they can choose their sample randomly (for example, by using a computer), they can be systematic (for example, taking every tenth name on the list), or they can be stratified (for example, they could divide the sample into different groups by age, class, gender or ethnicity, then randomly take names from each group). This is referred to as a 'probability sampling', because there is a chance that everybody on the list will get chosen.

Simple random sampling

Stratified sampling

The other main type of sampling is non-probability sampling, which is when the researcher does not have a sampling frame. There are different forms of non-probability sampling:

Snowball sampling

- Snowball sampling may be used when a sample cannot be easily located. Here, an initial contact leads to other respondents. For example, if a researcher wants to interview women about their experience of sex work, the researcher may make contact with one sex worker, gain his or her trust, and rely on this relationship to make contact with another sex worker to interview.

- Quota sampling is also common in market research undertaken by companies to find out about their customers. Here the researcher decides who they want to speak to and then they locate people who fit their criteria.

The choice of sampling method is often driven by access to a population. Hard-to-reach populations make probability sampling more difficult to achieve. Moreover, a sociologist's theoretical commitments also shape the choice of sampling method. Researchers committed to positivist inquiry will generally endeavour to achieve the scientific gold standard of probability sampling. However, even with this theoretical commitment they may be limited in scope due to issues of access.

> What advantages and disadvantages do you think each of the sampling methods described has? List as many as you can think of.

Probability sampling is more representative, so a researcher can be confident that they could **generalise** their findings to the wider population. By contrast, non-probability sampling is often used in earlier stages of research to generate ideas, but it cannot be generalised.

Once sociologists have circulated the survey to their sample, they also want to ensure that they get enough responses. The **response rate** is the percentage of the sample that completes the survey. The higher the response rate, the more valid the study. Researchers can use incentives (such as money) to try to get higher response rates, but this can make the research costly.

Quantitative researchers generally agree that a 50% response rate or more is good. Researchers doing qualitative research, by contrast, often use the term 'saturation' to indicate when they have gathered enough data. **Saturation** is said to occur when data is gathered to a point that no 'new' insight into the topic under investigation is emerging from the empirical material.

Case Study: Sex work: surveys

Jorgensen's study 'Badges and Brothels' (2018) conducted survey research on police officers' attitudes towards prostitution. Out of 3,516 people contacted, 314 responded to the survey. While most police officers believed that prostitutes had a hard start in life, most also held strongly negative views of prostitutes and were committed to strong policing. Eighty per cent of the sample believed that prostitutes were drug addicts, and more than two-thirds of officers believed that prostitutes deserved to be imprisoned. This research relied on a relatively low response rate of just under 10%. Such a low response rate is not uncommon when studying policing and, indeed, prostitution. However, researchers sometimes suggest that a low response rate can affect survey validity because the response may be biased (where it is skewed towards the views of those who respond, and does not account for the views of those who do not respond). Other researchers suggest a low response rate does not necessarily correlate to low validity when researching a relatively homogenous community (i.e. a population which shares common experiences).

Interviews

Questionnaires typically use close-ended questions to produce numerical, quantitative data through a structured format. In contrast, interview methods typically use open-ended questions to produce qualitative data in the form of words that can be analysed for meaning. Here the researcher focuses on a smaller number of respondents and asks them more detailed questions.

Qualitative researchers adopt two broad approaches to interviewing: semi-structured interviews or conversational/unstructured interviews.

Semi-structured interviews usually require an interview guide, which outlines an order of open and closed questions that research participants will be asked. Within the questions are probes that help the interview seek clarity in response (for example, 'Could you tell me more?', 'Can you give examples?'). While the interview is shaped by consistent overarching questions, these probes allow it to develop in different ways with participants.

Where semi-structured interviews provide some degree of flexibility, unstructured or conversational interviews allow even more opportunity to delve into the individual's experiences around the topic under investigation. These interviews are more free-flowing, and are often more relaxed, informal and conversation-like. In this respect, they can follow the direction of the participant, who has greater control over the interview. This can reveal more unique insights, and the complexity of the phenomena can be exposed in more depth. The interviewer will not allow the participant to go completely off topic, of course – they will ensure there is always some relevance to the social issue being researched – but conversational interviews are more likely to yield valid results because people usually say what they really feel when given the opportunity to speak freely. This style of interviewing is particularly good for sensitive topic areas, allowing the interviewer more flexibility to develop a rapport and bond empathetically with the participant in the conversation.

However, conversational interviews do have some disadvantages. Interviews may meander and get off track more easily. Interviewer bias may also present an issue because a relationship may develop between the two parties, causing the interviewer to influence the participant's responses. Finally, there is the problem of 'social desirability' – where people say what they think the interviewer wants to hear.

Case Study: Sex work: interviews

In their 2020 study 'The Relative Quality of Sex Work', Benoit et al completed face-to-face, semi-structured interviews with 218 sex workers in Canada. The participants described turning to prostitution due to an unstable job market (i.e. they had no jobs). Interestingly, it was the open-ended questions that enabled more free-flowing dialogue, like that of a conversational interview, and which perhaps surprisingly revealed that the prostitutes found sex work more satisfying than other jobs: it gave them more control, job satisfaction, and more money than other work. Despite these perceived benefits, respondents felt the job was stigmatised and had low status.

Observations

Like interviews, observations can be approached quantitatively or qualitatively (or both in the same study). They may take the form of non-participant observation or participant observation.

Structured (or systematic) observations are non-participant studies that yield numerical data. Usually, structured observations utilise an observation schedule to record pre-coded phenomena. For example, if a sociologist is recording the relationship between gender and coffee-shop use at certain times of day, they may have an observation sheet with the time down one side of the page and gender at the top. They then simply keep a record of who enters the coffee shop. They could add another column to record who pays for the coffee and perhaps (if they were close enough to hear) another column to record the type of coffee ordered (latte, flat white, Americano, etc.).

> If you were to conduct an observational study of boys' and girls' participation in a classroom, what might you want to record on an observation sheet?

Unstructured observations can also be non-participant. Here, the observer simply writes down what they see. This yields qualitative data. Researchers using unstructured observations may also be participants in the research process, either immersed in the social setting and known to those they are researching (overt), or 'undercover' (**covert**) observers. Studies in which the researcher takes part in observations are known as 'participant observations', but it is important to recognise that this can occur on a sliding scale where the researcher has greater or lesser degrees of involvement in the setting.

Participant observation is one method that characterises **ethnography** – the study of cultures and societies (ethnography means 'writing about cultures'). Ethnographic research developed from the discipline of anthropology, where researchers would embed themselves in another culture – usually somewhere other than the Global North – and write about its distinctive cultural practices. Such methods have been accused of exoticising and 'othering' the populations they studied (there is more on this in Chapter 5). Other methods involved in ethnographic research can include interviews and surveys.

It is important to note here that culture does not simply refer to groups living in a specific wider geographical space; it can be also be applied to groups inhabiting smaller locations or sharing habits and interests. We refer to 'sporting culture', for example, or 'café culture' or even to 'subculture'. These cultures are also the subject of ethnographic research, providing a deeper level of knowledge about people's lives. Where interviews are limited to what people say, and what they are willing to tell researchers, ethnographies allow sociologists to witness the interactions between people and observe them in their everyday lives and settings – to see the world through their eyes.

Some classic sociological research came from ethnographic studies. *Humphrey's Tearoom Trade* (1975) examined the lives of homosexual men engaging in sex in public places. Patrick's study *A Glasgow Gang Observed* (1973/2013) examined gang life. Barker's *The Making of a Moonie* (1984) examined life in a religious cult, and Becker's book *Outsiders* (1963/2008) examined the meaning of drug-taking.

Many contemporary sociologists continue to employ ethnographic methods that utilise participant observations. To explore this further, you could look up Goffman's work *On the Run: Fugitive Life in an American City* (2015), which examines the criminalisation of young Black men in an American suburb, and Garthwaite's work in *Hunger Pains: Life inside Foodbank Britain* (2016), which investigates what it feels like to turn to a food bank for help. Both researchers were deeply embedded in the cultures they were examining, and used participant observations alongside interviews to gather their data. Some researchers have even used ethnographic methods to explore the virtual world of the internet and online video gaming – for example, *Ethnography and Virtual Worlds: A Handbook of Method* (2012) by Boellstorff et al. Observational research raises numerous ethical issues, and we pick this up in Chapter 5.

Case Study: Sex work: ethnography

In *The Social Construction of Sex Work: Ethnography of Escort Agencies in Poland* (2019) Ślęzak completed non-participant observations across four escort agencies and followed this up with 42 unstructured interviews. She argued that pimps and prostitutes are typically regarded negatively and therefore their everyday lives and experiences are generally not heard. By establishing rapport throughout the duration of her study (2007–13) she was able to gain insight into the interactions between the sex workers and their clients, as well as the relationships between the escorts themselves.

Summary

You have learned about several different research methods employed by sociologists, divided into two broad types: quantitative and qualitative. The table below summarises the differences between the two approaches to help you identify the key features of each approach.

Qualitative	Quantitative
words, meaning	numbers, patterns
smaller scale (micro)	larger scale (macro)
studies opinions/beliefs	studies social facts
interpretivist, realist, constructionist	positivist, realist
unstructured, open questions	standardised, closed questions
generally uses non-probability samples	prefers random (probability) samples
aims to provide details of particular events and experiences; does not aim to generalise	usually wants to generalise to the population as a whole
looks at everyday meanings and interactions	looks for correlations or causation
uses naturally occurring data	researcher initiates data/draws from an artificial setting
researcher is immersed in the setting	researcher is distanced and detached, which removes bias

Sociological how-tos

To be a rigorous sociologist your research must be:

- evidence-based
- methodical – choose the research method best suited to the question asked
- open about the link between your chosen **conceptual framework** (your 'glasses') and the methods you use
- valid
- reliable.

CHAPTER 4
BE KNOWLEDGEABLE: ASKING QUESTIONS AND FINDING ANSWERS

In this chapter, we turn our attention to some key sociological questions by putting on our conceptual glasses and raiding our methodological toolbox, to generate both data and insights. We do this in three specific steps.

First, we explore the question of inequality. All societies are stratified and divided, so we ask: *How and why is society divided?* Here, we introduce the study of class, gender and ethnicity, and explore these divisions through an examination of education and health.

The next step starts with an exploration of the question: *What gives society order and why do some people break the rules?* This is a fascinating sociological question: we often take it for granted that our lives are orderly (most of us are fortunate enough not to live in a state of chaos), but what makes orderly society possible? Who makes the rules, and why do we obey them? In the second part of this section, we look at the rarer occasions when the rules are not followed – when norms and laws are broken, and when crimes are committed.

Finally, we examine a question of identity: *Who do we think we are, and what shapes our sense of self?* Here, using case studies of the family and religion, we examine the ways that cultures, beliefs and social norms shape our sense of identity and mould our choices.

How and why is society divided?

As COVID-19 took root as a global pandemic, it was described as uniquely non-discriminatory – everybody was at risk of catching the disease. However, while everyone was indeed at risk from the virus, some were more at risk than others. Some people were more vulnerable to infection. Others – for example, those in public-facing occupations or who lived in closely packed housing – were less able to protect themselves from it. Other groups were less able to access the care that would help them recover. Far from being a leveller, COVID-19 turned a spotlight on the pervasive and endemic inequalities that characterise social life: infection and recovery rates varied by age, gender, social class, ethnicity and location.

Several other findings illustrate the stark reality of inequality. For example, the Trussell Trust – the biggest charity operating a national network of food banks in the UK – reports year-on-year increases in the reliance on food aid. In the year before the first national lockdown in the UK (April 2019 to March 2020), the charity distributed 1.9 million three-day emergency food supplies to families unable to feed themselves – a figure 18% higher than the previous year. Figures released by the charity in November 2020 showed that the reliance on food banks increased by 47% during the first six months of the pandemic (April 2020 to September 2020). That equates to 2,300 emergency food parcels being distributed to households every day during this period. This startling figure does not even include numbers of people visiting the 800 independent food banks that operate in the UK.

While people became increasingly dependent on food aid, others had too much to eat. In 2020, 4.5 million tonnes of food were thrown away in the UK – this amounts to £700 a year for an average family with children (Smithers, 2020). During the pandemic, some households had the resources to stockpile food, and some estimates suggest that shoppers in the UK spent an extra £1.9 billion on groceries just before the first lockdown in March 2020. This not only resulted in a shortage of certain products in shops, but it also brought with it the risk of more food waste (Sillard, 2020). The stockpiled food also tended to be tinned products, which are typically lower-priced and so more affordable to people on lower incomes. The reduced availability of these products meant that some people found themselves unable to buy affordable food.

The examples above may appear exceptional – they refer, after all, to an unprecedented global pandemic. However, inequality is a permanent feature of social life. Let us explore another example. The London Underground is an extensive passenger train system that links up the various districts of the capital city. The network consists of 11 train lines and, as the 12th-busiest city rail network in the world, five million people are transported across London each day. Cheshire (2012) examined the life chances of people who lived near each tube station. An underground journey from Lancaster Gate to Mile End takes about 20 minutes on the Central Line, but you might be surprised to know that life expectancy between these two stations differs by 12 years. Between Oxford Circus and Docklands the journey time is a mere 14 minutes, but the difference in life expectancy is 20 years.

These stark contemporary inequalities do not simply relate to health. The UK (notably alongside the USA) is a highly unequal society when measured against any number of axes. The top 1% of the UK population owns 20% of all household wealth, the top 5% around 40%, and the top 10% own 50%. There is, therefore, what Dorling (2015) describes as 'a super-rich and a growing poor', and people in the latter group find their income position consistently squeezed. Society is thus characterised by the 'haves' and 'have-nots'. In fact, Burrows and Knowles (2019) make a further distinction for the super-wealthy, describing the 'haves and the have yachts'. At the other end of the economic scale, and in stark contrast to such wealth, are those who live in the condition of poverty.

Global data shows that the entire world is deeply unequal. Oxfam (2020) outlines what it calls a series of 'shocking' facts. For example, the world's richest 1% have more than twice as much wealth as 6.9 billion people all together, and the world's billionaires (who would fit in a double decker bus) have more wealth than 60% of the planet. In contrast, half of humanity lives on less than £4 a day.

Measuring poverty is complicated, and sociologists distinguish between **absolute poverty** and **relative poverty**. Those living in absolute poverty do not have access to the essentials needed to survive – they are living in a state of destitution or mere subsistence. This type of poverty is often regarded as only a historical concern in the UK, reminiscent of a time when there was no state support, when the poor were relegated to workhouses or starved on the streets. As such, it is often suggested that relative poverty is a more useful measure – this takes all households in a country and defines all those living on less than the median (middle) family wage as being in relative poverty.

The Social Metric Commission (2020) counted all households living on less than 54% of the average and suggested that 14.3 million people in the UK were in poverty (8.3 million people of working age – most of whom were working, 4.6 million children and 1.3 million pensioners). The 54% is, however, an arbitrary cut-off point, and moving the threshold down to 50% or up to 60% makes a huge difference – around 2.5 million people either way. Nevertheless, whichever scale is applied, the evidence of enduring relative poverty and widespread inequality in the UK is conclusive.

These types of inequalities are carefully but dramatically exposed in Wilkinson and Pickett's book *The Spirit Level: Why Equality is Better for Everyone* (2010). They established that rich but unequal societies have a very poor record compared to poorer but more equal societies in relation to many different factors, including physical health, mental health, drug abuse, education, imprisonment, obesity, **social mobility**, trust and community life, violence, teenage pregnancies and child wellbeing. Inequality, from their perspective, is far reaching, multi-faceted and not a good idea. But just how persuasive and pervasive are the ideas that inequality is bad and equality is good?

Sociologists must ensure that they are knowledgeable about the extent of inequality, and ask deeper questions about why inequality persists and whether it is desirable to have divided societies. The section below explores sociological evidence for inequality, division and difference, concentrating on social differences as measured by class, gender and ethnicity, and considering the empirical evidence through two case studies: education and health. This section documents the evidence for social inequality, but also suggests the value of an intersectional approach – one that recognises that different axes of inequality interact. You will see how difference and discrimination come in multiple forms, which can overlap, placing some groups in the most precarious of social positions and others in the most privileged.

Social class

The idea of social class probably makes some sense to you. It is strongly evocative – most people can distinguish between the common-sense ideas of what it means to be upper class, middle class and working class, and are usually able to describe their own social class position. Some people go so far as to suggest that class is a peculiarly 'British disease', and that the UK is the archetype of a class-ridden society.

If you were asked to describe what an upper-, middle- or working-class person was like, what would you say? You might make some suggestions about the type of job that person did, what clothes they wore, what leisure activities they engaged in, or what sorts of food they might prefer. Try it. You might find this exercise relatable and relatively straightforward to do – this is because social class has strong and subjective meaning.

Sociologists are interested in how people experience class, but they also want to objectively define the concept. Marx believed that modern, capitalist society is characterised by a binary (two) class division – between those who own the means of production (the bourgeoisie) and those that have to sell their labour (the proletariat). Objectively, then, for Marx a social class is a group of people who share a common relationship to the economy.

As useful as this conceptualisation is for revealing fundamental economic class divisions, it does not necessarily capture the nuance of people's lived experiences. For example, a university lecturer is a member of the proletariat (they work for a wage), but their life chances and experiences are very different from the administrators in the university – or the cleaners, the cooks and the technicians. For Marx, all these people are members of the same social class, but this is not sufficient to understand the ways in which people's lives are lived and mapped. Specifically, his model poses some difficulties for understanding and thinking about the massive growth of the middle class and the multiple ways in which middle-class people differ in terms of wealth, lifestyle and standing.

For this reason, the work of other sociologists has been useful. Weber, for instance, drew attention not just to the economic basis of social stratification (class), but also showed how societal position is shaped by social networks and political connections and standing. His discussion of class, status and party shows that social differences are complicated and multi-faceted. So, for example, members of the nobility may have seen a reduction in their economic power, but might still be regarded as occupying a position of high social class. Conversely, some celebrities may command great wealth but still not garner high social standing. Following Weber and Marx, Bourdieu (1984) showed how social class distinctions are expressed through multiple configurations of capital – not just money and wealth (economic), but also cultural values, habits and lifestyle choices (what music we listen to, our leisure activities, etc.), our social networks (friends, family and colleagues), and so on.

Savage (2015) used Bourdieu's insights to develop what he called the Great British Class Survey. This survey was conducted through the BBC, and the scale of interest from the general public was testimony to the importance ordinary people placed on social class. Incorporating questions about leisure, friends, income, wealth and cultural preferences, the online survey had an initial 160,000 respondents. It has now been visited over nine million times. The sample was skewed – more middle-class people responded than any other social group – but the results enabled the research team to develop a new seven-category classification to describe the ways in which Britain was divided in terms of social class.

Savage's seven categories, from left to right: precariat, traditional working class, emergent service workers, technical middle class, new affluent workers, established middle class, elite.

Savage observed that the class system is bookended by the wealthy elite at one end and the 'precariat' (those with low economic, social and cultural capital) at the other.

This was insightful, in that it revealed a chasm between the most privileged and the most deprived, and highlighted the need for a greater understanding of the experiences of each. The old working class and middle class had also fragmented, resulting in much more differentiation in the middle levels of society. The UK can therefore still be seen very much as a class society, but it is more unequal and divided at the extremes than it was 50 years ago, for example. These divisions are not only economic – they straddle cultural life and social networks, too.

There is now a growing body of work that studies these polar opposites: the closed elite and the stigmatised precariat. In *Getting By* (2015), McKenzie documented what life is like in a position of precarity. Her work, and that of Jones in *Chavs: The Demonization of the Working Class* (2016), emphasised the resilience, resourcefulness and hard work of the working class and pointed to the ways that their lives are often negatively presented by politicians and the media. The term 'chav', originally based on a Romani word and then co-opted as an acronym for Council Housed and Violent, for instance, has become a term of moralistic abuse of the White poor. These studies stand as important counters to the work of writers such as Murray (1996), who depicted the poorest in society as an underclass – feckless and lazy, and deserving of their lowly position. (There is more on this in Chapter 5.)

Returning to the example of food banks, it is interesting to note that the majority of people who use these facilities (39%) are the *working* poor – those on low incomes and struggling despite having jobs – not those who are 'lazy'. A study by McArthur and Reeves (2019) examined how British newspapers talk about the poor, and showed that this group is more likely to be stigmatised when there is a recession, turning attention away from the economy and focusing it on the character of those who suffer the most.

To be properly knowledgeable about social class differences, it is important that sociologists collect data to document changing patterns of class composition and to examine the impact that class has on life chances. This poses an operational problem – how should social class be measured?

The preferred method is to use occupation as a proxy measure. We can make a judgement about every single occupation in the UK, assigning each a social class position. In the UK, the most used model is the National Statistics Socio-Economic Classification (NS-SEC) (Office for National Statistics, 2020). This is not a perfect system, not least because it focuses on income rather than the social and cultural aspects of class, but it does allow the collection of data by dividing all occupations into class categories.

This influential schema was derived from the work of Goldthorpe and Hope (1974) (see also Goldthorpe, 2000) and usually applies seven class categories, as detailed in the table on the next page. This table does not include the eighth category of 'unemployed or never worked', as government research usually does not include this in its data analysis.

Goldthorpe and Hope's schema is used as the basis for all official data collection on social class in the UK (see pages 150–151).

Social Class I	Service Class (higher grade)
Social Class II	Service Class (lower grade)
Social Class III	Routine Non-Manual Employees
Social Class IV	Small Proprietors
Social Class V	Lower Grade Technicians and Supervisors
Social Class VI	Skilled Manual Workers
Social Class VII	Semi and Unskilled Manual Workers

Later in this section we will review some data that uses this type of classification to learn about educational and health outcomes, and later in the chapter we review the evidence about differences in crime. To conclude this review, we turn our attention to the question of social mobility – the extent to which it is possible to move between social classes and whether class origin determines where people end up in life. In 2020, the Social Mobility Commission produced a report entitled the *State of the Nation 2018–19*, which argued that:

> *Social mobility has stagnated over the last four years at virtually all stages from birth to work. Being born privileged in Britain means that you are likely to remain privileged. Being born disadvantaged, however, means that you will have to overcome a series of barriers to ensure that you and your children are not stuck in the same trap.*

Focusing just on occupation, the Great British Class Survey shows that members of the middle class are 80% more likely to secure professional jobs than those who begin life in the working class, and when working-class children secure a professional job, they earn 17% less than their middle-class counterparts. Friedman and Lauriston's (2020) work highlights the persistence of the class ceiling. They reveal that professions such as law, medicine and finance are dominated by the middle class, and while it is possible for people to be upwardly socially mobile, this mobility is restricted by one's class location. For example, someone from working-class origins may become upwardly mobile by going to an elite university and securing a job in a middle-class profession. However, their income will still be considerably lower than their middle-class peers in the same profession who have the same qualifications. These sociologists suggest that this may be because of class discrimination in the workplace, alongside other factors such as cultural capital (e.g. accent and clothing).

Overall, then, there are some important conclusions to be drawn:

- Societies are stratified by social class.
- Social class inequalities are complex and are widening.
- The class system is rigid. It is difficult to climb the social ladder, and those who start off in a privileged class position are unlikely to go down the ladder.

Gender

Since the passing of the Equal Pay Act (1970) and the Sex Discrimination Act (1975), it might be tempting to suggest that observable differences between men and women in terms of income, for instance, are the result of choice rather than overt discrimination. After all, in the UK, all children have the same educational rights, and many barriers to securing gender equality have been overcome. However, in order to be knowledgeable about inequality, it is important to interrogate assumptions like this. Before looking at the data about education and health more specifically, let's consider some of the ways that gender divisions are reproduced in the home and the workplace, and in terms of material wealth, in politics, and in cultural assumptions and representations. Note that in this section, we concentrate on gender differences as measured between men and women. There is currently insufficient data to examine the differences between men, women and people who categorise themselves as other or third gender.

Starting with employment and pay, statistics show that while the pay gap between men and women is narrowing, pay equity has not yet been achieved and the rate of change is now very slow. The official statistics from the Office of National Statistics (2019) show that for full-time workers, the gender pay gap – calculated as the difference between average hourly earnings of women compared to men doing the same job – is 8.9%. In 1997, the figure was 17.4%, but the percentage point has only dropped 0.6 since 2012. At this rate of change, it is estimated that it will take another 60 years before there is wage parity.

These differences also intersect with ethnicity. Longhi and Brynin (2017:8) showed that minority ethnic groups tend to earn less than White people, but the picture becomes more complex when gender is taken into consideration:

> Ethnic minority women generally earned more than White British women, with all Indian, all Chinese, British-born Black Caribbean and British-born Black African women experiencing notable pay advantages. Only two groups had a clear pay disadvantage: these were Pakistani and Bangladeshi immigrant women.

In terms of societal representation, despite securing the right to vote in 1918, women are still under-represented in the British parliament. In June 2020, there were 220 women members of parliament (MPs) – the highest number ever – but still only fractionally above a third (34%) of the whole House. Women are far less likely to be in senior management positions, and when women do manage firms (about 19% of global firms have a female manager), the workforce of that company tends to be predominantly female (Ortiz-Ospina and Roser, 2019). Feminists have blamed the **glass ceiling** for this discrepancy.

Gender inequalities are also visible in the division of labour in the home. Government data (ONS, 2016) shows that women carry out 60% more unpaid work – cooking, childcare and housework – than men. McMunn et al (2019) used data from the UK Household Longitudinal Study (UKHLS) to show that women do more domestic work than their male partners even when both work full time. Park et al (2013:134) reached an important conclusion:

> *Gender equality in terms of who does the bulk of the chores and who is primarily responsible for looking after the children has made very little progress in terms of what happens in people's homes. Men's uptake of unpaid domestic work is slow, and women continue to feel that they are doing more than their fair share. Whether women's 'double shift' – both doing a paid job and the bulk of family care and housework chores – is sustainable is an important question for the future.*

Feminists expose this **dual burden**, double shift or **triple shift** that women experience; studies have also shown that this picture varies by ethnicity, establishing the importance of intersectional analysis. Kan and Laurie (2016) argue that most research into the domestic division of labour has been ethnicity blind, and their study showed that several other factors shaped attitudes to housework. Women across all ethnicities undertook more household work than men, but the gap was highest amongst British Pakistani women, where 83% of the household work was the woman's responsibility.

There are other gender differences that characterise private home life, which can be illustrated by looking at rates of domestic violence. While men are subject to domestic violence, this remains a crime where women are the predominant victims. Data from the ONS (2019) shows that 2.4 million adults experienced domestic violence, of whom 1.6 million were women. Again, these data are more complex when ethnicity is included in the analysis, with women from the mixed ethnic group (20.0%) more likely than Asian (5.7%) or White women (7.2%) to report being victims of domestic abuse.

Differences between men and women are also visible in terms of cultural values and representation. We can explore these differences by looking, for example, at the ways that women and men are represented in video games or through the different ways they engage with social media. While there are now more women characters in video games, a reflection of growing female audiences, there is evidence that negative stereotypes still characterise this genre (Kondrat, 2015; Near, 2013). Women characters are often highly sexualised and are given less screen time. Studies of social media suggest that selfies on Instagram reflect gender stereotypes, with women more likely to pout and wear scant clothing, while men are more focused on their muscle presentation (Döring, Reif and Poeschl, 2016; Butkowski et al, 2019). These studies point to the continued pervasive ideals of exaggerated or emphasised femininity and hegemonic masculinity that set different standards for men and women to measure themselves against (see page 48). Elias and Gill (2018) reviewed beauty apps and showed that they reproduce demanding expectations that are classed and raced but also – more significantly – gendered. Women's bodies and faces, they argued, are subject to extensive surveillance and women learn that they can never look attractive enough.

Gender norms impact on men as well as women, and it is important to be knowledgeable about the ways in which inequalities shape the daily lives of men as well as women. Historically, sociological studies into gender inequality have centred on women, an emphasis that results from the important work of feminists, which focuses attention on the powerful impact of patriarchy. Male inequalities are not hidden, but they can sometimes be a secondary consideration. As you will see later in this chapter, men are more likely to commit crime, and they are more likely to commit suicide and to be homeless (86% of rough sleepers are men); men's health is poorer, they do not get the same level of support for paternity leave, they are subject to domestic violence, and often they do not fare as well in child custody cases (in 90% of cases custody is awarded to the mother). Traditionally male jobs, in manufacturing and construction for example, have also become more precarious. Taken together, these experiences are used by sociologists to shine a light on what is called a new crisis in masculinity.

The conclusions to draw here are as follows:

- Women continue to experience economic, political and cultural inequalities.
- Gender intersects with class and ethnicity, and this dynamic interplay helps explain nuanced experiences of inequality.
- Sexism and patriarchy are enduring expressions of power, and they impact life chances.
- Gender inequality has an impact on men as well as women.

Ethnicity

W.E.B. Du Bois (1903/1968) strongly argued that the most pervasive inequalities in the USA were associated with skin colour. He importantly drew attention to stratification by 'race' and the ways in which racism, in its various forms, shapes life chances.

As a sociologist, it is important to begin your study of racial and ethnic inequality by remembering that the inequalities that are recorded are not the outcome of biological differences between people, but are social constructs. The idea that it is possible to divide the world up into distinct racial groups has a long and dishonourable history, and has been used to legitimise enslavement and genocide. While there have been consistent attempts to prove that human 'races' vary in terms of physical, emotional, cultural and intellectual attributes, there is no evidence to support the idea that racial differences are underpinned by biology and genetics. Indeed, as scientist Steve Jones (1991) in a Reith lecture stated: 'The genetic differences between the snail populations of two Pyrenean valleys are much greater than those between Australian aboriginals and ourselves. If you were a snail it would make good biological sense to be a racist: but you have to accept that humans are tediously uniform animals.'

This idea of 'race' is inextricably linked to notions of White or European superiority, and can be traced back to European scientists such as Carl Linnaeus, who devised a schema of four distinct races with corresponding characteristics. Throughout the 18th and 19th centuries other 'scientific' attempts were made to establish difference – through phrenology, for example (the study of skull shape). Studies like this are now considered examples of **scientific racism**, but as you saw in Chapter 2, racism is a pervasive ideology that finds support in other forms, such as individual, interpersonal, cultural, structural and intentional expressions.

One important role of sociology is to explore how and why physical variations are singled out by communities as socially significant, and to document and challenge the differential treatment and opportunities that result from it. Some of the most visible examples of the consequences of this 'singling out' can be seen in the colonisation of land and slavery, in the genocide of Native Americans, in Nazi Germany where the idea of racial difference permitted the Holocaust, and in South Africa, where the idea of distinct and hierarchically different 'races' supported Apartheid. But racism can also be seen in everyday (micro) exchanges and through interactional practices.

Thus, sociologists stress that 'race' is not an objective or real category but rather a social myth – the product of history, economics and politics; a social construct, albeit one with very real implications and outcomes, which are played out through racism. Golash-Boza (2016) explains how racism operates as both an ideology (that continues to purport that physical differences can be measured and linked to social and cultural differences), and as micro and macro practices.

So dishonourable are historical attempts to measure race, that sociologists often try to avoid using the concept in studies of inequality. Instead, they may prefer to use the term 'ethnicity', which refers to cultural differences and similarities between individuals rather than biological ones (Hall, 1996). For example, ethnicity refers to identification with cultural values, language, practices and outlooks.

Sociologists do not deny the reality of racism, but they prefer to document and understand difference by focusing on how ethnicity shapes life chances. Using ethnicity as a way of differentiating between people arguably allows us to avoid judgements about the hierarchical positioning of each group, although it is important to acknowledge that cultural racism continues to operate (see page 42).

However, using ethnicity as a mechanism to understand divisions is not always straightforward. While people may self-select their ethnic grouping, these categories are socially constructed – shaped by wider sets of historical and social norms. As such, sociologists must recognise the usefulness of grouping people by ethnicity, but must also be mindful that such categories are often inadequate to capture the complexity of difference. They can also be inaccurate – even judgmental. For instance, to use the term 'British Asian' is to collapse a huge number of very different groups of people into a catch-all category. Another way that such inaccuracy and judgement operates is through research that documents the differences between non-White ethnic groups, but often groups all White people together.

Keeping all these points in mind, what do we know about inequality by ethnicity? The data suggests a very complex picture. Let's start by considering employment and poverty. In the UK, according to the 2011 census, 87% of the population are White and 13% belong to Black, Asian, Mixed or Other ethnic groups.

Government statistics (GOV.UK, 2021) showed that in 2019, employment rates varied by ethnic group, with 78% of White people employed, compared with 66% of people from all other ethnic groups combined. But there are nuances within this data. The lowest employment rate was in the combined Pakistani and Bangladeshi group (56%), and the highest rates were within groups designated as White Other (83%), White British (77%) and Indian (76%).

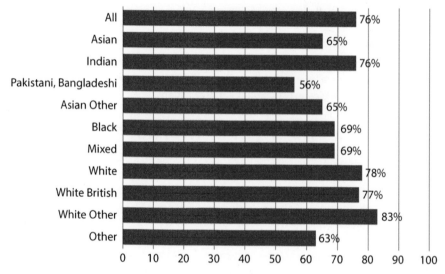

Figure 4.1: Percentage of 16–64-year-olds who were employed, by ethnicity, 2019 (GOV.UK, 2021)

Data from 2019 suggests that people from all minority ethnic groups except the Indian, Chinese, White Irish and White Other groups, were more likely than White British people to live in the most deprived 10% of neighbourhoods in England. Pakistani and Bangladeshi ethnic groups are again at the biggest disadvantage, being three times more likely than White British people to live in income-deprived neighbourhoods (GOV.UK, 2020).

Such patterns demand that we look at the ways in which ethnicity intersects with social class (GOV.UK, 2018), although the data relies on the 2011 census and this is rather dated. The data shows that 15.4% of people from the Indian ethnic group – the highest percentage out of all ethnic groups – were in higher managerial and professional occupations (the highest socio-economic group), followed by Chinese (12.8%). The lowest percentage was found in White Gypsy Travellers (2.5%) followed by Bangladeshi (4.2%) and then Mixed Caribbean/Black Caribbean (4.9%) communities.

In turn, this data intersects with gender: in every ethnic group, a higher percentage of men than women were in higher managerial and professional occupations; the biggest difference was in the Indian group, where 27% of men and 13% of women were in such occupations.

Overall, dividing the population by ethnic groups reveals significant differences and shows that:

- race is a socially constructed category
- categorising the population by ethnicity can help sociologists document contemporary inequality
- intersectional approaches reveal the importance of more nuanced analysis
- racism is an enduring expression of power and impacts on life chances.

Now that we have explored three axes of difference and have examined some of the data, we will turn to more detailed examination of inequalities in education and health, and begin to outline sociological explanations for these divisions.

Education: The myth of meritocracy?

Tony Blair, the Labour prime minister from 1997 to 2007, declared that 'education, education, education' was his political priority – a means to enhance social mobility and equalise opportunities. All political parties in the UK continue to support this position, as it is generally assumed that education enables meritocracy. It is expected that if educational opportunities are available for all, the association between class origin and educational attainment will weaken and be replaced by a strengthening relationship between educational attainment and class destination. This view assumes that an individual's social positioning reflects their ability and commitment to hard work rather than their access to privilege; that career success is based on talent and competency, rather than nepotism or social characteristics.

Functionalist sociologists, such as Davis and Moore (1945), argued that inequality in society was both inevitable and useful, and that differences in achievement were rightly linked to differences in reward. In most countries, the popular belief in meritocracy is strong and increasing. Mijs (2018) has established that more people than ever think that societal success is determined by hard work. This holds true for all social classes, with the working class almost universally supporting the idea.

This cartoon questions the idea of meritocracy. Do you think that the society you live in is meritocratic? What makes you think this?

'For a fair selection everybody has to take the same exam: please climb that tree.'

A belief in meritocracy remains even though, as we have seen, inequalities in income are at record levels and despite the persistence of unequal educational outcomes in early years, in school and in universities. In other words, as Mijs (2019) argued, there is no evidence of a questioning of inequality: more than ever, people believe in the meritocratic basis of success. We can see how this might fit with Marxist ideas – the belief in meritocracy drawing attention away from class exploitation. This was certainly part of the argument put forward by two classic Marxist scholars of education, Bowles and Gintis (1976/2008), who argued that the education system works to reproduce a skilled, hard-working and compliant workforce, which has internalised the norms and values of capitalism.

In the remainder of this section, we examine some educational inequalities in outcome and explore some of the ways that sociologists have questioned the idea of equal educational opportunity, and a meritocracy.

Before we look at education inequalities in the UK, it is important to put them in a global context. Oxfam (2020) detailed how 258 million children – one in every five – do not have access to schooling. This study also showed that these children are more likely to be girls – for every 100 primary school aged boys that cannot access school, there are 121 girls.

In the UK, year on year, official statistics reveal persistent educational inequalities (Clegg et al, 2017), and the performance gap between the richest and the poorest has remained consistently large since the mid-1980s. Consider income as measured by access to free school meals, for example. Data from 2017 establishes that 33% of children who qualified for free school meals achieved five or more GCSEs at grades A* to C (including English and Maths), compared to 61% of those who did not require free school meals.

Several broad patterns can be discerned when exploring ethnicity. British Chinese, Indian, Black African and Other Asian groups have disproportionately high numbers of high-scoring students compared to British Pakistani, Bangladeshi, Black Caribbean and other Black groups, which have disproportionately high numbers of low-scoring students. Comparing data from 1970 with data from 2000 shows that White students have, on average, fallen from being over-performers to under-performers. Overall, among students entitled to free school meals, all minority ethnic groups achieve greater success than White British students. (Strand, 2015).

It can also be noted that girls started to outperform boys in the 1970s. This difference has remained consistent, with an approximate 10% difference across the two genders achieving five GCSEs.

How can we explain these persistent differences? There is a huge body of sociological work focused on this question, and we explore some of the key ideas below. Explanations can be found both within and outside school, as well as in the way that parents exercise an influence on what happens in school.

Factors inside the school

Although schooling in the UK is free to all children up to the age of 18, not all schools offer the same experience. For those who can afford them, private schools (which educate about 6.5% of all students) often boast smaller class sizes, better equipment, and access to extracurricular activities. Children who attend private schools experience much good fortune (Friedman and Reeves, 2020; Reeves et al, 2017). They are more likely to attend elite universities (between 2010 and 2015, 43% of offers from Oxford and 37% from Cambridge went to privately educated students); 74% of judges came from this group and 32% of MPs – clearly disproportionate numbers.

However, the distinctions within schools do not relate only to whether they are state or privately run. A long and important history of research has established that not all students have the same experiences within state schools. This has established that:

- the quality of state schools can vary
- the classes in which students finds themselves can impact their access to learning (research has shown that setting and streaming in schools can affect teacher perceptions as well as what parts of the curriculum a student is taught)
- peers may influence the learning environment.

Important research has been carried out on how subcultures within schools can shape educational attainment. One of the most famous studies in this area is by a Marxist writer called Paul Willis (1977/1981), who vividly described how being situated in a peer group that was 'anti-school' and rejected the school's values had significant implications for a student's educational achievement. Boys in the 'anti-school' group disrupted lessons and played up to teachers as a means of securing status amongst their friends. Peer group influences can operate even in early years. Sellers (2019) found that young children's engagement with reading was in part shaped by their peers and whether reading enabled them to 'fit in' or made them 'stand out'.

Research tends to suggest that anti-school subcultures have a particularly strong impact on working-class boys. This can occur even when teachers try to raise aspirations and support these boys to reach their potential. For instance, Stahl (2014) followed 23 young, White, working-class boys in a London school and found that they regarded academic success as out of their reach; in fact, it was not even something they desired. They wanted to fit in, rather than stand out – to be seen as average/ordinary rather than 'better' than others.

Of course, peer pressure is also exerted and experienced by girls, who often gain status and popularity by refusing to be competitive and focusing attention on their clothing and sexuality. In other words, research shows the influence of hyper-heterosexual feminine norms and expectations, which in turn affects subject choices and classroom behaviour.

Smith used ethnographic methods (see page 69) to show how boys who were focused on displaying hegemonic masculinity did not engage with schoolwork. Indeed, they believed that engaging with homework was feminine. Smith (2007:192) concluded:

> All too often therefore, the main 'lesson outcome' is that schoolwork, a mental/intellectual pursuit positioned as 'feminine' in opposition to manual/physical labour, is something 'only girls do', and anyone displaying interest or enjoyment in study becomes a target for the kind of homophobic taunting rife in adolescent peer culture.

Smith's study also found that teachers were often complicit – condoning and accepting the differential engagement displayed by the boys. This leads to another explanation for unequal attainment: the extent to which teachers within any single school may, consciously or unconsciously, not always offer the same levels of support for all students, thus affecting educational performance.

Labelling theory examines how being treated as able/gifted or non-academic can impact a child's self-concept and become a self-fulfilling prophecy. If a child is *told* that they are able, they will *believe* that they are able, so will work harder and achieve more. For example, Francis et al (2020) examined the impact that putting students into sets based on levels of ability had on self-confidence. They demonstrated the cumulative impact of the self-fulfilling prophecy. Students placed in higher sets gained in confidence and subsequently improved their performance. This suggests that inequity is woven into school practices.

Booher-Jennings (2008) investigated labelling and gender by comparing the ways that teachers interacted with boys and girls, and how the messages were internalised. When boys failed tests, teachers put this down to their poor behaviour. In contrast, they thought that poor performance by girls was founded in low self-esteem. These different views affected how teachers interacted with their pupils and shaped the children's subsequent engagement.

Clearly, attitudes and values can have an impact not just on students' self-concept but also on other school experiences – which class they are put in and which subjects they are encouraged to study. Shifting the focus a little bit away from boys to girls, a study by Francis et al (2016) was insightful. The researchers found that young people made the association that 'girly girls' did not take or do well in science.

The impact of differential experience and treatment is also linked to ethnicity. Research suggests that boys of African Caribbean origin more often experience the negative consequences of labelling, streaming and lower teacher expectations. They find themselves systematically underrepresented in entry to the higher tiers in assessment at age 14 (Strand, 2012). This has a stronger impact on their final attainment than their family and economic background. These findings demand that attention remains focused on the ways that racism operates within schools (Gillborn, 2008; Mirza, 2009; Vincent et al, 2013).

Overall, then, the school that an individual attends, their peer group, their teacher expectations and prevailing social norms shape educational outcomes. These are all important insights, but it is equally important to put school into the wider societal context and explore the impact of factors beyond it, including material wealth and deprivation, cultural values and parental involvement in schooling.

Factors outside of school

Material factors undoubtedly shape educational achievement. Children from wealthier homes might have access to private tutors and a variety of resources; in contrast, those from poorer homes may find it harder to secure access to computers, books, a space to study, etc. The Sutton Trust (2019) showed, for instance, that 27% of 11–16 year olds had received private tuition – and in London that figure was 41%. This access to tutors was more likely if children came from richer families. These differences unsettle the idea of a meritocracy in important ways.

Case Study: The glass floor

An important **longitudinal study** conducted by McKnight (2015) is revealing. In this research, a cohort of children born in 1970 were tracked, to examine the relationship between family background, childhood cognitive skills and final success in the labour market. Two groups of children were followed – one group with relatively low levels of cognitive skills at the age of five, and one with higher levels of cognitive skills.

The report found that children from lower-income families, or those with less-advantaged social class backgrounds, did not perform as well in the cognitive tests as children from higher-income families or those from advantaged social class backgrounds. However, the study also showed that children from more advantaged social class backgrounds with lower cognitive skills still tended to succeed at school and in work, performing better than high-attaining children from less advantaged families. McKnight concludes that parents were able to 'game' meritocracy by scaffolding their children's education with private tuition, effectively constructing a glass floor that their children could not fall through.

Much research supports the idea that middle-class parents can influence their child's performance. Gillies (2005) showed that parents from this social class were keen to describe their children as unique and bright, even if they were not performing well in national tests. You can see here how labelling can operate within the family as well as school, and when supplemented with private tuition, help with homework and so forth, educational experiences are far from equal. It is here that the melding of home and school experiences can be seen. In another study, Triventi et al (2020) found that privileged families worked hard to secure educational advantage though their choice of schools, and so perpetuated inequality.

Scholars have also looked at the cultural influences that families endow, which can encourage stronger chances of success. For instance, Strand (2014) showed that despite limited access to economic resources, parental educational aspirations and support accounted for high achievement in some minority ethnic groups. This is a difficult area to study because it makes the dangerous assumption that some families do not support their children. Working-class and certain minority ethnic families are often blamed for 'failing' to support their children. Sociologists must always be careful when making or using inferences about cultural deprivation. There is more on this later in this chapter, and in Chapter 5.

To summarise, we have detailed a lot of information in this section, but only scraped the surface of the rich insights that sociology brings to understanding educational inequalities. What is clear is that inequalities continue to characterise education and sociological research is still necessary to reveal how schools, parents and wider society shape educational outcomes.

Health inequality: why do some people live longer than others?

Health inequality is another essential area of sociological research. All the available evidence suggests that differences in life expectancy (mortality rates) and illness prevalence (morbidity rates), both within the UK and between countries, continue to deepen. We will see the importance of thinking about the impact of absolute and relative poverty and, again, will show that an intersectional approach is vital for exploring health differences.

Before we examine the data for the UK, it is important to consider the global evidence. The World Health Organization (WHO) documents that 16,000 children under the age of five die every day. The risk is 14 times higher for children living in sub-Saharan Africa. The chances of women dying in childbirth – a minimal risk in the Global North these days – continues to be a real threat in some parts of the globe. In Chad, for example, the risk of maternal mortality is 1 in 16, compared to 1 in 10,000 in Sweden. Such inequalities do not only have an impact on just women and children. In terms of overall life expectancy, children born in

Sierra Leone can hope to live to the age of 50; children born in Japan can expect to live an extra 34 years – to an average age of 84.

One of the most influential writers on health inequalities in the UK is Michael Marmot (2015), who powerfully established the importance of studying social determinants of health. The conditions in which we are born, live, work and age, and our access to money and resources, all shape our chances of living a long and healthy life. Indeed, Marmot contended that these factors are more influential than the medical care we can access. His work has shown the fine-grained impact of social position on health – the higher someone is on the social scale, the better their health.

The impact of social position is evident in data from the Office of National Statistics (2020), which examines 2017 health outcomes in England by indices of deprivation, measured by income, employment and education, for instance. This shows that men living in the most deprived (MD) areas can expect to live until the age of 74, compared to 83.3 years for those living in the least deprived (LD) areas. Life expectancy for women is also shaped by deprivation, with those living in wealthier areas expected to live for seven and half more years than their more deprived peers (78.7 years versus 86.2 years).

There is some nuance evident here. Men who live in LD areas can expect to live longer than women in MD areas – in other words, deprivation intersects with gender. It is also important to add in other variables. The most deprived areas are in northern England, so comparing different geographical areas increases our intersectional knowledge. For example, women who live in Manchester can expect to live to the age of 79.5, compared to women who live in Camden who, on average, live until 86.5 (Kings Fund, 2020).

Social class has long been shown to have a significant impact on health outcomes. For instance, Engels (1841/1997), Marx's writing partner, wrote about the consequences of poor living conditions on illness, disease and death in the 19th century. Since the 1980s, several landmark reports have established the reality of health inequalities in the UK – and suggest that they are growing.

Again, we can use ONS data to examine life expectancy. The Registrar General's Classification of Class by Occupation for the years 2007–11 shows that people from Social Class I (see page 78) can expect to live for 5.9 years longer than those from Social Class XII, an increase from the 4.9-year difference documented in 1982–86. A year might seem like a small difference, but when referring to time lived, the finding is poignant.

Sociologists seek to understand these differences by focusing particularly on two main explanations:

- the impact of material/structural factors on health inequality (poverty, income, housing, pollution and working conditions)
- the extent to which lifestyle choices explain earlier deaths (diet, exercise, alcohol consumption and smoking).

These factors can be explored separately, but it is important to see the connections between them. Someone's income level shapes their access to leisure facilities and dictates the types of food they can afford to buy, for instance. Being poor can be very stressful and turning to cigarettes, for example, may help alleviate anxiety (Phelen, Link and Tehranifar, 2010). Acknowledging these connections allows us to be more sophisticated when trying to understand health differences, and suggests that simply trying to get people to change their lifestyle choices to improve health outcomes requires more than education.

While it can be instructive to examine the connections between structure and lifestyle, these explanations tend to ignore the health services and delivery of healthcare. To properly understand inequality, we also need to look at *access* to healthcare and whether patients are all treated fairly. The Kings Fund, for example, explains that certain groups of people – asylum seekers, refugees and Gypsy, Roma and Traveller communities – face discrimination and prejudice. Moreover, deprived areas tend to have fewer GPs per head of the population.

There are also differences in the way that GPs and other medical personnel treat patients. Middle-class patients have longer consultations and are more likely to be referred to consultants for further tests than working-class patients, who are more often seen as responsible for their ailments. Sointu (2017) undertook interviews with medical students to show the 'subtle, yet powerful' ways that ideas about 'good' and 'bad' patients develop and reinforce inequalities. Medical students were more likely to align with middle-class patients and define them as 'good', giving them more time and attention. Sointu also found that definitions of 'good' patients were underscored by ethnicity – a division we explore below. Overall, Sointu drew attention to the way that interactions between patients and doctors are classed and racialised.

A closer look at the statistics about health and gender reveal that while men die earlier than women, women are often described as generally sicker based on their more frequent use of healthcare services. How can we account for these differences? That women live for longer suggests that they will have more health problems in later life. However, we can also question whether the statistics are a good measure of objective health. Women are more likely than men to seek help and are far more likely to talk about their emotional and mental health. This suggests that the statistics may underestimate male health needs and that male suicide and earlier deaths of men might be preventable if they were more willing to seek help. You can see here how gender roles can help explain who seeks help and who gets diagnosed and treated.

However, feminist scholars suggest that women's health has been more consistently medicalised – their reproductive cycle, menstruation, pregnancy, infertility and the menopause are subject to medical diagnosis and intervention. If **medicalisation** accounts for the greater levels of *attention* given to women, rather than absolute differences in illness, it also points to the relative lack of attention given to men – another manifestation of gender inequality. Overall, feminist work suggests that patriarchal society impacts both women (greater surveillance and control) and men (who become more invisible).

What about health outcomes by ethnicity? You have seen that measuring ethnicity is complicated, but the data suggests some significant differences in health outcomes across ethnic groups. The poorest health outcomes are experienced by British Bangladeshi and Pakistani people, followed by British Caribbean and Indian people, with the best outcomes associated with British Chinese and White people. Such groupings point immediately to some problems of measurement: these broad categories, derived from self-reported classifications, are based on proxy measures of regional heritage rather than ethnicity, and therefore can mask heterogeneous experiences. Despite these problems, some persistent patterns emerge. For example, diabetes is almost four times more prevalent among British Bangladeshi men and almost three times more prevalent among British Pakistani and Indian men than it is among men in the general population. Differences by ethnicity can also be observed in the prevalence of mental health conditions. Rates of psychotic disorder are higher in Black men (3.2%) and Asian men (1.3%) when compared to White men (0.3%).

Case Study: Racism in health

Karlsen (2007) argues that understanding these differences in terms of biology or behaviour alone is flawed. Instead, ethnicity intersects with socio-economic factors. Nazroo's work (2003) is useful here, as he carefully explores these correlations and suggests that differentials in income, housing and employment play a strong independent role in accounting for health outcomes. However, he notes that socio-economic explanations are not sufficient, and argues that the impact of racial harassment and discrimination on health outcomes must also be considered. He finds the same when studying mental health inequalities (Nazroo, Bhui and Rhodes, 2020), arguing that structural, institutional and interpersonal racism underscore the risk of developing and being diagnosed with mental health problems. Specifically, the researchers contend that Black Caribbean and Black African people experience more psychotic mental illnesses because they face social and economic disadvantage. They are more likely be referred to mental health services by the police and face greater discrimination within the healthcare system. Racism operates both at the level of micro, interpersonal exchanges and as a product of discriminatory institutional practices.

Racism then, like poverty, stands as a 'fundamental' cause of health inequality, underscoring differences in opportunities, access to health services, and the levels of stress endured.

In this section, you have seen the importance of sociology in making sense of the intersecting socio-economic factors that shape our health chances and life expectancy, and have become knowledgeable about how class, gender roles, patriarchy and racism all shape health experiences and outcomes. In the next section, we turn to another central question for sociologists – that of social order.

What gives society order and why do some people break the rules?

Sociologists are often quick to ask why people break rules, why some members of society are 'deviant', and how social norms, institutions and structures might explain such rule-breaking behaviours. But to some degree, this overlooks the more obvious question: why do most people *follow* the rules? Underpinning this question is the notion of **social order**. What gives society order? Is social order necessary? Why do people conform to social order? By asking these questions, sociologists can more effectively address the additional questions of what causes social deviance and why social order may break down.

In this section we explore some of these questions posed above. We begin with an example to introduce this idea of social order through the 'rules of the road'. We then turn to the area of crime and deviance to examine who commits crime and why they do it.

What gives society order? The rules of the road

Imagine that there were no roads, that no one had to pass a test to drive a car, and that there were no safety checks to ensure that cars were roadworthy. Imagine there were no laws about wearing seatbelts, no speed limits and no traffic lights. It would be chaos.

Of course, most countries have roads, and rules that govern who can drive on them and how driving is conducted. These rules are made up of laws, but they also comprise two other types of rule that keep the roads safe: bureaucracy and social norms. Together, these three elements make societies and social order possible.

First are the formal rules of the road – the laws. People must drive within speed limits; they must stop at traffic lights when they are red. People who go faster than a speed limit or run a red light might get pulled over by police and given a fine or have points added to their driving licence. These laws are a mechanism of formal power and people can be punished by an authority for breaking them.

Behind these laws, as Max Weber explained, lies bureaucracy. In order to be allowed on the road, people must pass a driving test to ensure they are competent and safe. Cars must be manufactured to specific standards and undergo rigorous testing. Older cars have to undergo an annual check (a Ministry of Transport test – known as an MOT in the UK) to ensure they are still safe to drive. All drivers must have car insurance.

There are also more informal rules of the road – these form what Durkheim called the collective conscience. Think of a busy roundabout on a road in the UK. As a driver approaches the roundabout, the law says they must give way to the right and not enter the roundabout until there is a safe space for them to do so, but if traffic volume is very high, there may be no spaces. However, another driver may slow down or stop as they come round the roundabout, leaving a gap so that the waiting driver can get through; they may nod to the other driver to indicate that they are letting them pass. In a similar way, drivers may slow down and acknowledge other drivers to let them change lane safely. There is no *law* that says drivers have to let others through, but these are points of etiquette, or social norms – unwritten rules of social conduct that are created through interaction.

The social norms of driving can be illustrated with another example. After the Second World War, Germany was divided into East and West. Many East Germans drove slow cars called Trabants. In contrast, many West Germans drove BMWs, which were fast and accelerated quickly. The types of cars created different social norms in terms of road use, including different 'interpretations' of traffic lights. In East Germany, the social norm was for drivers to slow down if they saw the lights changing from green to amber, so that they could stop for a red light. In West Germany, the social norm was for drivers to accelerate to get through the amber light before it turned red. When Germany was unified there were significantly more car accidents at traffic lights than in the formerly divided counties!

Trabants in East Germany

There are also explicit forms of rule-breaking that take place on the road. For instance, many drivers do not strictly adhere to speed limits, but will brake as they approach a speed camera or if they see a police car up ahead. These behaviours suggest that we monitor our own practice and follow rules when we perceive that we are subject to surveillance (i.e. being watched).

The rules of the road are a good representation of the way that society is ordered at both macro and micro levels, revealing the following characteristics of social order:

- Rules are created by people in power and imposed on others in society.
- Social order nonetheless requires a collective conscience – the majority must buy into the rules in order for society to function without descending into chaos.
- People may bend and interpret rules, but they may be punished if they are caught.
- People create their own rules on a micro level to enable the functioning of society to operate even more efficiently, beyond the formal rules.
- Rules and norms can change.

Why do people follow the rules?

We will now explore each of these points further, as we examine the concepts of bureaucracy, power, ideologies, discourses, social norms and surveillance in relation to the question: Why do people follow the rules?

Bureaucracy

In his influential book *Crimes of the Powerful* (1976/2015), Pearce explains that social order is in fact imaginary. That is to say, it is a product of human construction – humans have created social order and the rules that underpin it. So, if we know that order is made up, why do we accept it and follow the rules, rather than doing as we please? In part, we accept a social order because we recognise that it is better to do so than to live in a state of chaos and anarchy. However, we do not simply follow an order because it makes sense to do so; we are also *obliged* to follow it because we may be punished if we do not. This leads to the question of the role of authority in society.

Weber suggested that we follow authority largely because of the bureaucratic organisation of society (see Chapter 2). Calling an organisation 'bureaucratic' is often a criticism, referring to the red tape we have to get through to achieve an end. This is because bureaucracies aim to be standardised and rational, and their processes are established through rules and procedures. The aim of a bureaucracy is to create a well-oiled machine. Bureaucracy can be seen in all aspects of modern social life.

Power through domination

Bureaucracies are the cornerstone of modern society, and their leaders – sitting at the apex of their hierarchy – are in positions of great power. Bureaucracies can be governments but also businesses and other large organisations. Weber said that bureaucracy generally leads to oligarchy: the rule of a few officials at the head of an organisation. He called this the 'dictatorship of the official'. When societies are dominated by very large organisations, there is a danger that there will be a concentration of economic, legal, political and social power in the hands of a few influential people. For example, Donald Trump was a business leader who extended his influence and became president of the USA. Weber was concerned with revealing this domination and how it characterised modern society.

Sociologists typically use the word 'domination' to refer to a situation in which people are subjected to power held by a few people. Some people will dominate others by force or even violence in order to maintain **social control**. For example, the powers of arrest held by the police enable them to use force to detain a suspected criminal – this may be a physical assertion of force, in which one person is dominated by another.

Power through ideology

Sociologists also talk about another form of power – one exercised not by domination or force, but through language and ideas. You came across this idea of 'ideological power' in Chapter 2. Ideologies are sets of ideas that present a particular, usually distorted, view of reality that serves the interests of those in power. For Marx and Gramsci, therefore, power is always exercised from the top down: held by a ruling class and wielded over people in subordinate classes and positions. Because power is limited to only a few people (e.g. a king over his country, a government over its people), these individuals could be overthrown. The minority in power therefore needs to find a way of governing the majority.

Those wielding ideological forms of power try to persuade the masses that their ideologies are in the best interests of the people. For example, religious ideologies might present a view of reality that justifies belief in a god and thus justifies the power of the Church to wield dominance over its congregation. Therefore, Marx called religion the 'opium of the people' because he thought that it drugged people into subservience to those in power (the bourgeoisie).

Ideologies often do not need to be enforced by violence, but instead become part of people's consciousness – they control people by making things seem natural and normal. Ideologies therefore maintain social order. For Neo-Marxists like Gramsci (1971) power is also achieved through consent. Gramsci coined the term 'hegemony' to explain how the ruling class dominated society by persuading people to share the same values and ideas. A belief in meritocracy (see page 85) is an example of an ideology – it maintains social order because people do not question inequality.

Discursive power

Others have argued that power operates in a more subtle and diffuse way than those described by Marxists. Foucault argued that power was not simply wielded by individuals or influential groups in a ruling class in a top-down fashion. Instead, 'power' (not domination) occurs from the bottom up. He points out how knowledge and power are interconnected, using the word 'discourse' to describe the way that some knowledges become powerful and the way that power is underscored by knowledge. For example, Foucault is not concerned with how medical doctors have power over us as individuals, but with the way in which certain forms of medical knowledge become dominant and therefore shape our conduct as individuals and order our lives. For example, the rise of psychiatry and psychology in explaining mental illness leads to what Foucault describes as a 'confessional society' where we divulge our inner feelings to experts who can then diagnose our inner thoughts and feelings and help us change our behaviour. He believed that discursive power had become more pervasive than a sovereign (top-down) view of power.

Thus far, we have explored three forms of power:

- Power through domination – sometimes by violence or force.
- Power through ideologies – this involves a ruling elite using language and ideas to gain control over the masses by producing false representations of reality, to garner consent.
- Power through discourse – this involves power that is not held by a ruling elite but instead operates through dominant stories (knowledges) circulating in society that tell particular truths about the world.

Sociologists may disagree about exactly how power is wielded, but the factor uniting these accounts is the belief that power is the reason why people follow the rules in societies.

Social norms

Unlike powerful institutions that can enforce laws, such as the military or the police, social norms maintain the social order in more subtle ways. Garfinkel (1967) distinguished between two categories of social norms to explain how social order is maintained – he called these 'mores' (pronounced mor-ays) and 'folkways'. Mores are norms that are regarded as moral principles shared by a social group. Some mores are regarded as stronger than others. The strongest mores are legally protected with laws or other formal norms. For example, stealing is considered immoral and is punishable by law (a formal norm). More often, mores are judged and guarded by public sentiment (an informal norm). For example, if someone does not give up their seat for an elderly or pregnant person on public transport, they are likely to be judged by other passengers, even though they have not broken a formal rule. Folkways are norms without moral underpinnings. They direct appropriate behaviour in the day-to-day practices and expressions of a culture.

For example, should you wear a shirt and tie or a T-shirt and trainers to an event? Mores and folkways stabilise the social condition and make it possible for people to manage their everyday lives. They also allow us to act in ways that seem rational to other people, creating shared understandings and routines.

Ethnomethodology studies the ordered properties of everyday conduct (see Chapter 2), and asks: How does social order enable people to carry out their day-to-day lives? What are the properties of such social order? How do people achieve, or struggle to achieve, such social order? Garfinkel carried out some well-known breaching experiments, which examined what happened when social order was broken down, either intentionally or accidentally. He detailed these in his book *Studies in Ethnomethodology* (1967). One example is that of the counsellor.

Case Study: The counsellor experiment

In this study, Garfinkel recruited ten university students, who were told that the Department of Psychiatry was doing a study into alternative, potentially more efficient, methods of counselling. Students attending the counselling sessions were told to provide the 'counsellor' (actually the experimenter) with some background to the serious problems they were having. They were then instructed to ask the counsellor approximately ten questions about their problem that could be answered with a yes or no response. The students were unaware that the counsellor's answers were entirely random, and not based on what they had said. As a result, the answers were often contradictory. For example, one student asked the counsellor for some advice regarding the change of study from physics to mathematics. The student was failing at physics but was not sure his grades in mathematics were strong enough either. The student asked questions such as whether he should change his degree subject, whether he should change his study habits, and finally whether he should quit his degree entirely and join the Air Force.

The student was recorded trying to make sense of the counsellor's answer, but the counsellor did not give any further response or clarification. The experiment showed that the students filled in the gaps: they made sense of seemingly incoherent responses with reference to the context in which the conversation was taking place: the norms that ordered the context and the assumptions about the other party. For example, in the discussion with the counsellor the physics student asked whether the counsellor thought he had sufficient incentive to get a degree in physics. The counsellor responded 'yes'. Then the student tried to make sense of this answer, noting that he agreed he could if he didn't have such a poor academic record. The student then asked whether the counsellor thought he might be able to successfully study at home and keep relations with his wife, to which the counsellor responded 'no'. This led to further questions about whether the student ought to find somewhere else to study, such as going into school ('no') or to the library ('yes'). After each response, the student tried to make sense of the counsellor's (random) advice.

Garfinkel concluded that we actively impose meaning from people's utterances and, in doing so, we rely on common-sense knowledge to make sense of what people say. When we try to decide what someone else means, we defer to an underlying pattern of behaviour or mores. We work hard to make sense of what is going on and we adapt to ensure that social order is maintained.

Garfinkel's breaching experiments also revealed a larger truism about social order. While the social order is fragile, it does not break because at the level of everyday interactions, we work hard to conform to the established order. The fact that the students in the experiment were quick to make sense of a seemingly nonsensical dialogue told Garfinkel that humans actively construct social order for their own sake and for others. Therefore, social order is performed, not given.

Erving Goffman similarly explored the resilience of the social order in his dramaturgical approach to social life (see pages 35–36). Through his studies of people's everyday interactions – what he called the 'interaction order' – Goffman revealed the ways in which people work to maintain order. When social order is disrupted, people often feel embarrassed, either for themselves if they have broken it, or for others (secondary embarrassment). For example, passing wind in public breaks the social norm. People typically feel embarrassed or may even try to blame it on someone else (or the dog). Goffman argued that our performances of identity are generally put on for different audiences, and we typically act in different ways in front of different sets of people based on our perceived expectations. This reveals how very orderly we are! We want to act in ways that maintain social order and we (generally) perform in accordance with social norms.

In a study entitled 'Performing counter-terrorism' (2020), Monaghan argued that the police engage in performances, or 'image work'. They actively exaggerate the threat of terrorism and present themselves as symbolic guardians against evil. Similarly, in their research into offenders' re-entry into society after a period of imprisonment, Smiley and Middlemass (2016) argued that clothing choice is used to give off certain impressions about the ex-offender's social status. They interviewed former prisoners about their clothing and what impression they thought their choices would have on others. Many ex-offenders described their reluctance to wear clothing that was issued to them on release by the Department of Correction (DOC). They saw DOC clothing as a 'stain' on their identity, limiting their ability to reintegrate and be accepted in society. Those who had the money to buy new clothes felt they integrated better into society and were able to manage the impressions of others to a greater extent. This indicates that individuals engage in impression-management strategies in order to re-enter the established social order.

Goffman's work, like Garfinkel's, focuses on the way that individuals maintain the social order in micro interactions. Foucault, however, goes further than this to explain why we engage in self-presenting behaviour that conforms to a wider set of social norms and order.

Surveillance and self-surveillance

Foucault's work helps sociologists to link power and norms. He believed that power operates through discourses that become dominant in society, establishing social norms that shape our behaviour. We do not simply follow rules because authorities tell us to; we actively monitor and regulate our own behaviour in accordance with wider sets of social norms. Foucault highlights the importance of surveillance, using Bentham's description of the panopticon as a metaphor for how power operates (see page 38).

Criminologists often talk about the connection between surveillance, visibility and social order. The social order is maintained by making people more visible. Visibility is a traditional theory of deterrence (Norris and Armstrong 1999; Norris, 2012); low visibility is associated with deviance and crime. Under this model, crime is considered a rational decision in which people engage in a 'visibility calculus' – they determine how to commit crimes in a low-visibility fashion (i.e. without being seen), reducing the risk of being caught and punished. For example, thieves may disable CCTV cameras before breaking and entering a property; a criminal may find an isolated space without cameras before assaulting a victim.

Sociologists have applied this metaphor of surveillance to many other areas of social life, in which we manage our own behaviours and engage in practices of self-surveillance, such as the example we used earlier of drivers reducing their speed around cameras and police cars.

In summary, you should now be able to see that:

- social norms maintain social order
- social order is inherently fragile and is constantly maintained by everyone
- we engage in practices of self-surveillance, which manage our actions and choices, and which also maintain social order.

In this section we have explained how the social order is produced and maintained, and why it is that people follow the rules. In the next section we turn our attention to the question of why people do choose to break rules.

Why do people break the rules?

There are different types of rules: formal and informal. Most of us are rule-following creatures. However, some people do break the rules and it is the sociologist's job to understand why. What social conditions make rule-breaking possible, or even necessary? People who break formal rules (criminal law) are considered criminals; those who break the informal rules of social order are referred to as deviant. Of course, these two terms, crime and deviance, are not mutually exclusive. While someone can commit a crime that is also considered deviant (murder or rape), someone may commit a crime that is not regarded as deviant (parking on a double yellow line or speeding to get to hospital in an emergency).

Likewise, someone may deviate from social norms without committing a crime (wearing a see-through top in the workplace or visibly picking their nose in a meeting).

In this section we are going to explore common explanations for why people break the law. We will discuss these in relation to the following:

1 'Born' criminals

2 Crime as a rational act

3 Crime as functional

4 Crime as a process of socialisation

5 Crime as a result of inequality and deprivation

6 Crime as resistance and liberation

7 Criminalisation

'Born' criminals

During the early part of the 19th century, it became popular to draw on psychiatry, anthropology and human sciences to understand why people committed crimes. This was called 'scientific criminology'. Cesare Lombroso was one of the founding fathers of positivist criminology, arguing that people were 'born' criminal (also described as being a 'habitual criminal'). This theory suggests that certain people are biologically predisposed to criminality. Lombroso said that there were criminal 'types' and that criminals were evolutionary throwbacks (what he termed 'atavism'). Lombroso and Ferrero (1895), studied the physical features of criminals and claimed that they shared certain distinctive anomalies, including a low forehead, prominent jaws and cheekbones, protruding ears, excessive hairiness and unusually long arms and believed that these 'anomalies' could be used to identify people with criminal tendencies.

Biological theories of crime influenced the eugenics movement, which sought to identify hereditary (born) criminals. In her book *The Criminal Brain* (2008), Rafter argues that because the born criminal was believed to pose a danger to society, responses such as indefinite imprisonment and euthanasia were viewed as ways to prevent criminal types from reproducing.

Lombroso and Ferrero's work also had implications for understandings of gender and crime. They argued that biology tends to prevent women from becoming criminals. They regarded women, like children, as morally deficient, but with natural feminine characteristics (maternal instincts, piety) that usually balanced this moral deficiency. However, if a woman lacked these feminine characteristics, she 'must be transformed into a born criminal more terrible than any man' (1895:151).

While early biological theories of crime have generally been discredited, biological science continues, even today, to try to explain criminality based on biological difference. For example, Wilson and Herrnstein's *Crime and Human Nature* (1985) argued that some people are born predisposed towards criminality. Mednick, Moffitt and Stack (1987) spoke of genetic factors that could predict criminal behaviour.

These biological views have also influenced the criminal justice system. For example, research by Moir and Jessel (1997) showed how women's hormones are often used to explain their criminal behaviour. Moir and Jessel give historic examples of women who were held responsible for crimes because it was assumed that they were suffering from pre-menstrual syndrome (PMS).

As sociologists, however, it is important to be wary of any explanation of criminality that tries to root it in a person's biology, because biological categories themselves are socially constructed. Any effort to reduce someone to their biology is described by sociologists as reductionist. Moreover, as Mills reminds us, the sociological imagination requires that we examine an individual act of crime in relation to broader issues of social structure rather than as a personal trouble.

Crime as a rational act

The view that crime is a rational act developed into several different theories that collected in the USA under the umbrella term '**right realism**' in the 1970s and 1980s, in an attempt to explain why people committed crimes. One example is the 'broken windows theory' developed by Wilson and Kelling (1982), which was underpinned by the assumption that people would be less likely to commit crime in an area if they thought they would get caught. Higher crime rates were found in areas that were subject to less surveillance. Broken windows that went unfixed were a signal that an area was not well surveilled, so criminals knew they were less likely to be caught. The decision to commit crime – or not – is therefore considered rational.

Statistics from the Office for National Statistics on Coronavirus and Crime illustrate the idea of crime as a rational act. The figures indicate a 32% decrease in crimes in the UK during the pandemic, particularly in crimes such as domestic burglary. We might theorise that this is because people spent more time at home during the pandemic, and it would not be a rational act for someone to break into a property to steal things when people were inside.

Crime as functional

In *The Rules of Sociological Method* (1895/2014), Durkheim argued that not only was crime a natural part of the social order, it was also inevitable and, indeed, functional. You may recall that Durkheim's view of social order was one of a collective conscience (see page 94), but he also said that not everyone in society would share this conscience. Because individuals are all unique, some people will still break the law.

Durkheim asked us to imagine living in a 'society of saints', where everyone behaved morally all the time. He said that even in this society, people would still be deviant because the standards of conduct would be so high that it would be impossible for everyone to measure up to them all the time. He went on to say that these deviations would be met with such strong disapproval that they would become criminalised.

Durkheim's view was that crime has a social function, and only becomes harmful when its rate is very high or very low. Some forms of deviance are seen as positive for Durkheim because they initiate social change. For example, when the Suffragettes broke the law it brought about social change in the form of voting rights for women. In addition to this, Durkheim saw punishment as being good for society because it reminded people to conform to social norms and it maintained the collective conscience. Without punishment, the collective conscience would lose its strength and ability to keep most people in society in line.

Crime as a process of socialisation

Socialisation is a process of behaviour regulation through which people come to learn and adopt society's values and norms. It takes place in the family (**primary socialisation**) and through other institutions (education, religion, etc.) or subcultural groups, such as friends (**secondary socialisation**).

Sociologists studying crime have argued that children can be socialised into criminal behaviour if their families engage in criminal activity. For example, an early study by Wilson (1987) argued that criminality runs in families. Farrington et al (2001) later argued that criminality in families predicts delinquency. They researched arrest patterns in families and showed that if close family members were involved in crime, it was possible to predict delinquency in children. The strongest predictor of delinquency was for boys whose father had been arrested. Taylor and Workman (2019) also argued that 'delinquents' could be re-educated and re-socialised so that they no longer saw crime as normal.

Other sociologists have developed theories of socialisation to examine how young people are socialised into crime outside of the family. Miller (2020) argues that gangs are an example where 'street socialisation' into crime takes place. In contrast, Messerschmidt (2005) argues that men are socialised into hegemonic masculinity, a term he adopts from Connell (2005). Messerschmidt argues that physical aggression is an important attribute of performing hegemonic masculinity, and that certain crimes can be seen as attempts to reproduce this. Dobash and Dobash's (1979) work revealed how hegemonic masculinity is linked to domestic violence – a means by which men display control over female partners.

As a sociologist, it is important to be careful when drawing on socialisation theories of crime, because they often accept the view that the individual committing the crime is a 'delinquent'. These theories claim that the person was socialised into delinquency, but do not consider how the crime itself is a socially produced category.

Crime as a result of inequality and deprivation

We began this chapter by discussing issues related to social inequalities as they impact education and health. It is also possible to apply this knowledge of inequality in order to understand crime. Many sociologists who research gangs (for example, Miller, 2020) discuss how these groups develop in areas with high instances of inequality and poverty. Gangs typically emerge in deprived neighbourhoods with high crime rates (Kirk and Papachristos, 2011).

Several sociologists have suggested that an individual's unequal position in society (deprivation) may explain why they break the rules (and law). Deprivation is a concept that should be used with care when trying to explain rule-breaking (we will explain why later), but below we outline some key studies and positions that try to explain crime in relation to deprivation.

Charles Murray and the underclass and crime

New right theorist Murray (1996) argued that society had an underclass, which he described as people who lacked employment, income and education. Murray also perceived the underclass as lacking intelligence. He criticised state welfare for encouraging a society of 'pathological welfare dependency', which he believed enabled this underclass not to work. Out of work and out of 'mainstream' society, members of the underclass were more likely to commit crime. Murray's is a 'culture of poverty' thesis that includes some of the earlier ideas concerning 'habitual' criminals that emerged from 19th-century positivism.

Cultural deprivation theories of crime

Much like the culture of poverty thesis, cultural deprivation refers to the idea that people break rules because they belong to a low-income subculture that is deprived of the means to achieve social success (see page 42). The idea that members of the working class have their own subculture, with distinct norms and values, can be criticised because it essentialises an entire class of people – that is, it sees everyone as the same when it is likely many people would not share the core characteristics said to describe this group. It reproduces derogatory stereotypes that can be seen as classist and racist.

Case Study: Crime and culture

A number of writers have shown how explaining crime by attributing it to particular cultures constitutes a new form of racism. We can see this problem unpacked in Phillips' (2019) study of Gypsy/Travellers and doorstep fraud. The statistics showed that Gypsy/Irish Travellers commit more fraud offences than other ethnic groups – they comprise 2% of those imprisoned for any (including non-doorstep) fraud offences while making up only 0.1% of the general population. Phillips makes a number of observations. First, the actual number of doorstep crimes amongst the Gypsy/Traveller community is still small, but it becomes exaggerated in public consciousness. Second, while there are aspects of Gypsy/Traveller culture that might make it more possible to commit crime (for example, a nomadic lifestyle means Gypsy/Travellers are less well-known to the local population and are less easy for police to track), it is too simplistic to accept this as the sole explanation for their disproportionate representation in the statistics. Rather, she argues that the discrimination faced by this group, both in terms of police and trading standards existing biases, and the likelihood of victim-reporting bias, explains why Gypsy/Travellers become known to the police and also might explain why this group might resort to crime because they face discrimination and are structurally excluded. Phillips, for example, notes that Gypsy/Travellers are disenfranchised and suffer deprivation on a number of different levels. For example, the UK Parliament's Commons Committee Report 'Tackling inequalities faced by Gypsy, Roma and Traveller communities' (2019) noted that these communities had the worst outcomes of any ethnic group in a wide range of areas, including education, health, employment, criminal justice and hate crime, but that little was being done to tackle longstanding inequalities. It is also important to note that these communities have also suffered a long history of racism and state exclusion.

There is another important issue to be drawn from this study. As Phillips notes, it is still only a minority of Gypsy/Travellers who commit crimes, so we can see here what sociologists call an **ecological fallacy** – when a statistical pattern (here, a slightly higher propensity to commit doorstep fraud among Gypsy/Travellers than other groups) is used to make a generalisation about all members of a group.

Robert Merton's strain theory and crime

Robert Merton (1938) was a functionalist sociologist who said that people broke the rules when they could not meet the expectations of society. His work considered how the 'American Dream', built on meritocratic ideals, created expectations that a good life was equally achievable for all. However, different opportunity structures (class, ethnicity, etc.) meant that not everyone could meet these expectations and that some people could only achieve success through illegitimate means.

Other sociologists have shown how societies with less welfare support exert a greater strain on individuals. Rudolph and Starke (2020) showed that countries with more welfare support, particularly in the form of unemployment benefits, had lower crime rates. Vanderpyl's (2019) research also shows that materialism and the pursuit of the American Dream is often cited by young prisoners as a reason for juvenile criminality.

Subcultures and crime

Some sociologists have argued that people break the rules of society because of their involvement in delinquent subcultures. For example, Cohen (1955), like Merton, said that working classes are deviant because they feel strained. They have status frustration because they cannot reach the success levels that society expects and normalises. However, Cohen said that people do not react individually (as Merton believed) but that they form subcultural groups together. These groups react to social norms by inverting them and creating delinquent subcultures that take on new, deviant norms such as truancy and vandalism. Members of the group adopt these new norms to gain recognition from one another. Here, people do not just break rules because they want money but because they want status.

Marxist theories of crime as a response to economic oppression

Marxists state that capitalism is criminogenic (it generates crime), because crime is the natural and inevitable result of living in a repressive and unequal capitalist system, where it is seen as a rational solution to an economic problem. Neo-Marxists also regarded crime as a form of resistance to economic oppression.

Left realists, marginalisation and relative deprivation

Jock Young and John Lea are often credited with developing a theory of crime called 'left realism' in Britain in the early 1980s. They supported the view that deprivation leads to crime, but they did not think of deprivation in absolute form. Instead, they argued that it was relative deprivation that would lead to rule-breaking. Relative deprivation is the feeling of being deprived in relation to other similar groups, or when one's expectations are not met. Advertisers and the media would have us believe that our lives will be wonderful if we have the latest designer merchandise, a new car, etc. This creates a society in which people feel deprived if they do not have these things. Young considered that the rise of consumer culture and the fact that people felt pressured to own the latest products, created a sense of expectation and deprivation. It is not just the poor who feel this sense of expectation, though – even members of the middle class and the elite can feel deprivation in comparison to their peers. This can explain **white-collar crime** – crime that is financially motivated. Young and Lea therefore argued that crime is generated by a combination of relative deprivation, the formation of subcultural groups and a sense of marginalisation (a lack of representation in positions of authority).

Crime as resistance and liberation

Feminists have critically examined the increase in women's crime rates over time. One theory is that since women have been liberated from the restrictive patriarchal social order, they have had more opportunities to commit crime. Adler (1975) is often credited with this liberation hypothesis, which suggests there has been a rise in violent female criminality attributed to 'ladette culture', or to what Young (2009) calls the emergence of the 'shemale' gangster. However, as Young noted, this notion of a surge in female involvement in violent crime is a media moral panic, and behind the hypothesis lies very little evidence. The girl gang members she interviewed were predominantly involved in low level violence and shoplifting, shaped by friendships rather than being gang-related. It is simplistic, therefore, to frame young women as hyper-violent female gangsters.

Gilroy (1982, 1987/2002) argued that Black criminality was a myth produced and perpetuated through negative stereotypes of African Caribbean and Asians, and could be explained as a response to anti-colonial struggles. These negative stereotypes were held by the police, resulting in a bias in police statistics concerning ethnic differences in offenders. It was not the case that groups were poorly socialised or more prone to crime.

Protests by the Black community that resulted in street-level conflict further fuelled the belief that Black people were more prone to criminality. However, as Gilroy wrote, these riots, as well as marches and demonstrations, throughout the 1970s, were forms of community self-defence in response to an oppressive social order and racial violence. Indeed, Gilroy referred to an example at a police disco in Hammersmith, London, where news was shared with officers that rioting had started. The officers' immediate response was to sing 'there ain't no Black in the Union Jack'. Senior officers silenced them, but nonetheless, such racist views demonstrate the police prejudice prevalent in Britain.

Criminalisation

Each of the theories above attempts to explain why people break the rules; however, none of them considers how the rules themselves are products of a social context that frames some acts as criminal and deviant and others as normal. Criminalisation is the process by which a group of people are socially constructed as criminals. We can turn to several examples here to explain how sociologists have developed this idea.

Labelling theory

In *Outsiders* (1963/2008), Becker argued that all social groups have rules and values, and if you contravene them you are labelled as a deviant outsider. Deviance is not directly related to a person's specific action, but rather it tells us the degree to which society determines whether what one does is normal or not. The person considered deviant is the person to whom a label has been applied successfully. People label deviant behaviour: certain acts only become deviant when people define them that way. The problem is that once someone is labelled as deviant, it becomes a self-fulfilling prophecy. A child labelled the 'bad' or 'naughty' one will be more likely to live up to that label.

The social construction of crime statistics

In England and Wales, the official statistics on crime come from two main sources: police-recorded crime and victim-reported crime (which comes from the Crime Survey for England and Wales, CSEW). In 'The Social Construction of Official Statistics', Coleman and Moynihan (2002) argue that official crime statistics do not simply present the facts about crime, but represent a series of complex decisions about what gets reported and what gets counted as a crime. In summarising complex information, statistics do not capture every intricacy. There are often simplifications and omissions: choices are made about how to define the problem being measured and how to go about measuring it. Many factors determine whether a criminal offence becomes part of the official 'crime rate'. For instance, members of the public or victims may choose not to report crimes. Perhaps they do not realise a crime has occurred (for example, in the case of fraud) or they may be powerless or frightened (as is often the case with domestic violence). They may feel that reporting the crime is too much hassle, or they may not trust that the police will act on the report.

Likewise, if a crime is reported, the police may exercise discretion over whether or not it gets reported. For instance, the police may let someone off with a warning instead of convicting them. Variations over time in levels of a particular crime may also be due not to actual variations in the crime, but rather variations in the police's decision to focus on particular crimes, who to subject to surveillance and who to prosecute. Police officers may also 'fiddle' the figures (for example, 'cuffing' – where the police do not record a reported crime).

Overall, statistics reveal that less than half of criminal incidences are reported to the police and only about 60% of reported crime is recorded by the police. This is referred to as the 'statistical iceberg', because only a small proportion of the true scale of crime can be seen, with much more hidden beneath the surface.

> Look back at Chapter 3. How might the information you have just read – about the challenges of and inconsistencies in recording crimes and crime rates – be linked to the disadvantages of using official statistics as a source of data?

The social construction of crime

Given that social processes determine whether something is considered a crime or not, some sociologists argue that crime is a social construct. Homosexuality, for example, was considered a crime in Britain until 1967, when it was legalised due to changing social norms concerning sexuality. Abortion, too, was regarded as a criminal act until 1968 when it was legalised under certain conditions in England.

Hardes (2020) showed how boxing avoided becoming a criminal act while duelling and prize-fighting were both criminalised. People sought to ban the practice, claiming that it promoted violence, so the rules and regulations governing boxing were adapted in order to sanitise and reinvent it as a sport (through the use of gloves, timed bouts and a definable, measured ring space, for example). Overall, this shows how boxing was constructed as a sport rather than as a criminal act of violence.

Criminalisation and inequalities

Race/ethnicity

Crime statistics indicate a disproportionate number of adults in the criminal justice system (CJS) in certain ethnic groups. Figure 4.2 is compiled from 2016 data and shows that the White population's presence in the CJS is lower than its overall population rate. Comparatively, the Black population is relatively small, but the arrested, prosecuted, convicted and prisoner population is higher.

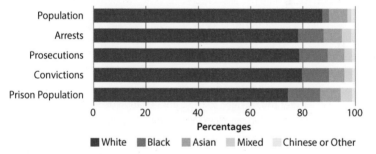

Figure 4.2: Ethnicity proportions throughout the CJS, 2016

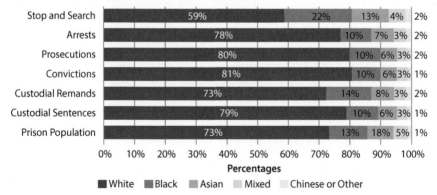

Figure 4.3: The proportion of adults throughout the criminal justice system in each ethnic group, 2018.

Figure 4.3 shows the most recent figures (2018), and also highlights the differences by ethnicity across all areas of the criminal justice system, from the processes that lead to arrest, such as stop and search, to imprisonment. However, the reference to the overall population size is not given in this chart. If you were to take the 2018 data at face value, it would appear that the relationship between ethnicity and crime is not as significant as in 2016. In removing the overall population size from the bar chart, the inequality and disproportionality within the CJS is hidden. The way that statistics are presented can completely change our interpretation of the relationship between crime and ethnicity. Sociologists are always alert to the way that the presentation of statistics changes over time.

There are difficulties in collating data about ethnic inequalities that stem from the way that communities are grouped for research purposes. Nevertheless, the evidence of inequality is compelling, and is revealed by looking more closely at stop and search. Government data from 2021 that collates the number of stop and searches between April 2019 and March 2020 showed that there were six stop and searches for every 1,000 White people compared with 54 for every 1,000 Black people. This means Black people are nine times more likely to be stopped and searched than White people.

Sociologists try to explain this disproportionality by considering wider social factors. We have already explored several explanations for ethnic differences in offending, including inequality and deprivation. However, social inequalities alone cannot explain the disproportionality of these statistics, and sociologists argue that police racism is another factor. Such racism is not simply a product of the beliefs and values of individual officers; it is deeply embedded in society and can lead to the criminalisation of Black and minority ethnic groups because it is grounded in negative stereotypes.

The Home Office argued that in fact the official data is skewed because most stop and searches take place in London, where a higher proportion of minority ethnic communities live. Furthermore, Waddington, Stenson and Don (2004) argued that it is important to consider who is available to be stopped and searched – that is, we should look at the 'daytime' population. When stop figures are compared to those groups *available* to be stopped, there is little difference proportionally by ethnicity. Critical race scholars like Bowling and Phillips (2002, 2007) strongly disagree with this, arguing that stop and search statistics indicate deeply embedded institutional racism. They also point out that Waddington's availability thesis ignores the structural factors that might make some people more 'available' to be stopped than others, such as unemployment, homelessness, school exclusion and evening and night work.

'Institutional racism' was a term adopted in Britain in the MacPherson Report (1999) following the death of student Stephen Lawrence in 1993. Lawrence was 18 years old when he was murdered in a racist attack in London by a gang of White youths. The report documented that the investigation into Lawrence's murder was marred by professional incompetence, a failure of leadership as well as institutional racism. The report defined institutional racism as 'the collective failure of an organisation to provide an appropriate and professional service to people because of their colour, culture, or ethnic origin. It can be seen or detected in processes, attitudes and behaviour which amount to discrimination through unwitting prejudice, ignorance, thoughtlessness and racist stereotyping which disadvantage minority ethnic people' (1999:49). There were several examples of incompetence, failures and institutional racism, including the fact that the police accused Lawrence's friend Duwayne Brooks (also young and Black), without evidence, of committing Lawrence's murder. Additionally, there was an inadequate collection of evidence at the scene, a two-day delay in setting up surveillance because police resources had already been committed to watching a Black alleged mugger, the patronising of Stephen's family, and a failure to make early arrests of the suspects or adequately search their premises.

Institutional racism is not confined to the UK. In her book *Are Prisons Obsolete?* (2003), Davis documented the history of mass incarceration in the United States and showed its links to controlling Black populations. She argues that certain 'criminal categories' were created in order to turn Black Americans into prisoners. The need to criminalise Black people was also tied to what she and others describe as the 'prison-industry complex'. The abolition of slavery meant that many former slave owners were in search of cheap or free labour. New laws made it possible to criminalise Black people, who then could be made to work without payment – a practice known as convict leasing. Many Black prisoners worked in brutal conditions while White prisoners were incarcerated but not required to work.

Gender

Studies on gender and crime have traditionally focused on why women are less likely to commit crime. They have either concentrated on why women have been more likely to escape detection or prosecution, or they have focused on the lack of opportunities for women to commit crime as they have historically been more confined to the domestic sphere. As Heidensohn (1996:175) put it, domesticity was a mechanism of 'detention'. Of course, this is not true of society today, and certainly most women in the Global North are free to choose whether they want to pursue a domestic life, a work life, or both.

However, if women do now have more freedom, how can we explain the continued over-representation of men in crime figures? There are a number of reasons for this. First, women are socialised to be conforming. Second, it is suggested that women are more likely to be let off by the police or have more lenient sentences because police and the judiciary regard women to be less likely to be involved in serious crime. This is known as the chivalry thesis (Chesney-Lind, 1978).

When women do break the law and are charged, they are seen as doubly deviant because they have failed to conform to gender expectations of appropriate femininity (Heidensohn, 1987). Weare (2013) also argued that women who murder are subjected to gendered norms concerning the act of killing. Since they are breaking the norms of being passive and gentle and caring, the law normalises their behaviour in other ways by reference to wider gendered social scripts. For instance, they tend to be labelled as either 'mad', 'bad' or as a 'victim' of a system that forced them to kill. This labelling can also result in more lenient sentencing, or sentencing that results in psychiatric treatment rather than imprisonment. These different examples reveal how gendered norms, and expectations of women criminals are deeply embedded in the CJS.

Moral panics

'Moral panic' literature also comes from the perspective that crime and deviance are social constructs. The term was made popular in Cohen's book *Folk Devils and Moral Panics: The Creation of the Mods and Rockers* (1972). Moral panics emerge when the general public develops a widespread anxiety, usually in relation to a certain condition, or to a group of people, who are seen to threaten social norms. The media plays a significant role in moral panics, because it sensationalises and exaggerates a particular issue and can direct attention away from other social issues. For example, Hall et al's (1978) work explained how the media created a moral panic around mugging and this directed attention away from wider economic austerity and towards young Black men.

Falkof (2020) argued that moral panics can best be understood as narratives that try to make sense of social change and insecurity, but which also have ideological motives. They are generally driven by a culture of anxiety and fear. Philips and Chagnon (2020) argued that a moral panic is often used to deflect attention from a genuine fear. For example, they examined the way that a moral panic is used to explain away the surge in university campus rapes. In the media, the focus on campus rapes was a described as 'witch hunt', deflecting attention away from the genuine cases that victims felt able to report following the MeToo campaign.

Invisible or hidden crimes of the powerful

We have already established that official crime statistics are not always valid and reliable. We have also shown how they are socially constructed, drawing attention to documented crime, which is also crime more likely to be committed by those who society treats more unequally. This is revealed by the fact that white-collar crime and corporate crime do not receive the same amount of police attention and do not figure so strongly in the official data.

A clear example of this discrepancy can be seen in the differential treatment of the crimes of benefit fraud and tax evasion. More attention is paid in the popular media and in police practices to benefit fraud despite the fact that statistics indicate that tax evasion occurs to a much greater extent. The Department of Work and Pensions (DWP) (2018/2019) estimated that £2.3 billion was lost to benefit fraud, constituting about 1.2% of all benefit spending. In comparison, Her Majesty's Revenue and Customs (HMRC) (2017/18) estimated that £35 billion was not collected in taxes, constituting 5.6% of tax revenues.

Look back at Charles Murray's piece on the underclass (page 104) and the discussion of moral panics above. What links can you draw between the ways that poor people who claim benefits are demonised while their elite counterpart's engagement in crime is overlooked? Consider how these crimes are disproportionately reported on in the media and how poorer people are often labelled as inadequate and lazy.

Summary

You should now realise that sociologists provide many explanations for the questions 'Why do we have social order?' and 'Who breaks the rules?' While the answers to these questions vary, they share some similarities.

We have a social order because:

- it makes living in a society, as groups of people, possible
- social order is sustained through bureaucracy, power, and social norms.

People break the rules because:

- they are subjected to social inequalities along axes of stratification (gender, ethnicity, social class)
- the rules are themselves products of social context that turns certain people into criminals and allows others to escape criminalisation.

Social order and rule-breaking are interrelated concepts, and they are both socially constructed categories. Sociologists have explored how those with power create a social order, comprised of rules and norms, that legitimises and maintains social inequalities. Those that break the rules of the social order often do so because they are otherwise powerless, or because they are seen as a threat to the social order and thus must be 'managed' efficiently by being labelled as deviant (within the media, for example), or by being criminalised.

Who do we think we are, and what shapes our sense of self?

In the final section of this chapter, we turn our attention to identity and cultural norms, values and beliefs. So far, we have explored how society is divided along different axes of inequality, and how society is ordered and why people break the rules. In this section, we want to delve deeper into the question of what makes us who we are and how our identity is socially formed. Focusing particularly on the family and religion, this section is framed around the following themes:

- socialisation
- culture: norms, values and beliefs
- identity and self-identity
- individualisation and consumerism.

Socialisation

As you have seen, sociologists distinguish between primary socialisation, which happens in the family, and secondary socialisation, which happens in other social institutions such as in education, healthcare, friendship groups, the workplace, and also – importantly for this section of the chapter – religious institutions.

Primary socialisation is the process through which children come to learn the culture of their family group. They learn how to think, believe, see, feel and act. The important point here is that we do not *instinctively* know how to behave; we learn how to conduct ourselves by mimicking our family's behaviour and by being disciplined when we do something 'wrong'. This serves an important social role in raising children to conform to wider societal expectations about behaviour and conduct. It also shapes who we think we are, how we act, and our social status.

The way in which parents dress their children, according to gender expectations, socialises those children into gender roles that are the product of wider social norms and expectations. Young (2005) went further than this, to suggest that such socialisation processes have a real impact on our bodies. Consider how girls' clothing often restricts free movement – girls are taught to sit with their legs crossed when they wear skirts. Young also notes that young children are given different toys to play with depending on their gender. Boys are more likely to play sport and engage in 'tinkering' and building with toys such as Lego, while girls generally have less opportunity to develop spatial skills as they are channelled into more sedentary play with toys such as dolls. Girls therefore develop bodily timidity and inhibition, which is revealed in lots of different ways. Young argues that this has enabled cultural stereotypes such as 'throwing like a girl', because girls often do not engage their full physical body when throwing a ball, but are more restricted in their movement.

Sociologists have also argued that socialisation in the family reproduces wider social inequalities (see page 121). Reeves (2015), for example, argued that middle-class families often encourage their children to play musical instruments, which he refers to as 'cultural socialisation'. Economically privileged families are more likely to engage in what Bourdieu calls highbrow and valued cultural activities, such as going to galleries and taking dance lessons. Primary socialisation, therefore, reproduces social class distinctions.

Secondary socialisation is the process by which children come to learn more specifically the cultures of wider society. We have used the word 'cultures' to emphasise the fact that many societies have multiple, dominant values, customs, beliefs and norms. Sometimes these are in conflict with one another. For example, children can be socialised in how to conduct themselves in an education setting. In school, we learn to be disciplined (to sit and listen); we learn about authority and about the consequences of not following the rules; we learn how to form relationships with peers and other adults outside our family unit; we learn that our position in life is the product of our ability and hard work (the myth of meritocracy).

Therefore, education plays an important social role in shaping our sense of self and identity. Functionalists would see this as the most effective way of integrating individuals into society and of enabling consensual order. One example is how we are socialised into becoming high-achieving individuals – we are tested as individuals, given praise or good grades for success – and this prepares us to live in a society where we are expected to perform and function as individuals.

In contrast, Marxists see this as an oppressive way of getting people to conform to and accept their place within a capitalist society. They refer to the **hidden curriculum** – the things that we learn in school that are not part of formal learning. For example, Bowles and Gintis (1976) showed how schools produce obedient and timetabled workers. Willis's famous study, *Learning to Labour* (1977/1981), also revealed how working-class boys were socialised in school to aspire to working-class jobs.

Feminists would add that schools socialise children into gender roles that are products of wider patriarchal social values. Booher-Jennings (2007), for instance, described how the process of 'learning to label' in schools occurs. She found that boys and girls were treated differently by teachers and that this reinforced gender roles, discouraging boys from engaging in educational work. Specifically, she found that teachers tended to explain boy's failure in school tests in terms of their poor behaviour, while in contrast they explained girls' failure in tests as a result of their lack of self-esteem.

> What other ways can you think of in which schools socialise boys and girls differently?

Culture: values, norms and beliefs

Sociologists define 'culture' as a social group's way of life. It exists before we are born and remains after we die. It includes not just values, norms, customs and beliefs, but also language, history and knowledge that are shared within a group and passed on from generation to generation.

Norms

As you have seen, norms define the behaviour that is seen as acceptable or unacceptable in society. In addition to this, social norms are underpinned by shared social values and beliefs. Norms are beliefs and values put into practice.

Beliefs

Beliefs are ideas about the world that we hold to be true. Sometimes our beliefs may not be based on evidence – for example, we might believe in a religious god or deity, in meritocracy or gender equality. Remember, however, that some beliefs are better seen as ideologies, perpetuated by the powerful in society. For example, the myth of meritocracy is designed to get people to believe that through hard work and effort it is possible to move up the social ladder. Beliefs therefore lead us to take on certain values that are deemed socially important.

Values

Often, we take values to be personal things – the standards or principles that we hold dear, which we deem as important, worthwhile or credible. Sociologists argue that values are held across society, but can also be specific to groups.

Values determine whether we perceive actions or behaviours to be right or wrong, good or bad. Values are therefore **normative**. Values also produce moral truths. We use our values to make moral judgments about people and behaviours. Shared values can bring us together, but they can also create social divisions when people cannot (or do not want to) meet the expectations that these values set.

We can see, then, the possibility of a clash of values when cultures have distinctly different sets of beliefs. This has led to a lot of discussion – and sometimes controversy – over how to manage **multiculturalism**. Some people believe that in any society, everybody should share the same values. This is a cultural assimilationist model of society, whereby people are expected to conform to the prevailing values. Others call for a more plural and tolerant model of difference, where cultural diversity is celebrated.

Multicultural societies have become more commonplace with global migration. This has also led to increased diversity of religious views and practices within nation states.

Some countries have embraced religious **pluralism** more than others. For instance, Indian society is formed of multiple religions and celebrates all religious holidays as national holidays for all citizens. France, however, is well known for its secular stance, which bans public displays of any religion (for example, head coverings). Who we think we are, and who we can be, is partly shaped then by how nation states respond to pluralism.

Identity and self-identity

We have explored how socialisation, culture, values, beliefs and norms all shape who we think we are. What this boils down to is the question of *identity*. Identity is often something that we associate with the individual. We believe that we can choose freely who we are and who we want to become. Our identity may be comprised of, and performed through, the clothes we wear, the food we eat or our hobbies. We often also think of a person's identity as their disposition towards life – whether they are optimistic or pessimistic, extroverted or introverted. Identity is also often linked to beliefs – political and/or religious.

Sociologists are interested in understanding how people's identities are products of wider social norms, or of cultural values and beliefs, and not simply a matter of personal choice. We form our identities and sense of self in relation to those whom we perceive to be similar to us and those who are different from us. Identities can therefore give us a sense of belonging or exclusion. Sociologists are also interested in how identities are made possible or restricted by social structures and access to different types of capital. One concept that will help with all this is Bourdieu's idea of **habitus**.

Bourdieu describes habitus as our socially engrained skills, habits and dispositions. Our habitus strongly shapes both who we are and who we imagine that we can be. However, it also prevents us from being whoever we want to be. Although we may seek to create our own identities, viewing ourselves as uniquely individual, Bourdieu explains that our identities are formed through the different capitals that we are endowed with and embody. To explain this, we can draw on Reay, Crozier and Clayton's work 'Fitting in or standing out' (2010), which examined what it felt like to be at university for a working-class student. Working-class students wanted to identify with the ways of being that characterised a middle-class university institution, but many felt like fish out of water, and had to undertake considerable identity work to have any chance of fitting in. So, to what extent is it possible to create and remodel one's identity? Sociologists argue that it is more possible in contemporary societies than in the past.

Individualisation and consumerism

Sociologists like Giddens argued that in late modernity our identities are no longer fixed and rigid, determined by our social locations such as gender, ethnicity, social class, family background or where we are born. Instead, we are free to create our own self-identity.

Late modernity is characterised by its disruption to tradition, customs and beliefs. Instead, it emphasises freedom, choice and individuality. With the spread of global capitalism, as people become more transnationally interconnected, as technology connects them through new virtual and economic networks, as manufacturing processes speed up, and as consumer society dominates, lives become more fast-paced and more fragmented. 'Choice' is opened up to us.

At the unit of the individual, there are significant new possibilities: ageing is no longer an inevitable part of the life cycle. Innovative technologies enabling youth-affirming surgeries can slow the ageing process. Consuming youth-promising products and engaging in healthy behaviours become part of everyday life.

We may also be able to choose where we live – a house, a flat, a converted barn or a converted church – and what vehicle we drive – motorbike, scooter, bicycle, car (and what type of car). We can choose who we fall in love with, who we marry, or whether we marry at all. Many of these options would not have been available historically. All these choices encourage the creation of our own self-identity. Giddens (1992/2013a, 1992/2013b) refers to the self as a **reflexive project** where we strive to become who we want to be.

This can be illustrated using the example of how family structures once had fixed, highly gendered, social roles. People were expected to get married, but marriage was for heterosexual couples, and within that marriage there were strict gender roles: men were breadwinners and women were confined to the domestic sphere. Today, we have much greater degrees of flexibility and far more opportunity to construct our life course.

Case Study: The family: changing roles and identities

The family is an important unit, within which we forge our sense of identity and belonging, but the family has undergone significant changes over the last 200 years. The traditional family in feudal England lived and worked together in **cottage industries**, and there was very little space for individuality. More than this, social roles were prescribed and there was no room for change or challenge.

This family type gave way to the modern 'nuclear' family that appeared in post-war Britain. The **nuclear family** was characterised by two adults (a heterosexual couple) and two children; the husband and wife stayed together for life and accepted rigid gender roles. This family type also, arguably, stymied the opportunity to develop a sense of individuality.

The ideals of the nuclear family continue to endure, as part of the set of values, institutions and laws that Gillis (1996) called the 'cultural imaginary'. In fact, two-thirds of UK families still conform to this type (ONS, 2019). However, despite the normalised nuclear family, diversification of family types is increasingly accepted. The nuclear family has been joined by lone-parent families, same-sex couple families, LGBTQIA+ chosen

families, extended families (multigenerational and multiple familied) and reconstituted families. There are also new 'spheres of intimacy' within families that consider pets to be family members, as Smart (2007) has argued. Marriage is no longer the only way to legalise a relationship, with common law and civil ceremonies becoming more commonplace.

Despite the diversification of family types, however, the significance of the family as a social institution and of marriage as a convention endures.

For example, Heaphy (2018) notes that before same-sex marriage was legalised, same-sex couples gave meaning to their relationships by following some of the conventions of heterosexual marriage, for instance by taking responsibility for one another's economic wellbeing, engaging in emotional and sexual monogamy, and agreeing a household division of labour. Rather than the diversification of family types pointing to a de-traditionalisation and a breakdown of the importance of the family, the family as a social institution was instead reformulated and reimagined through new, diverse family types. This is sometimes referred to as homonormativity, whereby same sex couples are socialised into heterosexual social norms.

Lindsay and Dempsey (2017) showed how lesbian couples usually draw on both mothers' surnames when naming their children to create family bonds, display family relationships and achieve societal legitimacy. In heterosexual couples, only 3% of parents chose to create a new surname, suggesting that the desire to individualise family identities is still rare. They conclude: 'In an era of family diversity…our research demonstrates that changes in social mores do not mean legitimacy concerns go away. Rather, they reappear in new guises.' (2017: 1032)

From this, we can conclude that there is much more space for individuality within the family, and many different ways to forge relationships and a sense of belonging, but also that conventions remain very strong.

Case Study: Social media: virtual identities

The fast-paced development of technology in recent years has created a new space through which identities can be built, and where a sense of belonging can be fostered. Our identities are enacted through social interactions with others. Today, we have many more opportunities to engage in social interactions – through social media such as Twitter, Facebook, Instagram, Snapchat, TikTok, as well as online video gaming. Goffman's (1959) work on the presentation of self helps us understand how identities can be created for different imagined audiences.

Because young people engage so extensively with social media, they arguably have greater capacity for self-expression. However, Elias and Gill (2018) suggested that there is much conformity through social media. They argued that beauty apps effectively enable people to change how they look in their photographs and post  what they perceive to be desirable images. This cannot simply be regarded as a form of narcissism; it shows how people feel compelled to create identities in line with wider social expectations about beauty. Beauty apps lead to what they refer to as 'optimal transformation through consumption' (2018:60).

However, Tiidenberg and Gómez Cruz (2015) present an alternative view. They argue that posting photographs of oneself on social media is an opportunity for self-affirmation and can also be used for awareness raising. The body positivity and 'Instagram vs. Reality' movements on social media are examples of people posting what they describe as 'authentic' images of themselves that have not been altered. Here, social media is a space where prevailing social norms can be resisted and challenged.

On the other hand, the capacity for self-expression is also bound by wider pressures to present to the world a socially desirable self. For example, engaging in the body positive movement could also be regarded as a strategic attempt to display oneself in a positive and socially desirable light: as someone 'authentic', genuine, compassionate and committed to social equality.

Sociologists have also drawn attention to the ways in which new relationships can be forged through digital platforms. For example, dating sites such as Tinder, Grindr, Plenty of Fish, Match.com and eHarmony have transformed the world of dating. Hobbs, Owen and Gerber (2017) draw on Bauman's work to show that internet dating gamifies and commodifies modern courtship.

Dating apps have revolutionised how we find partners, using algorithms on our smartphones. While in the past people tended to meet through interpersonal connections, love today often begins without any face-to-face introduction. Despite this, the authors reveal that most people using dating apps do indeed want to find a partner. Overall, social media provides an opportunity to experiment with identity, but it is also bound by prevailing social norms.

> Think about your own use of social media. Do you present yourself in different ways to different audiences? If so, how and why do you think that may be?

Sociologists argue that the decline in the influence of tradition and prescriptive social norms, coupled with the imperative that we each forge our own paths and identities, leads to individualisation – the idea that we focus on the self rather than on collective meaning and shared ways of living. As Bauman (2013) suggests, in late modernity everyone must ask themselves: Who am I? How should I live? Who do I want to become? We must be prepared to accept responsibility for the answers, he argues. Freedom, for the late modern individual, is a fate we cannot escape (except by retreating into the fantasy world or through mental disorders). As such, individual freedom is a mixed blessing. With all these choices come new possibilities. We can create our 'selves' in new ways that we may find liberating. But these choices can also be stifling. Giddens (1992/2013a, 1992/2013b) referred to these new societies as having a dual character: they hold possibilities for us, but they can also remain dangerously oppressive (see also Chapter 2).

Because identities are fragmented, we also have elevated expectations of all the things that other people are supposed to be. When dating, we might become picky about our partners – they may not live up to all the expectations we have of them, since love as a construct places so much burden onto one other person to be everything to us: friend, lover, confidant, therapist, parent to our children. In his work on intimacy in relationships, Giddens argued that we now see relationships as a means for self-development. When the relationship no longer serves our own self-interest, it breaks down. We can see then how this new possibility to be who we 'want' to be, may also lead us to new, unforeseen difficulties in our relationships with one another.

The family and changing social roles

Simone de Beauvoir (1831/1997) argued that women were constrained by ideologies of motherhood. She said that girls learned to become women through socialisation and that **gender identity** was shaped by key points in the female life course, such as puberty, menarche, heterosexual sex, coupledom, marriage, pregnancy and motherhood. All these socialised experiences affected women's orientation to the world. Motherhood, for example, limited women's freedoms. However, de Beauvoir argued that the 'mothering instinct' was not real – instead, social circumstances shaped how women felt about their children. Therefore, motherhood was not a choice, but a destiny written into a woman's social role, and strongly determined by their individual identity.

Not all women were equally subjected to this restrictive role of motherhood. De Beauvoir described motherhood as a 'class crime' – lower-class women were even more restricted in their choices to opt out of motherhood (no access to birth control, etc.). Women were thus socialised into feeling that marriage and motherhood defined them. This example shows that feminists like de Beauvoir did not believe that identities were freely chosen, but that they were determined through socialisation.

Contemporary feminists have argued that such an account of women's identity is dated. Pickard (2020) argued that women are not merely defined by the domestic sphere and motherhood. Instead, 'equality' in the workplace has led to employment also forming a central part of a woman's identity. This working identity exists alongside the identity of motherhood so that women now have hybrid  identities. This does not simply mean that women have been liberated from what feminists once described as domestic servitude. Instead, these new 'choices' available to women continue to be constraining. They ask women to take on board multiple roles that can be conflicting, contradictory and confusing. What should take priority – work or motherhood? How can a woman be both an excellent employee and an excellent mother?

Other sociologists, such as McRobbie (2009), note that women also have further pressures. Not only must they remain in employment and keep a household, but they must also display desirable feminine traits to be attractive to men – women must be 'reassuringly feminine'. All these different demands on women's identity results in their experience of what Pickard (2020) describes as a 'temporal ambivalence', because they are expected to do it all.

In her book *Heading Home: Motherhood, Work and the Failed Promise of Equality* (2019), Orgad argued that there is a gap between the promise of gender equality and women's experience of continued injustice. She interviewed highly educated London women who left paid employment to take care of their children while their husbands continued to work in high-powered jobs. In an online article with fellow sociologist Catherine Rottenberg (2020), Orgad also argued that the recent 'trad wife' phenomenon, where some women are choosing to give up their careers and retreat to the 'traditional' post-war housewife role, is partly due to the extraordinary social pressure women face in having to excel in a career then come home to a 'second shift' of unpaid labour of looking after the family.

The dated idea of segregated conjugal roles advanced by functionalist sociologists like Talcott Parsons, which saw the nuclear family as the ideal, with the man as the breadwinner and the woman as fulfilling the domestic, caring, expressive role, has seemingly come full circle. 'Trad wives' express their gendered housewife role as a choice: they see it as one choice out of many that women are now free to make. Others, including Orgad (2019) are more suspicious of this 'choice'. Are women free to choose or is the turn towards 'trad wives' symptomatic of wider societal pressures and demands that are, simply, too great for women?

It is important to remember that the number of women who choose to be 'trad wives' is tiny. The unemployment rate for women is 3.6%, which is less than the unemployment rate for men at 3.9% (House of Commons, 2020), and the majority of these women would not classify themselves as 'trad wives'. Additionally – and perhaps more importantly – not all women have this choice to give up work; some families do not have the financial resources to do so. In this respect it is a relatively middle- and upper-class phenomenon.

So, just how widespread is the ability to forge one's own identity? One of the greatest critiques levelled at Giddens and others concerning this theory of individualisation and reflexive identity projects is the question of who gets to define themselves and their identities. Who can afford cosmetic surgery, fashionable clothes or time off work? Forging one's identity is also premised on consumption and in turn on economic capital and resource. Are these possibilities open to everyone, or are some of us freer than others?

Feminists have argued that reflexive projects of the self are more accessible to White middle-class men. We discussed in the first part of this chapter the 'myth' of meritocracy. There is a similar myth at work here built on the idea of self-identity – that we can be who we want to be. Some of us have more financial freedom than others to create ourselves in new ways. Others are more strongly socialised into strict traditional and religious customs. Even taking these social axes out of the equation, those people with the most freedom and privilege are never 'free' to choose because they all still are subjected to social norms.

In Madigan and Munro's 'House Beautiful: Style and Consumption in the Home' (1996), postal questionnaires and qualitative interviews were used with residents of a Glasgow housing estate to explore their household consumption practices. These women consumers were not dupes of marketing; nor were they simply expressing themselves. Their choice in home décor was influenced by the media and advertising, and there were also aspects of conformity to classed and gendered ideals. Consider too the example of clothing choices explored in Chapter 1: these can never be considered individual, even if we like to think they are.

As we have established, individualisation can be stifling as well as liberating, and is inherently unequal. Another unintended consequence of the rise of individualisation is that it is highly unsettling. Sociologists like Durkheim argued that the rise of individualisation is matched by a weakening of social norms, but this has significant consequences for our feelings of security. In his work *Suicide* (1897/2005), Durkheim argued that anomie occurs when social norms break down, or when norms and values are no longer strong enough to keep society unified. Such a state of normlessness can lead to anxiety.

Sociologists like Giddens (1992/2013a, 1992/2013b) argue that the breakdown in social norms is characteristic of late modernity, which develops alongside the provision of more choice and individual freedoms. As the norms that guide us through life break down, they are replaced by endless possibilities and choices, and the imperative that we believe we must be 'individual'. Giddens described this process as invoking deep pressures on individuals that may lead us to a state of ontological insecurity – feeling destabilised in our sense of what the world is and what our existence means.

In modern societies, the world had an order that was prescribed by religion. Throughout the Industrial Revolution, religious social order broke down and was replaced by secularism; in consequence, people's sense of direction in life was less clear cut. The very 'meaning' of life that was once governed by a belief in god was replaced by individual accounts of life's meanings. As the world has evolved, and as more choices have become available, ideas about what is 'meaningful' change. This can be wonderfully liberating, but it can also be scary. We do not have a prescriptive moral compass to guide us. If we do not follow religious doctrine and rules, what rules do we live by?

When we ask ourselves 'Who am I?' or 'Who do I want to be?' we start to question ourselves and our identities, as well as the choices we have made. We look inwards, to our 'selves' to try to discover who we really are and who we want to become. This encourages an extreme form of introspection – we find that our 'true' self is impossible to find because we have so many competing identities. We then engage in what Giddens calls reflexive projects (see Chapter 5). The critical point is that our self-identity is always subject to change, since there are so many different roles we can fulfil, and so many competing social norms to align with. Giddens describes ontological insecurity as moral vacuity because there is no path to follow.

Warde's study 'Consumption, identity-formation and uncertainty' (1994) has become a sociological classic. In it, Warde considered how endless consumption produces anxiety due to the constant choices we must make – and the risk of making the wrong one. Choosing a brand of tomato ketchup may not seem that risky, but the prospect of choosing the wrong university course, the wrong career, or even the wrong life partner may cause extreme anxiety and force us to continually question our decisions.

This explains why people constantly look for ways to anchor themselves – a means by which they can predict their future. Despite the fragility of social order, we strive to maintain it in our everyday interactions. Some people find solace in trying to recreate a social order through a retreat into more traditional roles which, they argue, give them comfort. Others seek refuge in new forms of religion that try to give order to a world that might otherwise be perceived as chaotic.

One response to insecurity is to become closer to a group or collective that can provide us with security so that we do not feel alone or confused. Beliefs can offer a sense of relief from ontological anxiety. A system of beliefs tells us what to think and how to feel. It may therefore be comforting to be guided through life, particularly when life feels chaotic. In fact, Possamai-Inesedy (2002) argues that turning to religion can be viewed as a response to ontological insecurity by providing this social order.

Durkheim's traditional study of religion already tells us that religion serves a social function. It creates and reinforces social order by producing a collective conscience. It binds people together through its shared values. Acts of worship, particularly in groups, are important rituals that cement this social order by performing and communicating shared bonds.

Berger (1967/1990) also argued that religion had – and has – the capacity to provide meaning and a legitimate social order. In his work *The Sacred Canopy*, he argued that religion provided order within a world of chaos. While other sociologists argue that other belief systems (science, consumerism) can provide meaning, Berger believed there was something special about religion: its belief in the sacred offers a sense of wonder and amazement – the mysterious element of life.

We can look at the turn towards spirituality and New Ageism, and indeed fundamentalism, as possible responses to the rise in ontological insecurity – an interesting phenomenon in a predominantly secular society.

Case Study: Religion and spirituality: consuming and finding identity

Turner (2012) suggests that young people are influenced by the internet to participate in what he calls 'DIY religion'. They pick and mix different elements of religion to create their own religious identity and belief system. This might involve delving into aspects of practices such as yoga or Chinese medicine. New Age Movements (NAMs) from the  1980s onward also encompass an interest in supernatural powers such as spirits, aliens and mysticism. They are also related to the movement of the Global North towards the cultural appropriation of 'eastern' practices of yoga, Thai Chi and reflexology, to name just a few (Cant, 2020). New Ageism is often seen as a rejection of the promises of scientific progress where salvation is not found in an external source, but instead in working on oneself. We can see how NAMs might resonate with Giddens' idea that the self is a reflexive project and also Foucault's notion of self-surveillance.

In *Easternization of the West* (2008), Campbell argues that such practices are part of a globalised consumerist world order that allows us to engage with alternative ways of living. Many people, in states of anxiety, are searching for meaning in other traditions. This meaning, however, is culturally appropriated and reframed in 'westernised' contexts through consumerism. Bauman (1997) argues, much like Turner's DIY approach, that in a postmodern era religion is better understood as something that is chosen, along with one's identity, and can be changed, rejected, adopted and mixed. Lyon argues in his book *Jesus in Disneyland: Religion in Postmodern Times* (2000) that faith and spirituality continue to flourish despite the breakdown in the traditional religious order.

He argues that in part this is due to the role that consumerism plays in enabling new forms of spirituality to flourish in the global marketplace. Lyon's work is also related to other sociological accounts, which argue that as societies became modern, people became less bound to close-knit communities with a religious institution at their centre. People now move around more than ever, there is growing social diversity, and greater religious pluralism. As such, we are more exposed to different religions and we can now try them on for size.

Voas (2009) coined the term 'fuzzy fidelity' to refer to people who had a pick-and-mix approach to religion, such as those who choose to marry in church despite not holding religious beliefs.

Davie's *Religion in Britain since 1945: Believing without Belonging* (1994) was critical of the argument that there had been a decline in religion. She stated that 'believing...persists while belonging continues to decline – or to be more accurate, believing is declining (has declined) at a slower rate than belonging'. (Davie 1990:455). Her point is that traditional Christian religion has declined, but that there has been a rise of post-Christian spirituality. Partly this is due to a spread of New Age and post-Christian spirituality. The Church as an institution – as a place of belonging, with regular attendance – is said to have declined in favour of more individualised forms of spirituality.

In research by Tromp et al (2020), statistical measures were applied to the European Values Study for 20 European countries (1981–2008) to examine Davie's earlier thesis that there had been a deinstitutionalisation of Christianity coupled with an increase in spiritual forms of belonging. They found much evidence for the spiritual forms of belonging. While some people have sought connection through New Ageism and new spiritual modes of belonging, sociologists have argued that the late modern age is also associated with the rise of religious fundamentalism. Fundamentalism is seen as a way of re-establishing a claim to truth that has been lost. Religious fundamentalists believe the contemporary breakdown of religion is damaging to the social order and a precursor to the breakdown of social values.

Giddens also argues that fundamentalism is a reaction to the undermining of traditional social norms. Moreover, Brown describes fundamentalism as a 'coping strategy' for our 'lost condition' in postmodernity (2020:35). Davie (2013) argued that fundamentalists create islands of certainty around themselves to protect them from a world of social and cultural chaos. Underpinning what they regard as the breakdown of religion, norms and values is the quest for truth, when truth is evasive – that is, when the very idea of 'truth' has been unsettled. Lyotard describes this condition as the decline in the metanarrative (see Chapter 3).

Pentecostalism is one example of religious fundamentalism. Appearing in the USA in the early 20th century, it has since become a global phenomenon. This form of Christianity emphasises the power of the Holy Spirit in affecting people's lives. People who convert to Pentecostalism accept Jesus Christ as their own personal saviour. This step involves many conversion rituals where people are 'born again'. Pentecostalism is an example of a globalised form of fundamentalism. It arguably tells us something about our desire to form a concrete identity in a world seemingly in flux, and to feel a sense of belonging in a world characterised by anomie.

In summary, we can see that our sense of who we are is shaped by either our connection to, or our separation from, the beliefs and values of the society or community in which we live.

Our sense of who we are and who it is possible to be are shaped by broader social structures, formed through socialisation, reinforced and destabilised by changing social norms and values. Importantly, as individuals, we constantly seek a sense of societal anchorage and belonging.

We must, however, reflect on the ways that norms, values and beliefs can be oppressive but also liberating. Sociologists recognise the importance of belonging but also the ways in which being a member of a community or group can produce inequalities and social exclusions.

Summary

In this chapter, we have taken three important sociological questions and subjected them to sociological analysis to become more knowledgeable. To be properly knowledgeable, you need concepts and data, but this goes beyond simply acquiring ideas and facts. You must ensure that your data collection is ethical, that you check for bias and try to acknowledge when you might have been blinkered to other questions and perspectives. This insight demands the capacity to be reflexive – a fundamental disposition that we explore in the next chapter.

Sociological how-tos

To be knowledgeable, you must:

- understand how society is inherently unequal and know about the different axes of social stratification
- acknowledge that axes of social stratification are intersectional
- recognise the importance of social order
- understand why some people break the rules
- use and critically interrogate official data and measures
- appreciate how socialisation, social norms, cultural beliefs and values shape our identity
- recognise the impact of social change on normlessness, and how this may lead to anxiety
- situate the rise of New Age Movements, spirituality and religious fundamentalism alongside an appreciation of ontological insecurity and the need to belong.

CHAPTER 5
BE REFLEXIVE: TURNING THE SOCIOLOGICAL IMAGINATION ONTO SOCIOLOGY ITSELF

The arrival of the travelling funfair to any town or village brings excitement for many – a temporary change to the landscape; an out-of-the-ordinary experience. Many fairgrounds include a House of Mirrors. Here, you find yourself reproduced multiple times in multiple ways. Mirrors above you, beneath you, and around you enable dazzling, kaleidoscopic ways of seeing yourself: you are duplicated, repeatedly, as far as you can see, from every angle, in various forms and sizes. Some of the mirrors are distorted, providing unusual, humorous and sometimes shocking reflections; others are more appealing.

We draw on this imagery to introduce you to the idea of reflexivity in sociology. Reflexivity demands that sociologists continually subject their work to critical reflection. However, unlike the reflections produced by the house of mirrors, which confront the viewer with a fleeting and unusual look at themselves, sociologists must *always* hold up multiple mirrors to their own practice.

Being reflexive is essential for good research practice and good sociology. In this chapter, we explore how sociologists examine their own positionality, constantly acknowledging how their own values and biases shape their work. These factors do not mean that sociology is not scientific and cannot be objective and value-free – far from it. Rather, reflexivity supplies important checks and balances: it puts a sociologist's work in context and allows others to critically assess their findings. We will show the importance and value of turning mirrors not only onto ourselves as individual sociologists, but also onto the discipline, allowing us to revisit and rewrite ideas and history, and to identify new lines of sociological enquiry.

What is reflexivity?

Reflexivity is not the same as being reflective. The latter involves thinking about any data or findings and being confident in drawing certain conclusions from them. Reflexivity is a far more active, self-orientated process. It involves thinking about and examining the role of the individual (the sociologist) within the research process. It requires sociologists to ask themselves who they are as individuals, what draws them to research questions, and what theoretical 'glasses' they are wearing when they approach their research. This is called an appreciation of 'positionality'.

Reflexivity means questioning your own assumptions – being able to understand, analyse and evaluate yourself as an active participant in the thinking and research process, acknowledging personal values and beliefs, and being mindful of your own limitations. Therefore, reflexivity requires an openness and an acceptance that you are part of any research that you engage in and any knowledge that you generate.

Reflexivity as part of the human condition

Being reflexive – being able to make sense of ourselves, our place in society and appreciating the impact that we have on others – is a human capacity. Many sociologists have described how this capacity shapes both social life and our sense of self. For instance, in *Human Nature and the Social Order* (1902/1992), Cooley described the 'Looking Glass Self'. He explained how our unique sense of identity, our concept of self, comes from reflecting on how we think we are seen or perceived by others.

Mead's work was an extension of this idea. He distinguished between the 'I' and the 'me' within each person. In his book, *Self and Society* (1934), Mead wanted to show that our sense of self and individuality is not predetermined – we are not born with it. Selfhood instead comes through social interaction and conscious, personal reflection and thinking. He argued that the 'me' is the socially constructed part of ourselves, produced through our social interactions: the 'me' can think about, describe and conceive of itself. Goffman's (1959) description of the 'front stage' performance of the self is equated with the 'me', and Merton's concept of the self-filling prophecy – how being labelled positively or negatively becomes a true reflection of who we are – it is a reflexive construction (see Chapter 2 for more details on both these ideas).

For Mead, the 'me' is that part of the self that constantly reflects on the 'I'. The 'I' is the more instinctual essence of humanness (the part that acts and reacts). It is through this interaction of the 'I' and 'me' that our sense of self develops. These insights within interpretivist sociology show how reflexivity is a distinctive human capacity that in turn underscores social life, social order and society.

For sociologists such as Giddens (1992/2013a; 1992/2013b) this disposition has never been more important. He argued that the contemporary age is best described as 'reflexive modernity'. While we have always drawn on our reflexive capacity to make sense of ourselves and the social world, we have also been able to draw upon traditional modes of thinking and acting, and habitual ways of being in the world. This is what we might call practical knowledge – a predisposition to act in particular ways. Thus, we draw on our socialisation and shared values to make sense of who we are and the social world around us, and these habits guide and shape our choices and decisions and give us a sense of security. They are essentially un-reflexive, conventional ways of thinking, feeling and acting in relation to the social world.

Giddens argues that the speed of recent social change has led to the breakdown of traditional structures such as marriage and the family; it has seen the unsettling of gender norms and class boundaries, and has involved a review of shared values. Together, these changes have produced a situation where our taken-for-granted, habitual ways of living and acting are no longer as robust or useful: they cannot so easily help us navigate the complexity of social life. As such, we must draw more consciously on our capacity to be self-aware, conscious and, hence, reflexive. It is helpful to consider this, as it shows that reflexivity is a human capacity and that we draw upon this ability more now than people ever did in the past. But what does all this mean for sociology and its claims to be a science?

A mirror on our own research practice: ethics and positionality

Being reflexive means different things to different sociologists. Within positivism, for example, there is a commitment to objective and value-free research practice (see Chapter 3, pages 58–9 and 70). It is assumed that sociology can mimic the natural sciences. This does not mean that positivist researchers are un-reflexive: they may have thought long and hard and reflexively about their research question and methods, but once research has begun there is an assumption that the position and influence of the researcher can be controlled (i.e. they can distance themselves from the research and remain objective and unbiased).

In contrast, reflexivity is regarded as central to the whole research process within interpretivist sociology. Here, sociologists believe that it is not possible to ever be completely value-free, so they must continually check their practice and be aware of their influence on it. Some researchers even keep field note diaries and journals to reflect on their own biases throughout the research process.

Research ethics

To illustrate the importance of reflexivity, we examine the importance of ethics and also whether it is possible to be a sociologist and maintain a political position at the same time. Being reflexive is central to ensuring that research is ethical. All sociological work is bound by ethical guidelines (you can find these on the British Sociological Association website). At the core is a commitment to ensuring the anonymity (privacy) of and consent to participate by any research participants. These principles sound relatively easy to achieve on paper, but the reality of research means that a sociologist must be constantly reflexive about whether these golden rules are being upheld.

Why might it be difficult to preserve anonymity and consent in research studies?

There are potentially serious ethical and legal issues in the use of covert ('undercover') research, where the researcher's identity is not revealed to participants. Sociologists may use covert methods when they feel they would be unable to gain informed consent from the people they are researching. In these cases, it is essential that anonymity is preserved (Roulet et al, 2017; Spicker, 2011). Calvey (2019) argued very strongly that his six-month ethnographic study of bouncers in Manchester nightclubs had to be carried out covertly because of the nuanced insights it produced, particularly in relation to violence. Without covert research, he felt his sociological imagination would be stifled. He suggested that bouncers are portrayed in the popular imagination as aggressive and violent, and that they may emphasise these characteristics if interviewed openly. While Calvey did witness violence, this was not the only aspect of the life and experience of bouncers that his work was able to reveal.

Preserving anonymity, a key ethical principle, means that sometimes valuable data cannot be shared or used. Cant and Sharma (1998) were engaged in research with complementary therapy associations, in the course of which they faced this very issue. The field of study was small, and most people knew one another, which had the effect of potentially compromising anonymity when publishing the data. During the study, some participants also shared information that was controversial, even indiscreet. This data had to be destroyed, even though it was insightful. Here, reflexivity is linked to being both ethical and professional.

Reflexivity is also needed to secure the wellbeing and safety of participants and to ensure that the experiences of those being studied is not altered. This has been a criticism levelled at some anthropological studies, which undertook ethnographic research studying people of the Global South but through the lens and interests of scholars from the Global North. Indeed, we must take seriously the very fact that the term 'research', as Smith (2013) notes, is one of the 'dirtiest words in the indigenous world's vocabulary'. Linked to histories of colonialism and imperialism, 'research' has been carried out on those without power by those who have it. The ways in which knowledge was collected on 'others' and then represented requires reflexive examination, even retrospectively.

Even qualitative research, which is often framed as reflexive, has had a role in the history of colonialism – one that has claimed to be scientific in its representations of the 'dark-skinned other' as Lincoln and Denzin write: 'Colonizing nations relied on the human disciplines, especially sociology and anthropology, to produce knowledge about strange and foreign worlds.' (2005:1). In doing so, these nations and researchers were implicated in the 'othering' of the people they studied.

Lincoln and Denzin highlight the ways that research can be unethical and have a dangerous impact on those being studied, but there are other practical issues to consider in the research setting. First, researchers need to be reflexive about the effect of their presence on the people they are studying; respondents may change their answers and actions because they know they are being questioned or watched. Reflexivity allows a sociologist to check for these types of alterations.

Second, reflexivity in research ethics also needs to address the researcher's own safety and integrity, which can also be unsettled in the research process. This is referred to as 'going native', when the researcher is completely immersed in the community they are studying, so that they can no longer view it objectively. (Perhaps you can see that the semantics here are problematic. Using the term 'native' to describe this process reinforces a colonial hierarchy that assumes the researcher is more objective and rational than those they study.) In Venkatesh's (2008) study of gangs, he admits that he crossed the line, increasingly viewing his respondents as friends, and consequently finding himself in dangerous situations. The same occurred in Goffman's work *On the Run: Fugitive Life in an American City* (2015), a study where she examined the lives of African American men in a poor Black neighbourhood in Philadelphia. The work details the interactions between the men and the criminal justice system. Goffman explains how she was involved in many dangerous situations, some possibly criminal. She even recounts how she had to dispose of many of her field notes in case she was called into court to provide evidence against her research respondents.

It is also important to think about researcher's values and how they impact or influence their research. Does this matter? Can sociological research ever be completely value-free? This is a tricky idea, because inevitably our own interests and values shape our research interests. Some sociologists have been motivated to undertake their research because they want to change and improve the world that they study.

The writings of Karl Marx have undoubtedly had far-reaching political and economic consequences – his ideas were not simply contained in his books but were used to stimulate social movements. Social change was his ambition, and he even used the word 'manifesto' as a title of one of his books. So, can we describe his work as sociological if it is driven by political interest and is value-laden? We suggest that sociologists can do this by being very open and clear about these dimensions in their work.

Weber and Du Bois both drew attention to the importance of acknowledging researcher **subjectivity** and positionality, and the difficulty – if not impossibility – of researching at a distance, or taking a 'view from nowhere' (Nagel, 1989). Rather, we are always located somewhere, and we cannot withdraw ourselves entirely from this social location. We can, however, acknowledge this positioning and make sure that we check any interpretations of the data we generate.

For example, Du Bois was an intellectual, but also a civil rights activist. He aimed to challenge White privilege and racism, and made no apologies for this position. However, he also undertook systematic and careful research to support his position. From a different position, Oakley (2016) felt that claims to **objectivity** in research were naïve and detrimental for the people that sociologists choose to study. For her, the role of the researcher was not simply to document and analyse, but also to listen and support the people being interviewed. In each of these cases, the relinquishing of some objectivity is not at the expense of good sociological enquiry.

Such viewpoints celebrate the importance of positionality in research. To be fully reflexive is to be open about our biases and our aspirations. This is also the basis for standpoint theory, which argues that all knowledge emanates from a social position. It is helpful to understand a researcher's position because we are then alert to the aspirations and limitations of their work. More than this it is imperative that marginalised groups ask subjectively important questions, otherwise these questions would not be raised, and their insights are even more valuable as a result.

As sociologists we also need to ask: Who can speak for whom? Who has the power to do research? And who ends up being the 'researched'? Alice Goffman's work has been critiqued in terms of its positionality in relation to those she studied. As a middle-class White woman studying the lives of poor young Black men, a power imbalance is evident. Parry (2019) openly challenged Goffman, asking: 'Should privileged, White outsiders tell the stories of poor minority communities?' We see the importance once again of reflexivity which is bound up in Bejarano et al's (2019) call to acknowledge White privilege, and the hierarchies of power and inequality that sociologists may reproduce. This leads us to another consideration.

> In Goffman's research her positionality was her ethnicity and social class. Can you think of how other socio-demographic characteristics might shape the relationship between the researcher and their participants?

Turning the mirror onto sociology itself

Being reflexive demands not just an examination of conduct in a research project and the sociologist's own values and aspirations; it should also consider the positionality of the wider discipline. This requires a critical examination of certain assumptions in sociology – how problems are defined and an exploration of which research questions tend to be included or excluded. We need to turn the sociological imagination onto sociology itself.

Removing the blinkers

In Chapter 2, we showed how neither Marx, Durkheim nor Weber – all White men – prioritised questions of gender and ethnicity. As such we can examine (after the fact) how their sociological knowledge production was limited. We can see that at this time, rather than simply reflecting the social world, sociology also made some questions and issues invisible. It was a product of, and complicit with, colonialism and patriarchy.

While there were women writing about social issues at the time the founding fathers were developing the sociological project, questions of gender difference were not considered of central importance. Indeed, it was only in the 1970s that feminist writers called out sociology for its **gender blindness**. Much of the research up until this point had focused on the public and male domains. So, for example, there was research about paid work but not about housework. Little attention was given to women's paid work either, or their work as mothers. When measuring social class, women were often categorised according to their husband's occupation. Assumptions about women's roles were largely unchallenged. For instance, functionalist descriptions of family life uncritically accepted that women were naturally better carers and should handle the **emotional labour** in the home.

Nor did sociology at this time give sufficient attention to the power relations between men and women, and many predominantly female experiences went undocumented, remaining invisible to sociological scrutiny. Therefore, feminists demanded that the 'black box' of the home be subject to sociological investigation, focusing attention on domestic violence, for example. It is interesting to note that the poorer educational attainment of girls in comparison to boys was not a subject considered worthy of study – yet, when the situation reversed, the problem of boys' 'underachievement' was a cause for considerable concern (see Chapter 4).

Mainstream sociology was thus seen to be **malestream**. It had either ignored women or had fit them into male rules of thought and male areas of interest. Second wave feminism demanded a revolution in sociological thinking, and in turn has had to be reflexive about the ways in which its own research focussed on the experience of White, middle-class, heterosexual women. It was through drawing on its reflexive ability that sociology has been able to assess its own bias, its own prescriptive lines of questioning and enquiry. In this way, sociology has subjected its own thinking to internally generated critique.

This does not mean that sociology has entirely succeeded in tackling women's issues. It is interesting, for example, that books about women are still often described as feminist books, rather than sociology books – there remain subtle but pervasive gendered characteristics to sociology. As Skeggs argues:

> Feminism has inscribed sociology, cutting into its complacency and comfort zones, carving out new areas and challenging old ones. Very little of traditional understandings of gender is left unscathed from feminist critique, yet whether this critique has re-inscribed the discipline of sociology is a different matter. (2008:672)

Sociology continues to describe (colonial) modernity as a White masculine enterprise, but nevertheless, we can see that sociology has the ability to engage in continuous examination of its limits and its weaknesses. The work of feminists was critical and reflexive. It challenged the gender blindness of sociology and continues to recognise the limitations of its own questions.

This reflexive process is on-going, as sociologists interrogate the continued usefulness of their concepts, such as male and female, masculine and feminine, in understanding more recent challenges to these binaries. These reflections require a sociology that can accommodate transgender and intersex into its theorising and research – for example, through queer theory (see page 48).

Gender is not the only blinker that sociology has had to reflexively address. A strong debate rages about how to best measure class, for instance, and indeed whether social class is a useful concept anymore. In light of widening inequalities, it is evident that the concept of class is far from redundant, but sociologists are right to suggest that its explanatory power needs to be checked. Beck (1992), for example, argued that new global risks give a different way of thinking about social relations where class differences would be diminished. Certainly, with evidence of ecological disasters and global pandemics, where no one is immune from personal trouble, it is helpful to be reflexive about just how far class as a concept can go. At the same time, as we have seen in this book, class continues to shape our life chances.

It is also the case that social class has been used unreflexively to explain certain phenomena. Murray (1996) famously used the term the 'underclass' to describe people who were unemployed and living in poverty. The term itself can be regarded as derogatory and Murray attached a moral judgment to the term, suggesting that this underclass was characterised by undesirable behaviour, including unemployment, violence, crime, drug dependency and having children out of wedlock.

Murray's work shares similarities with cultural deprivation theories, which suggest that members of the working class share distinctive norms and values that do not support 'success'. Working-class children are seen to be 'deprived' of opportunities. The problem with cultural deprivation theories is that they demonise and 'other' the working class in the following ways:

- They do not apply a sociological imagination to consider how the characteristics described – unemployment, crime, single parenthood, etc. – are public issues that are products of broader social structures and socio-economic inequalities.
- They homogenise an entire group, treating the working class as a single entity with shared characteristics.
- They do not give enough attention to the classism evident in society – for example, the school curriculum tends to favour the middle class. Sociology students often learn

the difference between **restricted** and **elaborated codes** of speaking, but this fails to reflect on the way that certain ways of speaking are valued and normalised and others are not.

- It contradicts evidence that reveals that working-class families are successful and thriving. For example, McKenzie (2015) describes how a negative, one-dimensional perspective of working-class lives is often seen through the lens of the middle class.

Such representations are damaging to members of the working class – they devalue their lives and lead to negative understandings and stereotypes.

Race and ethnicity is another area of investigation that has often been marginalised in sociological study, and which is still predominantly taught separately rather than being central to the canon (Joseph-Salisbury et al, 2020). Sociology also continues to present modernity as a characteristic of White, Western societies.

Hence, Bhambra (2010) called for a re-examination and a re-articulation of key sociological ideas. Far from modernity being simply a product of the Renaissance, the French Revolution and industrialisation, she reminds us that this history neglects significant wider global changes such as the impact of the Haitian Revolution on our changing ideas and aspirations (see page 41). She also demands that enslavement is recognised for its exploitative and central role in the advancement of the Global North. Without such reflexive insights, sociology could have remained blinkered to its colonial and Eurocentric assumptions. This mode of thinking requires us to interrogate the sociology curriculum and assess why so many Black scholars are not given greater prominence in the teaching of sociology.

More than this, some sociological theories can be described as racist. For example, MP David Lammy was rightly critical of the inclusion of dated research in sociology textbooks that suggested Caribbean fathers and husbands were largely absent from their families. He argued that this produced ignorant stereotypes about Black Caribbean family engagement with the British education system. It treated all Black Caribbean families as a homogeneous group and ignored contradictory evidence: single parenthood is not a family formation particular to Black Caribbean families. It also silenced the fact that many Black Caribbean students have extremely high attainment and experience educational success.

There is a deeper point here. Clearly, sociologists and indeed sociology have their own inherent biases, but we must also acknowledge that the wider social context makes it possible for some knowledge to emerge while other knowledge is silenced or marginalised. Some insights from the philosophy of science go some way to explaining this.

The philosophy of science and why reflexivity is important for sociology

At different times, in different histories, we see differing and changing ideas about what knowledge is considered desirable and indeed possible. This is what Kuhn (1962/1970) called a **paradigm**. This is simply a framework within which members of a scientific community understand the world, informing the types of questions they ask and thus restricting understandings of the world.

Kuhn argued that the development of the sciences occurs through scientific revolutions. This happens when one world view replaces another. We can see this in the example of the discovery that the world was round, not flat as had long been believed, or when Einstein's physics replaced Newton's. Kuhn suggested that a revolution happens when new discoveries are made and then the evidence overwhelmingly supports it, so that the existing paradigm can no longer explain it.

Foucault's (2005) work on shifting **epistemes** draws on a similar point – he explains that our knowledge about the world is shaped by existing dominant knowledges (discourses). The development of knowledge about crime, for example, shows that in different periods of time, or epistemes, our knowledge about what 'crime is' has been different.

While Kuhn and Foucault were coming from different perspectives, they shared a similar view that different periods in history have different sets of dominant knowledge, which shaped interpretations of the world. We can think reflexively about sociological knowledge using these insights – remember, the knowledge sociologists produce is always bound by the social context in which they find themselves. The capacity for reflexivity demands that we are mindful of this and are always prepared to challenge our own rules of thought.

Extending the remit of sociology: the new cutting edges?

We conclude this chapter with a few examples of how a reflexive sociology enables us to extend our imagination through developing responses to five important areas of sociological concern: the sociology of the body; the connections between sociology and biology; the sociology of animal and human relations; science and technology; and the sociology of the environment.

The sociology of the body

It was not until the last quarter of the 20th century that sociology properly extended its imagination to the question of the human body (Shilling, 2005). With some exceptions, until this point, the body was seen largely as the preserve of biologists and medics – a physical entity rather than a social one. However, our reflexive capacity has enabled the body to become a key focus of sociological enquiry, with valuable work examining the ways that bodies are socially constructed and socially regulated rather than biologically predetermined.

For example, sociologists have examined the way that the body becomes a project to be worked on through dieting, fitness regimes, tattooing, piercing or cosmetic surgery. These body projects are viewed as reflections of personal identity that can be created and recreated; they are shaped by social norms and structures such as consumerism, capitalism, neoliberalism, the media and subcultural groups.

In relation to surveillance, sociologists have shown how we regulate our bodies in accordance with wider sets of social and often medical norms. Fletcher (2014), for example, undertakes a sociological critique of the way that bodies are measured by doctors. She shows that the increased use of the body mass index (BMI) is one of the reasons we now describe Britain as suffering from an epidemic of obesity. BMI categories are constructed on an assumption that one can determine whether someone is 'overweight' or 'obese' from a simple calculation based on weight and height. The reality is that these categories are arbitrary, humanly constructed – and based on White European men. BMI does not account for the differences between bodies. Many elite athletes, for instance, are classified as obese due to their muscle mass density. Likewise, someone with a 'normal' BMI may not necessarily be healthy. BMI has also been shown to overestimate health risks in Black populations and underestimate health risks in Asian populations. These examples show how new sociological insights can help explain how we respond to our own bodies, but also reveal the ways that our bodies are socially judged.

Sociologists have also drawn attention to the way that certain bodies have been stigmatised. Goffman (1963) explored how some bodies become 'abnormal' as they are seen to deviate from wider social norms. As a result, a body may be socially labelled as deviant and stigmatised if it requires a wheelchair or prosthesis, for example, or if is not slender enough, is scarred, overly tattooed or pierced.

> Can you think of any other ways that bodies may be stigmatised and labelled as socially deviant?

Consider, too, the ways that, historically, norms around Whiteness have been stigmatising for non-White bodies, and how norms around gender have been stigmatising for trans bodies. These insights have spawned some important insights such as the work of Oliver (2017), a sociologist who argued that disability must be subjected to a sociological imagination in order to appreciate that 'personal troubles [are] directly linked to public issues…and the personal troubles of disabled people…[are] often caused by the disabling barriers of society and not our tragic impairments'.

Bio-social studies and socio-biology

One of the most interesting shifts in sociological thought has been the development of biosocial studies and socio-biology. This is particularly intriguing, because sociologists have historically been careful to avoid biological explanations for human behaviour. Biological explanations are believed to emphasise individual characteristics as reasons for human behaviour rather than considering how public structures shape us. Biological explanations therefore tend to go against the sociological imagination.

Such biological thinking has been shown to lack empirical foundation and has been associated with dangerous movements such as eugenics. It has been used as a rationale to contain or execute certain peoples in the past (enslavement and the Holocaust, for example). With such a dishonourable history, it is easy to see why sociology might shy away from engaging with biological ideas.

However, as Meloni notes, there has been a biological turn in sociology where 'sociology is becoming more open to biological suggestions, just at a time when biology is becoming more social' (2017:594). There are benefits to developing a biosocial perspective. For instance, sociology has informed the study of epigenetics – the examination of how our social experience can activate or elaborate certain genetic markers. Kuzawa and Sweet (2009) show how the experience of racism can have an impact on maternal biology, transmitting stress in the uterine environment with a measurable impact for the next generation of children. Similarly, Meloni (2017) suggested that the impact of enslavement can still be biologically seen in the lower birth weight of children from descendants of slaves in comparison to the birth weight of babies born to women of the same ethnicity but without slave ancestry in their families. These are powerfully reflexive ideas but must also remain open to sociological critique.

The sociology of animal-human relations

Peggs (2012) argued that until very recently sociology, with its focus on the 'humanly' produced social world, ignored the study of animals. This is rather an oversight considering how entwined animals are in our human world – we use them to support our work, we often eat them, we use animal products to make clothing, and we have them as our beloved pets. Having a sociology of animals enables us to think about the consumption of animals, animals as leisure, and to identify the crimes and abuse associated with animals and animal rights (Irvine, 2008).

This is still a new area for sociology, but it is one with great promise. For example, Charles (2014), shows just how important close relations with one's family pets can be:

Animals are clearly experienced as a source of emotional support, comfort and security for their human keepers, which lends credence to the idea that they may provide a sense of ontological security. (2014:726)

Haraway's (2003) earlier works in this area used the term 'companion species' to describe human relationships with animals, but also with non-human species such as technology. Interestingly, her work has informed the field of Science and Technology Studies, which we turn to next.

Science and technology studies

Science and Technology Studies (STS) has grown out of sociological thinking and has meshed with other disciplines to form an area of study in its own right. Sociologists working in STS argue that science is socially constructed, and that technologies actively shape our lives in new ways.

Technology informs human behaviour as much as human behaviour shapes technology. Consider how your mobile phone beeps when it runs out of battery. You run to get your charger and plug it in. The phone has directed this action. Latour (1996) argues that the mobile phone is an actor – that is, it acts, and thus has a level of agency. There is no *motivation* behind its action, but it is still the source of the action. This is an interesting yet controversial thought; historically only humans have been credited with agency.

Lupton's (2020) work has applied STS insights to wearable devices such as fitness trackers. She argues that these devices break down the boundaries between humans and technology, referring to the 'thing-power' of wearables, where these technologies assert agency over the wearers, influencing and perhaps even altering human behaviour.

> What other examples can you think of where technology acts upon you? Can you think of other wearable devices that influence or alter how you behave?

Haraway (2006) introduced the important concept of a cyborg to capture the ways that technologies and physical bodies have become intimately entwined. Think about pacemakers, artificial limbs, cochlear implants, contact lenses – these technologies transcend the boundaries between the idea of an organic 'natural' body and the artificial world, the human and the inhuman or animal, the physical and non-physical.

The sociology of the environment

Can a reflexive sociology help us tackle the environmental problems that we increasingly face? Irwin (2013) argued that sociology is crucial, because environmental damage is largely human made and the solutions lie in human responses. Despite this, sociology was largely silent on environmental issues throughout the 20th century. From the 1980s, however, sociology became central to the environmental justice movement that sought to address climate change, deforestation, pollution and over-population. It aimed to link these issues to everyday social life and lived experiences.

In his classic study, Bullard (1983) showed that waste incinerators in the USA were more likely to be situated in Black than in White communities. In doing so, Bullard highlighted environmental racism – while African Americans made up 25% of Houston's population, 90% of waste facilities were situated in their communities and near their children's schools.

More recently, in the UK, Aryee et al (2020) have focused on the impact of fracking on local communities, in particular the emotional harm that local residents can experience and the criminalisation of environmental protest. Other research from America has revealed the exploitation of poorer communities by fracking companies. Such communities agree to have the fracking technology situated near their homes through the promise of greater income; however, fracking can cause significant social stress including environmental damage and poor health outcomes (Sangaramoorthy et al, 2016).

Summary

In this chapter we have introduced you to the importance of being reflexive. Reflexivity can – and should – be invoked by sociologists to ensure four key things:

* that their research practice is ethical
* to acknowledge that sociological research is shaped by researcher values, sometimes deliberately so
* to enable creative consideration of the limitations and blinkers that shape sociological knowledge production
* to continue to be relevant and useful and explore new topics.

Sociological how-tos

To be reflexive you need to:

* be ethical in your research practice
* be mindful of your own positionality
* assess whether there are other questions that you should be asking
* ask which voices are unheard, silenced or erased.

CHAPTER 6
BE TRANSFORMATIVE: BRINGING ABOUT CHANGE IN YOURSELF AND OTHERS

At the start of this book, we introduced you to a key disposition that characterises sociology: the ability to be imaginative, to see the connections between personal troubles, triumphs and truths, and broader social structures. As you have seen, this disposition needs to be supplemented by other key capacities. To be a sociologist you need to be conceptual, rigorous, knowledgeable and reflexive. These are all characteristics of sociology – and of sociologists.

There is one final disposition central to the discipline – the ability to be transformative. Studying sociology fosters change and enables us to put ourselves in others' shoes. It requires us to ask difficult questions, but also enables us to suggest solutions that might improve people's lives. Therefore, we find that we have travelled full circle, back to imagination, to capture the idea that sociology can imagine a better world and can work towards building it.

To describe the transformative potential of sociology, we will look at how it can change our view of who we are and who we aspire to be. We then move on to examine how studying sociology can increase our empathy and compassion, which we argue is central for active citizenship. We then progress to examine the ways that sociology has transformed the social world it studies, through both its impactful research and through changing civic consciousness. In other words, we describe how sociology can be both public and humane. Finally, we pull these transformative potentials together to explore how sociology can prepare you for a variety of jobs, not least by enabling you to become a critical and analytical thinker.

Transforming yourself

Sociology is the study of society and the individual's place in it. By exploring the relationship between the self and wider society, sociology will inevitably change some of your existing ideas. It will require you to interrogate your social position, your life experiences, and who you think you are. You will recall that in the first chapter, we described how Charles reappraised his own privileged position and recognised that his journey in life had been easier because of his family connections and wealth. This revelatory capacity is what makes sociology both terrible and magnificent – as Mills (1959/2000) explained, we can see the social world anew and this is both extraordinary and unsettling, both empowering and disquieting. Featherstone (2015) went as far to say that without sociology we are lost: the discipline helps us 'find and situate' ourselves in the social world. While this can be unsettling, it is better to have the insights that sociology affords than to remain blinkered.

Giddens also argued that it is better to have studied sociology than not to have had the opportunity:

> Sociology is a path of self-exploration, at least if explored with enthusiasm. You will find that the world doesn't look quite the same as before, or your own place in it. (2015:39)

It might be helpful here to share some personal stories about how we, the authors, were transformed by sociology.

Case Study: Sarah

I was brought up in a mining community in Yorkshire and started studying sociology at the age of 14, when a fabulous new teacher introduced the subject to my comprehensive school. This was 1980, and sociology was new to the school curriculum, only having been introduced in 1972. It was not long before I was able to use my newly acquired sociological language to interrogate and challenge some aspects of my life. My family was traditional – as the daughter, I was expected to offer considerable help around the house. I recall a moment of epiphany when hanging out the wet sheets on the line, battling with the wind, while my brother sat watching Saturday morning television. I realised that I needed to, and could, challenge my family mores and prescribed gendered roles. Keen to explore law as a career, I wrote a letter to the Law Society for advice about which A Levels to study. The response, encased in a heavy, cream manila envelope with the Law Society's golden crest emblazoned on the back, advised that law was not a profession well-suited to women. This was in 1984. Sociology again helped me make sense of this reply, understanding it as profoundly patriarchal.

I left my mining community at the age of 18 to study sociology at Durham University – another town built around mining. The miner's strike was still in full swing and I was immediately drawn to the sociologies of working-class lives and jobs, as well as more practical activism. I studied *Coal is our Life* (Dennis, 1956) and it illuminated my own: I was able to draw parallels with the respondents' narratives, seeing how my *personal troubles, truths, and triumphs* were tied up with class, industry and community. This was revealed in other ways. At the time I went to university, undergraduate intake was still reserved for a minority and Durham, with its predominantly public-school applicants, was a shock to the system – social class differences were acutely visible and palpable to me for the first time. I found that fellow students immediately asked which school I had attended and then turned their backs, never to speak to me again, when I innocently declared 'Ridgewood Comprehensive'. My schooling made me a nobody in their eyes. Throughout, sociology was my touchstone, the place I could go to make sense of these experiences. It also resonated with the way I thought about the world.

Having always been a person that asked questions and wondered why things were as they were, sociology fitted with my enquiring disposition and helped me to make sense of the world though multiple perspectives, to question injustices, and to envision how the world might be different. This 'finding a home' within sociology is a common experience for many who have chosen to study the discipline (Back, 2015).

Case Study: Jen

Like all of us who each have different journeys into sociology, my pathway was different, but it was here that I, too, found a home. I did not have formative experiences in the way that Sarah describes. I went to an all-girls grammar school, and I was indoctrinated into a worldly belief in meritocracy – a bit like our fictional character Charles in Chapter 1. I did not start out studying sociology either. I decided to study a subject in which I thought I could more easily find a 'job' and I opted to do a coaching and teaching degree in sport with the aim of becoming a PE teacher. Never in my wildest dreams did I think I would become a sociologist.

I gradually felt disconnected from my sports degree, though, and had a deep sense of dissatisfaction with sport science that focused on biological and psychological explanations for sporting success and failure. My pathway into sociology was influenced significantly by the sub-field of sport sociology, which revealed how success and failure in elite sports were shaped by wider social norms and values that dominated sport. My eyes were opened to thinking about how issues such as 'athlete burnout' could not merely be understood as a limitation of an athlete (a personal trouble) who was overtraining, but instead were linked to unrealistic and dangerous demands produced by elite sporting institutions, that expect athletes to adopt an 'athlete identity' that is rigid, compliant and dangerously disciplined.

This led me into the parent discipline of sociology, where I have since taken my sociological imagination and applied it to many different areas of life that have helped me explain and reframe different personal troubles (and truths and triumphs) as public issues. This has had a hugely transformative effect on me, not least because now I am a sociology lecturer and not a PE teacher! Bauman (2014) describes being asked why sociology is so important to him as a question he finds challenging, and also embarrassing. He does not have a clear answer, but says that sociological thinking just became a 'normal' status for him, a way of being in the world. This really resonates with me because I, too, did not know that I could see the world in another way. Once you have seen the world through a sociological lens it is very hard to see it otherwise.

Transforming your relationship to society

Sociology does not just transform ideas about yourself and your own place in society, it connects you with other people and, in doing so, increases levels of understanding and fosters empathy. While Weber argued that verstehen was an important methodological tool – putting yourself in other people's shoes was the proper way to study the social world – it is also, we argue, an outcome of studying sociology. With its focus on inequalities and social justice, sociology can instil compassion alongside producing valuable knowledge.

This potential is illustrated by the insights of the American philosopher John Dewey. He argued that through conversations about things that individuals and groups want and hope for, people can start to understand their shared interests and develop a social consciousness. He called this a 'social intelligence' (Dewey, 1916).

We can see then that sociology can foster this capacity through the very things it studies. This leads us to the idea of active citizenship. To be able to fully participate in society, community and political life, it helps to be able to think critically, to evaluate ideas that you come across on social media and in other conversations. Studying sociology gives us this capacity because it demands respect for the people it studies, it privileges research evidence, and aims for a holistic understanding of social issues. If being an active citizen requires these competencies, then sociology provides them. Becoming an active citizen does not involve simply increasing your understanding of others and your personal role in society, but it also demands the development of self-perception, self-reflexivity and self-criticality.

Nussbaum (2020) also argued that subjects such as sociology are central to education for democracy, as they enable us to take an active, conscious role in society. Reflecting on the changing social world, in which we are increasingly focused on profit and our individual experiences, subjects such sociology have never been more important. She says this:

> What we want is a nation that is not just a gain-generating machine, but one in which the people make laws for themselves, expressing their autonomy and their equality in so doing. Let me also stipulate that: this nation takes equality seriously, giving all citizens equal entitlements to a wide range of liberties and opportunities, and guaranteeing to all at least a threshold level of a group of key material entitlements.

For Nussbaum, the next generation needs to be educated about economic distribution and social equality, about race and gender relations, about how our quality of life, especially health and education, can be improved. Specifically, she calls for the following to be central to education:

- *The ability to deliberate well about political issues affecting the nation, to examine, reflect, argue and debate, deferring neither to tradition nor authority.*
- *The ability to think about the good of the nation as a whole, not just that of one's own*

local group, and to see one's own nation, in turn, as a part of a complicated world order in which issues of many kinds require intelligent transnational deliberation for their resolution.

• *The ability to have concern for the lives of others, to imagine what policies of many types mean for the opportunities and experiences of one's fellow citizens, of many types and for people outside one's own nation.*

Sociology, we contend, has the capacity to foster such an education: in fact, Nussbaum could be describing much of the sociology curriculum! The role of sociology in enabling democracy is rooted in the exchange of ideas rather than the production of a blueprint. It does not matter than there is often disagreement in sociology – differing viewpoints encourage debate and make us think.

This does not mean that sociology cannot be objective. It means that sociologists can make politically driven suggestions if they are clear about the ideas that underpin their research and are prepared to consider alternative viewpoints (reflexivity). Holmwood (2015:50) succinctly describes this capacity, seeing sociology as 'an expression of democratic citizenship and as centrally concerned with facilitating public debate over pressing social issues'.

More than this, sociology provides insights that can be used to tackle long-standing social problems. Shah (2020) argues that global problems of environment, mass displacement, mental illness, poverty and inequality need social sciences for effective solutions. Without sociology, how can we navigate multiple data sets and produce workable solutions?

Transforming society: public and humane sociology

Being compassionate and humane is not just a personal disposition; the actual work of sociologists can make both small and significant differences to people's lives. In other words, sociology should have an applied capacity. Research findings do not just shine a light on social problems; they can also enable a researcher to suggest policies and practices that can change the world being studied. To explore this further, it is helpful to understand the ideas of **public** and **humane sociology**.

Public sociology refers to the capacity of the sociologist to enter, and transform, the lives of the non-sociologist, to engage with audiences beyond sociology. It can do this in several ways. Giddens (1987) outlines how sociology can enter the lay world and make a difference, describing this process as a **double hermeneutic**. Sociological concepts and ideas about social class, race relations, gender divisions or divorce, for example, are shared beyond the sociological community. They become part of the everyday language that we use, and importantly can bring about unforeseen and sometimes unintended changes. Because the public can think, make choices and be reflexive, they can also use sociological knowledge to revise their own practices and ideas. In this way, sociology can create the very social world it describes. For example, more widespread discussion of LGBTQIA+ experiences and lives may provide people with more understanding and confidence to express their own sexuality.

Indeed, sociology has positive and practical consequences. Burawoy (2005), when President of the American Sociological Association, strongly advocated for a public sociology. For him, sociology should not just be read by other sociologists, but should be shared and applied so that it can make a bigger difference. He believes that sharing sociology permits an open dialogue in which both sides – sociologists and non-sociologists – deepen their understanding of public issues and of each other.

Burawoy therefore actively encourages sociologists to engage with issues that are of significant public and political concern, to use its rigorous research methods and its conceptual apparatus, not just to describe the social world, but to think about what society could be like. Not all sociologists support this idea; some are concerned that if sociology has a political and applied focus, its value freedom and objectivity is harder to defend. We do not take this view. Rather, we see the importance of the transformative role that sociology can exercise.

We are particularly drawn to the manifesto for critical humanism written by Plummer (2013), where he calls for humane sociology. In the context of the ecological crisis, food shortages, widening global and national inequalities, and continued enslavement, the world needs a discipline that takes a position and seeks to build a better future. He describes the cost of human progress:

> Currently, there are some seven billion of us and we are fast growing…In the twenty first century we have become increasingly hi tech, media based and global. We rightly worry that we have degraded out environment catastrophically over our short history here on Planet Earth. We have lived through many major vast civilizations – from Sinic (or Chinese) to Islamic (or Arabian) to African and Western. The western world often acts as if it is a dominant world even as it is very small when compared with the rest of the world (only one in eight humans live in North America and Europe!). The Past Ghosts of our history always haunt us. Today, we are now organized into some 200 countries, with seven or eight major religions (and thousands of smaller ones), and some 6,000 languages. Difference and schismatic tension always pervades us, though it creates a vast global chain of interconnections. Half of us live in cities, often brutalized; 85% of us own nothing. Most of us live under an economic system of global capitalism that provides prosperity for a few while damaging many more. Indeed, many groups – women, the poor, ethnic and sexual minorities of all kinds – often get violently excluded leading wasted lives. (2013:490)

Plummer regards sociology as a necessary antidote – a discipline tasked with ensuring that the human world remains intact for future generations and can learn from its own mistakes.

This means that sociologists must engage in meaningful research, but also make their work accessible. Plummer advocates for sociological knowledge to be powerful, directed towards societal improvement, and easy to read! This capacity has never been more important – in Bauman's words: 'Sociological wisdom is needed more than at any other time in modern history' (2015:33). Impactful sociological work can operate in several ways. It can:

- produce research findings that contradict common sense and scientific assumptions
- improve the workings of society, both at a technical and interpersonal level
- influence policy and legislation.

We will illustrate each of these impacts with examples drawn from across several areas of sociological research.

Medical sociology: pregnancy and childbirth

We start with the work of Ann Oakley (2016) and her long-standing interest in childbirth and motherhood, which spanned her academic career (1973–2013). The Science Museum in London has an exhibition that charts the changes to childbirth and the move from home to hospital births. For many years, women found the experience of hospital birth disempowering – they described being treated as if they were birthing machines rather than choice-making actors. Oakley's work documented women's frustrations, those of mothers and midwives, and called for medical intervention only when necessary. In the Science Museum's exhibition, the most recent history shows birthing pools and bean bags, birth plans drawn by expectant mothers, and a retreat of medical paraphernalia. The museum places Oakley's books at the centre of the exhibit – her work regarded as a key catalyst for these changes.

Oakley used her feminist sociological imagination to enact real change for real women in real time. Medical sociology more generally, as the largest sub-discipline within sociology, has undertaken research in many different areas. For example, research on the doctor-patient relationship and lay health perspective has enabled the patient's voice to be heard. Sociology is central to understanding inequalities in health outcomes (drawing attention to social and economic causes, as you saw in Chapter 4). Additionally, important work has questioned the medicalisation of social life and the ways that some health conditions are stigmatised and receive less medical attention. Sociology therefore has had a tremendous impact on the way that medical care is organised and delivered, and the ways that doctors and other health professionals are taught.

Computer technology

In Chapter 2, we explored how interpretive sociology developed from the work of Weber and, in turn, produced several schools of thought, including symbolic interactionism and ethnomethodology. One important and applied outcome of ethnomethodology was

conversational analysis. This focuses on the verbal and non-verbal exchanges that occur between people – not just everyday conversations, but those that occur between doctors and their patients, lawyers and their clients, etc. This important area of research revealed the power dynamics embedded in conversations.

There has been another practical impact of this research. In their book *Computers and Conversation*, Luff, Gilbert and Frohlich (1990) explore how conversational analysis was instrumental in the development of computer linguistics. Conversational analysis showed the importance of turn-taking, utterances and interruptions in conversation, and demonstrated how these elements should be acknowledged and accounted for when humans interact with computers. Computer programs need to be built so that they can be a flexible and responsive interface. For example, humans often misunderstand one another and engage in repair work or seek clarifications, and these capabilities also need to be built into computers. Other work, such as that conducted by May-Chahal et al (2014), has combined sociological research methods with informational technology to develop a range of original software tools designed to tackle the risks to children posed by new media.

Inequalities in education

In Chapter 4, we outlined the extensive divisions that continue to characterise educational attainment and introduced you to several research studies. These pieces of research do make a difference to how schools are run and the way that teachers teach. In one example, Archer, Moote and MacLeod (2020) looked at girls studying physics at A Level. Seventy-five per cent of students taking A Level physics come from 25% of schools, and only 20% of A Level physics students are girls. These researchers said that the dominant explanation given by the Institute of Physics (IOP) was that girls themselves were the 'problem' – they did not aspire to study physics. Archer et al argued that the IOP needed to change its narrative concerning how they communicated physics to girls. Through a partnership, they moved from the 'deficit' model that blamed girls to a model that was more empowering and advocated girl's involvement in the subject.

Migration and asylum

One of the most pressing social problems today is the impact of mass human migration. Human beings have always travelled and have often been forcibly displaced, particularly during and after war. Human displacement remains a significant problem today, characterised by an exponential growth in the number of people seeking asylum in other countries. The conflict in Syria began in 2011 and by 2015 refugees were arriving in Europe at an unprecedented rate – some estimates suggesting that a million people had risked their lives, fleeing in flimsy boats. The rate of movement has been described as a refugee crisis (Refugee Council, 2020), and sociology has been involved in much important research concerning this topic area (Mayblin, 2014). Many refugees face destitution, homelessness and sometimes deportation, even when they have secured passage to a place of safety. Schuster (2015), for example, conducted research in Afghanistan, Morocco and Uganda to detail the impact of deportation and to enable the voices of migrants to be heard. Mayblin, Wake and Kazemi (2020) importantly raised the public consciousness and advocated for better human rights by drawing a link between the current refugee crisis and colonialism.

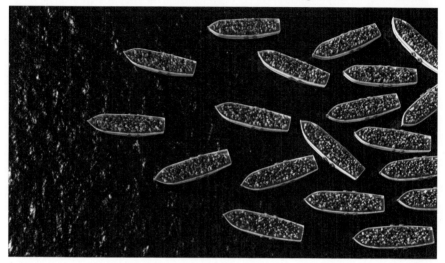

Stop and search

Racism is a hugely troubling social inequality that needs to be tackled – in all areas of society, and significantly in the criminal justice system. We have explored the disproportionate arrests, prosecutions and imprisonment of minoritised communities (see page 109), and how Bowling's work has been central in transforming police practices of stop and search. In 2009–10, Bowling was appointed as the sole external advisor to the Equality and Human Rights Commission (EHRC), and his research was foundational to their Stop and Think (2010) report that demonstrated how stop and search was unlawful. This report has been used to influence police practice. Bowling also spoke at the hearing of the Metropolitan Police Authority consultation on the 2011 Police and Criminal Evidence Act (PACE), which ensured that stop and searches continued to be recorded by police.

Social class

To be able to document and respond to social class differences, sociologists need evidence, and the work of Goldthorpe and McKnight (2006) has been central to this. Their class schema (see page 78) is used extensively throughout Europe, Australasia and North America to assess the impact of social class on life chances and to chart social mobility.

Savage's (2015) Great British Class Survey has also made a significant impact on public debate and public consciousness about social class. It has spawned an important body of work on the precariat and the elite and has revealed how class impacts on our chances in complex ways. Friedman and Laurison's (2020) work on the class ceiling is being used by employers, trade unions and government to understand the cultural barriers that stymie social mobility and to explore how these barriers might be overcome.

Decolonising the curriculum

In Chapter 5, we investigated how sociology has often failed to fully integrate the study of race and racism into its analyses. Instead, sociologists too often treat these central questions separately, almost as secondary topic areas. However, the reflexive capacity of the discipline means that sociology has recognised these limitations, even if there is still much more to do. Sociologists have been central to the campaign to 'decolonise the curriculum'. This is a campaign that demands that teaching and learning both within and beyond sociology is representative, accessible, and inclusive.

For the last two decades it has been acknowledged that curricula within schools and universities reproduce the work of White scholars who already have a privileged position. It is now increasingly recognised that the teaching of sociology itself needs to be rethought and reimagined. The sociological canon, its theories, methods and writers, need to be held to account and checked – for its White privileged perspectives and approaches, and for the uncritical ways that the history of sociology is usually told. To decolonise the curriculum, however, it is not enough to simply integrate thinkers of colour. Bhambra et al (2018; 2020) have argued that the university itself must be recognised as a colonial and capitalist project. This would mean resisting coloniality inside and outside of the classroom, including closing the awarding gap (the differences in degree classifications by ethnicity), recruiting more minority ethnic academic staff, and challenging the ways in which the institutions unconsciously reinforce racism.

To date, sociology has been at the forefront of campaigns to promote and take up this challenge within academia and this is why we include this example in the transformative chapter. Meghji (2021), for instance, explains that sociology was born when global colonisation was at its height and therefore is replete with colonial rules of thought and colonial ways of thinking. Sociology was itself implicated in the reproduction of colonialism, and it continues to be Eurocentric in its approach. His work brings together the work of underrepresented sociologists and explores how sociology must strive for inclusivity and equity. Decolonising the curriculum is very much a work in progress, but sociology has shown commitment to this project, and is a disciplinary leader.

Transforming your career

Studying sociology requires the dispositions that we have outlined. The exciting thing is that these dispositions are transferable. You can apply them in all walks of life, and within different occupations. As the British Sociological Association says:

> Studying sociology involves continuous interplay between matters of concern in society and concepts and theories of society. The requirement to reason and critically analyse the workings of society makes sociology an effective medium of intellectual development in the course of an undergraduate degree or other programme of study. Employers recognise this.

The final three words in this quotation are perhaps the most important. Employers like employees who have studied sociology because they are analytical, critical, considered and creative: skills that suit so many workplaces. As such, sociology students go on to work in the public services as teachers and social workers. They find employment in the criminal justice system as lawyers, police and probation officers, prison officers, etc. They can use their research skills in marketing and public relations work, or as social researchers working for the civil service and local and central government, or within the private sector. They also remain in universities undertaking funded research and teaching the next generation of sociologists as well as many other students following paths where sociology is regarded as centrally important (law, medicine, social work, the police, etc.). Sociologists often want to work within the charitable sector, supporting those who are disadvantaged and vulnerable. Sociologists go into politics to be at the cutting edge of policy change. It is interesting to note that both Michelle Obama and Martin Luther King Jr. studied sociology!

The ability of a sociologist to understand and use multiple theories and be able to judge and navigate complex sets of evidence, means that they are excellent and analytical communicators. Sociologists work as journalists, and in human resource management. Because sociology studies anything and everything that people do, we can see that sociologists can find work in almost all areas of employment. We understand how the social world and employment is changing, and this makes us adaptable. The American Sociological Association makes this very point on its website:

> We have all been asked at one time or another, 'What are you going to do with a sociology degree?' The answer is that the sociology degree serves as an excellent springboard for a variety of careers in many diverse fields…the 21st century labour market is fast-changing, the jobs you apply for as a graduate may not even exist yet. To navigate the 21st century means being able to keep up with the changing world.

Overall, then, sociology can be transformative for your career. Studying sociology gives you the ability to judge and evaluate evidence, understand the diversity and complexity of social life, make reasoned and theoretically informed arguments, collect information in a rigorous and ethical way, work on your own and with others, and be imaginative, agile and reflexive. There are few subjects that bestow such wide-ranging and important lifelong skill sets.

Summary

This chapter is an optimistic conclusion to our discussion of the key dispositions that make a sociologist and a hopeful vision for the future of sociology. We hope that our passion for the subject has shone through the pages of this book and that you can see the enduring importance of a sociological education. In the final pages, we put on our rose-tinted glasses and leave you with a sociology of hope and optimism.

Sociological how-tos

To be transformative you need to:

- be empathetic and humane
- be open to the ways that sociology can enable you to think and act differently
- be knowledgeable of the skills and capacities that studying sociology affords – which will be useful for both personal transformation and to make a difference in other people's lives.

AN ENDING: A SOCIOLOGY OF HOPE AND REASONS TO BE OPTIMISTIC

We said at the start that there was never a more important time to study sociology and to be a sociologist. We have introduced you to the key dispositions that characterise sociology: imagination, conceptual thinking, rigorous methods, knowledgeability, ethical reflexivity and a commitment to bringing about change. We have shown that sociology studies the most pressing social concerns – inequality and poverty, environmental damage, and human displacement (asylum seeking) – and that it provides some solutions. It is perhaps inevitable, and not at all surprising, that sociology is often described as the study of social problems.

However, this is not all that sociology does. We want to conclude the book by thinking about a sociology of hope. This is the sociology that studies what works well in society – the sociology that looks to showcase community spirit and conviviality, cohesion and cooperation. This sociology studies that which makes society good and it celebrates the positive sides of human life, focusing on social interaction, shared values and mutual care. In this concluding section, we put on our optimistic, rose-tinted glasses.

For all the important sociological work that describes difference and prejudice, there is also work that draws attention to what Gilroy (2004) called conviviality – the instances where communities are different but integrated and supportive, a sociology of everyday ties, acceptance and belonging. In an article about social polarisation (Koch et al, 2020), Cant's case study of Margate showed that alongside the very real articulation of racism, there were simultaneous attempts by people to challenge racist sentiments and build community. For example, while some Margate residents resented locally residing Roma populations, other residents were keen to call out the racism and actively resist it by encouraging inclusive community activity such as street parties, which would bring diverse groups together. It is therefore important to also document moments such as this when communities come together. Neal et al (2019), for example, looked at what brings communities together, how people find commonality rather than difference, and showed that an ethnically diverse society enables social interaction and shared practice.

We have described the rise in dependency on food banks, and the increase in food insecurity and hunger. At the same time, it is possible to see the emergence of grass-roots, community-driven, volunteer-based organisations that collect food donations and administer them to those in need. We must have some criticality in studying these initiatives – they do 'fill in' for the state, and judgements are made about who can and cannot access their help (Williams et al, 2016) – but there is also evidence of solidarity and care. Volunteering is an example of altruism and philanthropy, as well as self-interest and curriculum vitae (CV)-building, and it is important to give sufficient voice to the former. That people give their time is worth celebrating and understanding.

In Chapter 2, we described the gig economy and how this can lead to precarious work and a sense of hopelessness. However, sociological studies have also shown how workers come together to support one another when dealing with difficult work practices. Gregory (2020) described how gig workers forge new communities of support: they turn to one another for care in an economy that does not care for them. This sociology recognises and celebrates human compassion. Similarly, Tassinari and Maccarrone (2020) described the ways in which gig workers collectively organise to resist exploitative working conditions. These collective modes of resistance can have practical consequences: for instance, in February 2021, the UK Supreme Court ruled that all Uber drivers were entitled to minimum wages and holiday pay.

The COVID-19 pandemic was a global challenge, but it also inspired mutual aid: neighbours bought food for one another and checked in on those who were feeling isolated. Rainbows appeared in windows and people stood on their doorsteps to clap for carers, giving thanks to the National Health Service (NHS). This was a moment when the collective human capacity for empathy and compassion was reproduced across communities. As Marston, Renedo and Miles (2020) document, community participation was crucial in the pandemic and people stepped up:

> Community participation is essential in the collective response to coronavirus disease 2019 (COVID-19), from compliance with lockdown, to the steps that need to be taken as countries ease restrictions, to community support through volunteering. Communities clearly want to help: in the UK, about 1 million people volunteered to help the pandemic response and highly localised mutual aid groups have sprung up all over the world with citizens helping one another with simple tasks such as checking on wellbeing during lockdowns. (2020:1676)

Sociology is central to the identification of the ingredients that help communities cohere, to see similarities as well as differences, and to disseminate these findings to bring about positive social change. There is important work that documents what encourages connections, for instance. Gladwell (2006) describes how 'little things make a difference', and how societal changes can have a positive impact on everyday life. In particular, he describes the importance of 'connectors': those people in any community that know large numbers of other people and do enormous work linking people together, creating ties and bonds.

In *Sociology for Optimists*, Holmes (2016) describes how humans have the resilience to respond to social problems and can collectively enact social change. She is referring to the agency that we all have, and which we can all use, to make a difference. She argues that optimism must be a central part of the sociological toolkit and asks that sociologists document and understand what brings about happiness, satisfaction, enjoyment, fun and wellbeing. In her book, she details several studies that show how people come together, even in times of adversity, and can find the space for joy. Holmes goes as far as to say that fun might even have the capacity to be revolutionary.

For example, she describes research by Helena Flam, who studied communities in central Europe when the communist regime was coming to an end. The climate was violent and many people lived in fear of reprisals, yet Flam documented how the community worked together to build joyful gatherings. Everyday events were turned into a form of celebration – such as taking pets (including dogs and goldfish) and favourite things (such as casseroles!) for collective walks to express peaceful solidarity. This is a lovely image.

Holmes also introduces us to Clark's book, *Inhuman Nature: Sociable life on a Dynamic Planet* (2010), which explores human responses to climate change and environmental crises. Clark describes how in 2004, when the Boxing Day tsunami caused widespread devastation and loss of life across Southeast Asia, the community reached out to one another; tourists and locals battled together to survive and help each other. This is an instance of collectivism in a time of crisis, and there are many other examples of communities coming together during war, natural disasters and terrorist attacks.

There are also all the occasions when people come together to campaign for social change. Sociologists often describe these as social movements, and examples include Black Lives Matter, Occupy and Extinction Rebellion. There is something awe-inspiring about the way that these movements unite people, often across all axes of social stratification, including generational and global divides. They enable the formation of collective identities. These extraordinary moments and movements also reveal the human capacity to help and care for one another in (extra) ordinary times, and to find direction and happiness.

Sociologists like Furedi (2004) and Ahmed (2010) have criticised optimistic visions of sociology, arguing that happiness is a dark figure of modernity, a product of consumerism, and a tool to justify oppression. While, of course, sociologists must be wary of the concept of happiness and subject it to a sociological imagination, this should not limit us only to such negative renderings of personal experiences (Cieslik, 2015). We have already argued that sociologists should not only examine personal troubles but should also subject to the sociological imagination personal truths as well as triumphs. A focus on triumphs has two implications: it allows us to look at the social inequalities that enable some people to flourish and be triumphant, but it also demands that we examine the social structures that enable a good and happy life. In this respect we can see the positive, hopeful features of our social world rather than being blinkered by conceptual glasses that tend to see the darkness of the social world rather than the light.

To look for the everyday, happy, supportive networks is not to ignore inequality or prejudice, nor does it absolve the state from providing support, and nor does it blame communities that do not find such resilience. It does, however, give sociology the scope to examine and showcase hope and optimism. Having a critical but optimistic outlook means that we can be hopeful about the transformative potential of sociology – and this feels like a good place to close this book.

REFERENCES

Adler, F. (1975). *Sisters in Crime: The Rise of the New Female Criminal*. New York: McGraw-Hill.

Ahmed, S. (2010). *The Promise of Happiness*. London: Duke University Press.

Althusser, L. (2006). 'Ideology and ideological state apparatuses (notes towards an investigation)'. *The Anthropology of the State: A Reader*, 9(1), pp. 86–98.

American Sociology Association. Career Centre [online]. Available at: https://www.asanet.org/career-center [Accessed 29/12/20].

Anderson, B. (2020). *Sociology On and Beyond the Covid-19 Crisis. An Online Symposium* [online]. Available at: https://www.youtube.com/watch?v=AU1qcXAf6kM [Accessed 04/01/21].

Archer, L., Moote, J. and MacLeod, E. (2020). 'Learning that physics is "not for me": Pedagogic work and the cultivation of habitus among advanced level physics students', *Journal of the Learning Sciences*, 29(3), pp. 347–384. doi: 10.1080/10508406.2019.1707679

Aryee, F., Szolucha, A., Stretesky, P.B., Short, D., Long, M.A., Ritchie, L.A. and Gill, D.A. (2020). 'Shale Gas Development and Community Distress: Evidence from England'. *International Journal of Environmental Research and Public Health*, 17(14), pp. 50–69.

Back, L. (2015). 'Living Sociology' In K. Twamley, M. Doidge and A. Scott (eds). *Sociologists Tales. Contemporary narratives on sociological thought and practice*. Bristol: Bristol Policy Press. pp. 83–99.

Baker, S. (2017). 'A glamorous feminism by design?'. *Cultural Studies*, 31(1), pp. 47–69.

Barker, E. (1984). *The Making of a Moonie*. Oxford: Blackwell.

Baudrillard, J. (1983). *Simulations*. New York: Semiotext.

Bauman Z. (1997). *Postmodernity and its Discontents*. Oxford: Blackwell.

Bauman, Z. (2013). *Liquid Modernity*. New York: John Wiley & Sons.

Bauman, Z. (2014). *What Use is Sociology?* Cambridge: Polity Press.

Bauman, Z. (2015). 'Sociology as science/technology of freedom'. In K. Twamley, M. Doidge and A. Scott, eds. *Sociologists Tales. Contemporary Narratives on Sociological Thought and Practice*. Bristol: Policy Press, pp. 29–35.

Bauman, Z. and May, T. (2019). *Thinking Sociologically*. London: John Wiley & Sons.

Beck, U. (1992). *Risk Society: Towards a New Modernity*. London: Sage.

Becker. H.S. (1963/2008). *Outsiders: Studies in the Sociology of Deviance*. New York: Simon and Schuster.

Becker, H.S. (1973). 'Labelling theory reconsidered'. *Outsiders: Studies in the Sociology of Deviance*. New York: The Free Press, pp. 177–212.

Bejarano, C.A., Juárez, L.L., García, M.A.M. and Goldstein, D.M. (2019). *Decolonizing Ethnography: Undocumented Immigrants and New Directions in Social Science*. London: Duke University Press.

Benoit, C., Smith, M., Jansson, M., Healey, P. and Magnuson, D. (2020). 'The Relative Quality of Sex Work'. *Work, Employment and Society*, 35(2), pp. 239–255

Berger, P. (1967/1990). *The Sacred Canopy: Elements of a Sociological Theory of Religion*. New York: Random House.

Bhambra, G.K. (2007). *Rethinking Modernity: Postcolonialism and the Sociological Imagination*. London: Springer.

Bhambra, G.K. (2010). 'Sociology and Post-colonialism: Another "Missing" Revolution?'. In Burnett, J., Jeffers, S. and Thomas, G. (eds) *New Social Connections*. Palgrave Macmillan: London. pp. 125–140

Bhambra, G.K., Gebrial, D. and Nişancıoğlu, K. (2018). *Decolonising the U125-140niversity*. London: Pluto Press.

Bhambra, G.K., Nisancioglu, K. and Gebrial, D. (2020). 'Decolonising the university in 2020'. Identities: 1–8.

Boellstorff, T., Nardi, B., Pearce, C. and Taylor, T.L. (2012). *Ethnography and Virtual Worlds: A Handbook of Method*. Princeton: Princeton University Press.

Booher-Jennings, J. (2008). 'Learning to label: socialisation, gender, and the hidden curriculum of high-stakes testing'. *British Journal of Sociology of Education*, 29(2), pp. 149–160.

Bourdieu, P. (1984). *Distinction: A Social Critique of the Judgement of Taste*. Cambridge: Harvard University Press.

Bowles, S. and Gintis, H. (1976/2008). 'Schooling in capitalist societies', *Schools and Society*, pp. 41–44.

Bowling, B. and Phillips, C. (2002). *Racism, Crime and Justice*. London: Pearson Education.

Bowling, B. and Phillips, C. (2007). 'Disproportionate and discriminatory: Reviewing the evidence on police stop and search'. *The Modern Law Review*, 70(6), pp. 936–961.

British Sociological Association. Sociology careers. Available at: https:www.britsoc.co.uk/what-is-sociology/sociologist-careers/ [Accessed 29/12/20].

Brown, G.W. and Harris, T. (1978/2012). *Social Origins of Depression: A Study of Psychiatric Disorder in Women*. Abingdon: Routledge.

Brown, W. (2020). *States of Injury: Power and Freedom in Late Modernity*. Princeton: Princeton University Press.

Bullard, R.D. (1983). 'Solid waste sites and the black Houston community'. *Sociological Inquiry*, 53(2-3), pp. 273–288.

Burawoy, M. (2005). 'For public sociology'. *American Sociological Review*, 70(1), pp. 4–28.

Busfield, J. (1988). 'Mental illness as social product or social construct: a contradiction in feminists' arguments?'. *Sociology of Health and Illness*. 10(4), pp. 521–542.

Butkowski, C.P., Dixon T.L., Weeks, K.R. and Smith M.A. (2020). 'Quantifying the feminine self(ie): Gender display and social media feedback in young women's Instagram selfies'. *New Media and Society* 22(5), pp. 817–837.

Butler, J. (1990). *Gender Trouble: Feminism and the Subversion of Identity*: New York: Routledge.

Burrows, R. and Knowles, C. (2019). 'The "HAVES" and the "HAVE YACHTS": Socio-Spatial Struggles in London between the "Merely Wealthy" and the "Super-Rich"'. *Cultural Politics*, 15(1), pp. 72–87.

Calvey, D. (2019). 'The everyday world of bouncers: a rehabilitated role for covert ethnography'. *Qualitative Research*, 9(3), pp. 247–262.

Campbell, C. (2015). *Easternization of the West: a thematic account of cultural change in the modern era*. Abingdon: Routledge.

Cant, S. (2020). 'Medical pluralism, mainstream marginality or subaltern therapeutics? Globalisation and the integration of "Asian" medicines and biomedicine in the UK'. *Society and Culture in South Asia*, 6(1), pp. 31–51.

Cant, S. and Sharma, U. (1998). 'Reflexivity, ethnography and the professions (complementary medicine) watching you watching me watching you (and writing about both of us)'. *The Sociological Review*, 46 (2), pp. 244–263.

Cant, S., Savage, M. and Chatterjee, A. (2020). 'Popular but peripheral: the ambivalent status of sociology education in schools in England'. *Sociology*, 54(1), pp. 37–52.

Castells, M. (2011). *The Rise of the Network Society*. New York: John Wiley & Sons.

Charles, N. (2014) 'Animals just love you as you are: Experiencing kinship across the species barrier'. Sociology, 48(4), pp. 715–730.

Cheshire, J. (2012). 'Lives on the Line: Mapping Life Expectancy Along the London Tube Network'. *Environment and Planning A: Economy and Place*, 44(7). pp. 1525–1528

Chesney-Lind, M. (1978), 'Young Women in the Arms of the Law' and 'Chivalry Examined: Women and the Criminal Justice System' in Bowker, L.H.(ed) *Women, Crime and the Criminal Justice System*, Massachusetts: Lexington Books. pp. 171–217.

Cieslik, M. (2015). '"Not Smiling but Frowning": Sociology and the "Problem of Happiness"'. *Sociology*. 49(3), pp. 422–437.

Clegg, N., Allen, R., Fernandes, S., Freedman, S. and Kinnock, S. (2017). *Commission on Inequality in Education*. London: Social Market Foundation.

Cohen, A.K. (1955). *Delinquent Boys: The Culture of the Gang*. New York: Free Press.

Cohen, S. (1972/2002). *Folk Devils and Moral Panics: The Creation of the Mods and Rockers*. London: Psychology Press.

Coleman, C. and Moynihan, J. (2002). 'The Social Construction of Official Statistics'. In Y. Jewkes and G. Letherby, eds, *Criminology: A Reader*. London: Sage. pp. 96–104.

Comte, A. (1853/2009). *The Positive Philosophy of Auguste Comte, Volume 2*. Cambridge: Cambridge University Press.

Connell, R.W. (2005). *Masculinities* (2nd ed.). Berkeley: University of California Press.

Cooley, C.H. (1902/1992). *Human Nature and the Social Order*. Piscataway: Transaction Publishers.

Crenshaw, K. (1991). 'Mapping the Margins. Intersectionality, identity politics, and violence against women of color', *Stanford Law Review*, 43(6): pp 1241–1299

Davie, G. (1990). 'Believing without belonging: Is this the future of religion in Britain?' *Social Compass*, 37(4), 455–69.

Davie, G. (1994). *Religion in Britain Since 1945: Believing Without Belonging*. New York: John Wiley & Sons.

Davie, G. (2013). *The Sociology of religion: A critical agenda*. London: Sage.

Davis, A. (2003). *Are Prisons Obsolete?* New York: Seven Stories Press.

Davis, K. and Moore, W.E. (1945). 'Some principles of stratification'. *American Sociological Review*, 10(2), pp. 242–249.

De Beauvoir, S. (1831/1997). *The Second Sex*. London: Verso.

Dennis, N. (1956). *Coal is Our Life: An Analysis of a Yorkshire Mining Community*. London: Eyre & Spottiswoode.

Department for Business, Energy and Industrial Strategy. (2018). *The Characteristics of those in the Gig Economy*. London: DBEIS.

Dewey, J. (1916). 'What pragmatism means by practical'. In *Essays in Experimental Logic*, Chicago: University of Chicago Press, pp. 303–329.

Dobash, R.E. and Dobash, R.P. (1979). *Violence Against Wives*. New York: The Free Press.

Döring, N., Reif, A. and Poeschl, S. (2016). 'How gender-stereotypical are selfies? A content analysis and comparison with magazine adverts'. *Computers in Human Behavior*, 55, pp. 955–962.

Dorling, D. (2015). *Injustice. Why Social Inequality Still Persists*. Cambridge: Policy Press.

Du Bois, W.E.B. (1899). *The Philadelphia Negro: A Social Study* (No. 14). Publications of the University of Pennsylvania, Series in Political Economy and Public Law. Boston: Ginn and Company.

Du Bois, W.E.B. (1903/1968). *The Souls of Black Folk: Essays and Sketches*. Chicago: A. G. McClurg; New York: Johnson Reprint Corp.

Durkheim, E. (1897/2005) *Suicide: A Study in Sociology*, translated by J.A. Spaulding and G. Simpson. London: Routledge.

Durkheim, E. (1895/2014). T*he Rules of Sociological Method: And Selected Texts on Sociology and its Method*. London: Simon and Schuster.

Ekins, R. and King, D., (1999). 'Towards a sociology of transgendered bodies'. *The Sociological Review*, 47 (3), pp.580–602.

Elias, A.S. and Gill, R. (2018). 'Beauty surveillance: The digital self-monitoring cultures of neoliberalism'. *European Journal of Cultural Studies*, 21(1), pp. 59–77.

Elliott, A. (2013). *Reinvention*. Abingdon: Routledge.

Engels, F. (1841/1997). *The Condition of the Working Class in England*. Harmondsworth: Penguin.

Falkof, N. (2020). 'On Moral Panic: Some Directions for Further Development', *Critical Sociology*, 46(2), pp. 225–239.

Fanon, F. (1961/2007). *The Wretched of the Earth*. New York: Grove Press.

Farrington D.P., Jolliffe, D., Loeber, R., Stouthamer-Loeber, M. and Kalb, L.M. (2001). 'The concentration of offenders in families, and family criminality in the prediction of boys' delinquency'. *Journal of Adolescence*. 24(5). pp. 579–96.

Featherstone, M. (2015). 'Why Sociology?' In K. Twamley, M. Doidge and A. Scott (eds), *Sociologists Tales. Contemporary narratives on sociological thought and practice*. Bristol: Policy Press.

Fletcher, I. (2014). 'Defining an epidemic: the body mass index in British and US obesity research 1960–2000'. *Sociology of Health and Illness*, 36(3), pp. 338–353.

Fernando, S. (2010). *Mental Health, Race and Culture*. London: Macmillan International Higher Education.

Francis, B., Archer, L., Moote, J., de Witt, J. and Yeomans, L. (2016). 'Femininity, science, and the denigration of the girly girl'. *British Journal of Sociology of Education*, 38(8), pp. 1097–1110.

Francis, B., Craig, N., Hodgen, J., Taylor, B., Tereshchenko, A., Connolly, P. and Archer, L. (2020). 'The impact of tracking by attainment on pupil self-confidence over time: demonstrating the accumulative impact of self-fulfilling prophecy'. *British Journal of Sociology of Education*, 41(5), pp. 626–642.

Friedman, S. and Reeves, A. (2020). 'From Aristocratic to Ordinary: Shifting Modes of Elite Distinction'. *American Sociological Review*, 85(2), pp. 323–350.

Friedman, S. and Laurison, D. (2020). *The Class Ceiling: Why it Pays to be Privileged*. Bristol: Policy Press.

Foucault, M. (1975). *Discipline and Punish*. Abingdon: Routledge.

Foucault, M. (2005). *The Order of Things*. Abingdon: Routledge.

Furedi, F. (2004). *Therapy Culture: Cultivating Uncertainty in an Uncertain Age*. London: Routledge.

Gabriel, S., Naidu, E., Paravati, E., Morrison, C.D. and Gainey, K. (2020). 'Creating the sacred from the profane: Collective effervescence and everyday activities'. *The Journal of Positive Psychology*, 15(1), pp. 129–154.

Garfinkel, H. (1967). *Ethnomethodology*. Upper Saddle River: Prentice Hall.

Garthwaite, K. (2016). *Hunger Pains: Life Inside Foodbank Britain*. Bristol: Policy Press.

Giddens, A. (1987). *Social Theory and Modern Sociology*. Cambridge: Polity Press.

Giddens, Anthony. (1992/2013a). *The Transformation of Intimacy: Sexuality, Love and Eroticism in Modern Societies*. London: John Wiley & Sons.

Giddens, Anthony. (1992/2013b). *The Consequences of Modernity*. London: John Wiley & Sons.

Giddens, A. (2015). 'Why Sociology Matters'. In K. Twamley, M. Doidge and A. Scott, eds, *Sociologists' Tales: Contemporary Narratives on Sociological Thought and Practice*. Bristol: Policy Press, pp. 35–41.

Gillborn, D. (2008). Racism and Education: *Coincidence or Conspiracy?* Abingdon: Taylor & Francis.

Gillis, J. (1996). *A World of Their Own Making*. Boston: Harvard University Press.

Gillies, V. (2005). 'Raising the Meritocracy: Parenting and the Individualization of Social Class'. *Sociology*, 39(5), pp. 835–853.

Gilroy, P. (1982). 'The Myth of Black Criminality'. *The Socialist Register*, 19 [online]. Available at: https://socialistregister.com/index.php/srv/article/view/5474/2373.

Gilroy, P. (1987/2002). *There Ain't No Black in the Union Jack: The Cultural Politics of Race and Nation*. London: Routledge.

Gilroy, P. (2004). *After Empire: Melancholia or convivial culture?* Abingdon: Routledge.

Gladwell, M. (2006). *The Tipping Point: How Little Things can make a Big Difference*. New York: Little, Brown.

Goffman, E. (1959). *The Presentation of Self in Everyday Life*. Garden City, NY: Doubleday.

Goffman, E. (1963). *Stigma: Notes on the Management of Spoiled Identity*. New York: Simon and Schuster, Inc.

Goffman, E. (1961). *Asylums: Essays on the Social Situation of Mental Patients and Other Inmates*. New York: Anchor Books

Goffman, A. (2015). *On the Run: Fugitive Life in an American City*. New York: Picador.

Golash-Boza, T. (2016). 'A critical and comprehensive sociological theory of race and racism'. *Sociology of Race and Ethnicity*, 2(2), pp. 129–141.

Goldthorpe, J.H. (2000). 'Social class and the differentiation of employment contracts'. In J.H. Goldthorpe, *On Sociology: Numbers, Narratives, and the Integration of Research and Theory*. Oxford: Oxford University Press.

Goldthorpe, J.H. and Hope, K. (1974). *The Social Grading of Occupations*. Oxford: Clarendon.

Goldthorpe, J.H. and McKnight, A. (2006). 'The economic basis of social class'. *Mobility and Inequality: Frontiers of Research in Sociology and Economics*, pp. 109–136.

GOV.UK. (1999). 'The Steven Lawrence Inquiry: Report of an Inquiry by Sir William Macpherson of Cluny' [online]. Available at: https://assets.publishing.service.gov.uk/government/uploads/system/uploads/attachment_data/file/277111/4262.pdf [Accessed 5/01/21]

GOV.UK. (2020). 'Ethnicity facts and figures: People living in deprived neighbourhoods' [online]. Available at: https://www.ethnicity-facts-figures.service.gov.uk/uk-population-by-ethnicity/demographics/people-living-in-deprived-neighbourhoods/latest [Accessed 28/12/20].

GOV.UK. (2021). 'Ethnicity facts and figures: Employment' [online]. Available at: https://www.ethnicity-facts-figures.service.gov.uk/work-pay-and-benefits/employment/employment/latest [Accessed 19/2/21].

Gramsci, A. (1971) Selections from the Prison Notebooks. London: Lawrence and Wishart.

Greer, G. (1994). The Whole Woman. London: Black Swan.

Green A.I. (2002). 'Gay but not queer: Toward a post-queer study of sexuality'. Theory and Society. 31(4), pp. 531–45.

Greenfeld, L. (2013). Mind, Modernity and Madness. Cambridge: Harvard University Press.

Gregory, K. (2020). 'My life is more valuable than this: Understanding Risk Among On-demand Food Couriers in Edinburgh'. Work, Employment and Society. 35(2):316-331. Available at: https://doi.org/10.1177/0950017020969593 [Accessed 22/12/2020]

Hall, S. (1996). 'New ethnicities'. In Hall, S and Morley, D (eds). Critical Dialogues in Cultural Studies. London: Routledge pp. 441–449.

Hall, S., Critcher, C., Jefferson, T., Clark, J. and Roberts, B. (1978). Policing the Crisis: Mugging, the State, and Law and Order. London: MacMillan.

Haraway, D. (2003). The Companion Species Manifesto: Dogs, People and Significant Otherness. Chicago: Indiana University Press.

Haraway D. (2006). 'A Cyborg Manifesto: Science, Technology, and Socialist-Feminism in the Late 20th Century'. In J. Weiss, J. Nolan, J. Hunsinger and P. Trifonas, eds. The International Handbook of Virtual Learning Environments. Dordrecht: Springer.

Hardes, J.J. (2020). 'Governing excess: Boxing, biopolitics and the body'. Theoretical Criminology, 24(4), pp. 689–705.

Hartmann, H.I. (1979). 'The unhappy marriage of Marxism and feminism: Towards a more progressive union'. Capital and Class, 3(2), pp. 1–33.

Heaphy, B. (2018). 'Troubling traditional and conventional families? Formalised same-sex couples and "the ordinary"'. Sociological Research Online, 23(1), pp. 160–176.

Heidensohn, F. (1987). 'Women and crime: Questions for criminology' in Carlen, P., and Worrall, A. (eds). Gender, crime and justice. Milton Keynes: Open University Press, pp. 16–27.

Heidensohn, F. (1996). Women and Crime. London: Macmillan

Henriksen, T.D. (2020). 'Do Prostitution and Social Vulnerability Go Hand in Hand? Examining the Association Between Social Background and Prostitution Using Register Data'. Sociological Research Online, 21(4), pp. 121–132.

Hines, S. (2019) 'The feminist frontier: on trans and feminism'. Journal of Gender Studies, 28:2, pp.145–57.

Hobbs, M., Owen, S. and Gerber, L. (2017). 'Liquid love? Dating apps, sex, relationships and the digital transformation of intimacy'. Journal of Sociology, 53(2), pp. 271–284.

Holmes, M. (2016). Sociology for Optimists. London: Sage.

Holmwood, J. (2015). 'Sociology as Democratic Knowledge'. In K. Twamley, M. Doidge and A. Scott, eds. Sociologists Tales. Contemporary narratives on sociological thought and practice. Bristol: Policy Press, pp. 49–55.

Humphreys, L. (1975). Tearoom Trade: Impersonal sex in public places. Piscataway: Transaction Publishers.

Irvine, L. (2008). 'Animals and sociology'. Sociology Compass, 2(6), pp. 1954–1971.

Irwin, L. (2013). Sociology and the Environment: A Critical Introduction to Society, Nature and Knowledge. New York: John Wiley & Sons.

James, C.L.R. (1938). The Black Jacobins: Toussaint L'Ouverture and the San Domingo Revolution. London: Secker & Warburg.

Jones, S. (1991). 'The language of the genes'. The Reith Lectures. London: BBC. Available at p00gq073 [Accessed 07/04021].

Jones, O. (2016). Chavs: The Demonization of the Working Class. London: Verso.

Jorgensen, C. (2018). 'Badges and Brothels: Police Officers' Attitudes Toward Prostitution'. Frontiers in Sociology, 15(3), p. 16.

Joseph-Salisbury, R., Ashe, S., Alexander, C. and Campion, K. (2020). 'Race and Ethnicity in British Sociology' [online]. Available at: https://es.britsoc.co.uk/bsaCommentary/wp-content/uploads/2020/06/BSA_race_and_ethnicity_in_british_sociology_report_pre_publication_version.pdf [Accessed 24/12/2020].

Kan, M.Y. and Laurie, H. (2018). 'Who is doing the housework in multicultural Britain?'. Sociology, 52(1), 55–74.

Karlsen, S. (2007) Ethnic Inequalities in Health: The impact of racism [online]. Available at https://raceequalityfoundation.org.uk/wp-content/uploads/2018/03/health-brief3.pdf [Accessed 23/10/19].

King, A. and Smith, D. (2018). 'The Jack Wills Crowd: towards a sociology of an elite subculture'. The British Journal of Sociology, 69(1), pp. 44–66.

Kings Fund. (2020). 'What are health inequalities?' [online] Available at: https://www.kingsfund.org.uk/publications/what-are-health-inequalities [Accessed 27/12/2020].

Kirk, D.S. and Papachristos, A.V. (2011). 'Cultural Mechanisms and the Persistence of Neighbourhood Violence'. American Journal of Sociology, 116, pp. 1190–1233.

Koch, I., Fransham, M., Cant, S., Ebrey, J., Glucksberg, L. and Savage, M. (2020). 'Social polarisation at the local level: a four-town comparative study on the challenges of politicising inequality in Britain'. Sociology, 5(1), pp. 3–29.

Kondrat, X. (2015). 'Gender and video games: How is female gender generally represented in various genres of video games?'. *Journal of Comparative Research in Anthropology and Sociology*, 6(01), pp. 171–193.

Kuhn, T. (1970). *The Structure of Scientific Revolutions*. Chicago: University of Chicago Press.

Kuzawa, C.W. and Sweet, E. (2009). 'Epigenetics and the embodiment of race: developmental origins of US racial disparities in cardiovascular health'. *American Journal of Human Biology: The Official Journal of the Human Biology Association*, 21(1), pp. 2–15.

Lambert, C. (2020). 'The objectionable injectable: recovering the lost history of the WLM through the Campaign Against Depo-Provera'. *Women's History Review*, 29(3), pp. 520–539.

Latour, B. (1996). 'On actor-network theory: A few clarifications'. *Soziale Welt*, 47(4), pp. 369–381 [online]. Available at http://www.jstor.org/stable/40878163 [Accessed 19/11/20].

Lazreg, M. (2009). *Questioning the veil: Open Letters to Muslim Women*. Princeton: Princeton University Press.

Lincoln, N.K. and Denzin, Y.S. (2005). *The Sage Handbook of Qualitative Research*. London: Sage.

Lindsey, L. (2016). *Gender Roles. A Sociological Perspective*. Abingdon: Routledge.

Lindsay, J. and Dempsey, D. (2018). 'Surnaming children born to lesbian and heterosexual couples: displaying family legitimacy to diverse audiences'. *Sociology*, 52(5), pp. 1017–1034.

Littlewood, R. and Lipsedge, M. (1997). *Aliens and Alienists: Ethnic Minorities and Psychiatry*. London: Psychology Press.

Lombroso, C. and Ferrero, G. (1895). *The Female Offender*. New York: Appleton & Company.

Longhi, S. and Brynin, M. (2017). *The Ethnicity Pay Gap* [online]. Available at: https://www.equalityhumanrights.com/sites/default/files/research-report-108-the-ethnicity-pay-gap.pdf [Accessed 27/12/2020].

Luff, P., Gilbert, N.G. and Frohlich, D. (1990). *Computers and Conversation*. London: Academic Press.

Lupton, D. (2020). 'Better understanding about what's going on: young Australians' use of digital technologies for health and fitness'. *Sport, Education and Society*, 25(1), pp. 1–13.

Lyon, D. (2000). *Jesus in Disneyland: Religion in Postmodern Times*. Cambridge: Polity Press.

Lyotard, J.F. (1984). *The Postmodern Condition: A Report on Knowledge*. Minneapolis: University of Minnesota Press.

MacDonald, R. and Giazitzoglu, A. (2019). 'Youth, enterprise and precarity: or, what is and what is wrong with the "gig economy"'. *Journal of Sociology*, 55(4), pp. 724–740.

MacPherson, W. (1999). 'The Stephen Lawrence Inquiry: Report of an Inquiry' [online]. Available at: https://assets.publishing.service.gov.uk/government/uploads/system/uploads/attachment_data/file/277111/4262.pdf [Accessed 1/04/21].

Madigan, R. and Munro, M. (1996). 'House Beautiful: Style and Consumption in the Home'. *Sociology*. 30(1), pp. 41–57.

Marmot, M. (2015). *The Health Gap*. London: Bloomsbury.

Marston, C., Renedo, A. and Miles, S. (2020). 'Community participation is crucial in a pandemic'. *The Lancet*, 395(10238), pp. 1676–1678.

May-Chahal, C., Mason, C., Rashid, A., Walkerdine, J., Rayson, P. and Greenwood, P. (2014). 'Safeguarding cyborg childhoods: Incorporating the on/offline behaviour of children into everyday social work practices'. *British Journal of Social Work*, 44(3), pp. 596–614.

Mayblin, L. (2014). 'Asylum, welfare and work: reflections on research in asylum and refugee studies'. *International Journal of Sociology and Social Policy*, 34(5/6), pp. 375–391.

Mayblin, L., Wake, M. and Kazemi, M. (2020). 'Necropolitics and the slow violence of the everyday: Asylum seeker welfare in the postcolonial present'. *Sociology*, 54(1), pp. 107–123.

McArthur, D. and Reeves, A. (2019). 'The rhetoric of recessions: how British newspapers talk about the poor when unemployment rises, 1896–2000'. *Sociology*, 53(6), pp. 1005–1025.

McKenzie, L. (2015). *Getting By: Estates, Class and Culture in Austerity Britain*. Bristol: Policy Press.

McKnight, A. (2015). 'Downward mobility, opportunity hoarding and the "glass floor"'. Social Mobility and Child Poverty Commission.

McMunn, A., Bird, L., Webb, E. and Sacker, A. (2019). 'Gender Divisions of Paid and Unpaid Work in Contemporary UK Couples'. *Work, Employment and Society*. 34(2), pp. 155–173.

McRobbie, A. (2009). *The aftermath of feminism: Gender, culture and social change*. London: Sage.

Mead, G.H. (1934). *Self and Society*. Chicago: University of Chicago Press.

Mednick, S.A., Moffitt, T.E. and Stack, S.A. (1987). *The Causes of Crime: New Biological Approaches*. Cambridge: Cambridge University Press.

Merton, R. (1938). 'Social Structure and anomie'. *American Sociological Review*, 3(5), pp. 672–682.

Meghji, M. (2021). *Decolonising Sociology*. Cambridge: Polity Press.

Meloni, M. (2017). 'Race in an epigenetic time: Thinking biology in the plural'. *The British Journal of Sociology*, 68(3), pp. 389–409.

Messerschmidt, J. (2005). 'Men, Masculinities, and Crime'. In M.S. Kimmel, J. Hearn and R.W. Connell (eds), *Handbook of Studies on Men & Masculinities*. Thousand Oaks: SAGE Publications, Inc., pp. 196–212.

Mills, C. W. (1959/2000). *The Sociological Imagination*. Oxford: Oxford University Press.

Mijs, J.J. (2018). 'Inequality is a problem of inference: How people solve the social puzzle of unequal outcomes'. *Societies*, 8(3), p. 64.

Mijs, J.J. (2019). 'The paradox of inequality: income inequality and belief in meritocracy go hand in hand'. *Socio-Economic Review*, pp. 1–29. https://doi.org/10.1093/ser/mwy051

Mijs, J.J. and Savage, M. (2020). 'Meritocracy, elitism and inequality'. *The Political Quarterly*, 91(2), pp. 397–404.

Miller, J. (2020) 'Passing on gang culture in the theatre of the streets: "They'll grow out of it, then our age will grow into it and then we'll grow out of it"'. *Journal of Youth Studies*, 23(8), pp. 1086–1101

Mirza. H. (2009). *Race, Gender and Educational Desire: Why Black Women Succeed and Fail*. Abingdon: Routledge.

Moir, A. and Jessel, D. (1995). *A Mind to Crime: The Controversial Link Between the Mind and Criminal Behaviour*. London: Michael Joseph.

Monaghan, J. (2020). 'Performing counter-terrorism: Police newsmaking and the dramaturgy of security'. *Crime, Media, Culture: An International Journal*. doi: 10.1177/1741659020966370.

Mousteri, V., Daly, M. and Delaney, L. (2020). 'The gig economy is taking a toll on UK worker's mental health'. Available at: https://blogs.lse.ac.uk/businessreview/2020/01/18/the-gig-economy-is-taking-a-toll-on-uk-workers-mental-health/ [Accessed 22/12/2020].

Murray, C.A. (1996). *Charles Murray and the Underclass: The Developing Debate* [online]. Available at https://www.civitas.org.uk/pdf/cw33.pdf [Accessed 28/12/20].

Nagel, T. (1989). *The View from Nowhere*. Oxford: Oxford University Press.

Nazroo, J.Y. (2003). 'The structuring of ethnic inequalities in health: economic position, racial discrimination, and racism'. *American Journal of Public Health*, 93(2), pp. 277–284.

Nazroo, J.Y., Bhui, K.S. and Rhodes, J. (2020). 'Where next for understanding race/ethnic inequalities in severe mental illness? Structural, interpersonal and institutional racism'. *Sociology of Health and Illness*, 42(2), pp. 262–276.

Near, C.E. (2013). 'Selling Gender: Associations of Box Art Representation of Female Characters With Sales for Teen- and Mature-rated Video Games'. *Sex Roles*, 68 (3), pp. 252–269.

Neal, S., Bennett, K., Cochrane, A. and Mohan, G. (2019). 'Community and conviviality? Informal social life in multicultural places'. *Sociology*, 53(1), pp. 69–86.

Norris, C. (2012). *Routledge Handbook of Surveillance Studies*. Abingdon: Routledge.

Norris, C. and Armstrong, G. (1999). *The Maximum Surveillance Society: The Rise of CCTV* (Vol. 2). Oxford: Berg.

Nussbaum, M. (2020). 'The struggle within: How to educate for democracy' [online]. Available at: https://www.abc.net.au/religion/martha-nussbaum-education-for-democracy/11191430 [Accessed 23/12/2020].

Oakley, A. (2016). 'Interviewing women again: Power, time and the gift'. *Sociology*, 50 (1), pp. 195–213.

Oakley, A. (2016). 'The sociology of childbirth: an autobiographical journey through four decades of research'. *Sociology of Health and Illness*, 38(5), pp. 689–705.

O'Reilly, K. (2009). 'Going "Native"'. *Key Concepts in Ethnography*, London: Sage. pp. 88–93.

Office for National Statistics. (2016). 'Women shoulder the responsibility of unpaid work' [online]. Available at: https://www.ons.gov.uk/employmentandlabourmarket/peopleinwork/earningsandworkinghours/articles/womenshouldertheresponsibilityofunpaidwork/2016-11-10 [Accessed 28/12/20].

Office of National Statistics. (2019). 'Domestic Abuse' [online]. Available at https://www.ethnicity-facts-figures.service.gov.uk/crime-justice-and-the-law/crime-and-reoffending/domestic-abuse/latest [Accessed 28/12/20].

Office of National Statistics. (2019). 'Gender Pay Gap' [online]. Available at: https://www.ons.gov.uk/employmentandlabourmarket/peopleinwork/earningsandworkinghours/bulletins/genderpaygapintheuk/2019 [Accessed 27/12/2020].

Office for National Statistics. (2020). 'The National Statistics Socio-economic classification (NS-SEC)' [online]. Available at: https://www.ons.gov.uk/methodology/classificationsandstandards/otherclassifications/thenationalstatisticssocioeconomicclassificationnssecrebasedonsoc2010 [Accessed 28/12/20].

Office for National Statistics. (2020). 'Domestic Abuse during the coronavirus (COVID-19) pandemic, England and Wales: November 2020'. Available at https://www.ons.gov.uk/peoplepopulationandcommunity/crimeandjustice/articles/domesticabuseduringthecoronaviruscovid19pandemicenglandandwales/november2020 [Accessed 25/03/21]

Office for National Statistics. (2020). 'Health state life expectancies by national deprivation deciles, England: 2016 to 2018' [online] Available at https://www.ons.gov.uk/peoplepopulationandcommunity/healthandsocialcare/healthinequalities/bulletins/healthstatelifeexpectanciesbyindexofmultipledeprivationimd/2016to2018 [Accessed 28/12/20].

Oliver, M. (2017). 'Disability History, Bleeding Hearts and Parasite People' [online]. Available at: https://blogs.kent.ac.uk/dhmkent/2017/12/11/disability-history-bleeding-hearts-and-parasite-people/ [Accessed 22/12/20].

Orgad, S. (2019). *Heading Home: Motherhood, Work and the Failed Promise of Equality*. New York: Columbia University Press.

Orgad, S., and Rottenberg, C. (2020), 'Tradwives: The women looking for a simpler past but grounded in the neoliberal present'. The Conversation [online]. Available at https://theconversation.com/tradwives-the-women-looking-for-a-simpler-past-but-grounded-in-the-neoliberal-present-130968 [Accessed 01/04/21].

Ortiz-Ospina, E. and Roser, M. (2019). *Economic Inequality by Gender* [online]. Available at: https://ourworldindata.org/economic-inequality-by-gender [Accessed 25/03/21].

Osborn, K., Davis, J. P., Button, S. and Foster, J. (2018). 'Juror Decision Making in Acquaintance and Marital Rape: The Influence of Clothing, Alcohol, and Preexisting Stereotypical Attitudes'. *Journal of Interpersonal Violence*, 36(5–6)

Oxfam. (2020). 'Five shocking facts' [online]. Available at: https://www.oxfam.org/en/5-shocking-facts-about-extreme-global-inequality-and-how-even-it [Accessed 28/12/20].

Paoletti, J.B. (2012). *Pink and Blue: Telling the Boys From the Girls in America*. Bloomington: Indiana University Press.

Park, A., Bryson, C., Clery, E., Curtice, J. and Phillips, M. (eds.). (2013). *British Social Attitudes: the 30th Report*. London: NatCen Social Research [online]. Available at: www.bsa-30.natcen.ac.uk [Accessed 29/12/20].

Parliament, UK. (2019). House of Commons Committee Report: 'Tackling inequalities faced by Gypsy, Roma and Traveller communities' [online]. Available at: https://publications.parliament.uk/pa/cm201719/cmselect/cmwomeq/360/full-report.html [Accessed 23/2/21]

Parry, M. (2019). 'Alice Goffman's first book made her a star. It wasn't enough to get her tenure' [online]. Available at: https://www.chronicle.com/article/alice-goffmans-first-book-made-her-a-star-it-wasnt-enough-to-get-her-tenure/ [Accessed 04/01/21].

Patrick, J. (1973/2013). *A Glasgow Gang Observed*. Castle Douglas: Neil Wilson Publishing.

Pearce, F. (1976/2015). *Crimes of the Powerful*. London: Pluto Press.

Peggs, K. (2012). *Animals and Sociology*. London: Springer.

Phelan, J.C., Link, B.G. and Tehranifar, P. (2010). 'Social conditions as fundamental causes of health inequalities: theory, evidence, and policy implications'. *Journal of Health and Social Behavior*, 51(1), pp. 28–40.

Phillips C. (2019). 'The trouble with culture: A speculative account of the role of gypsy/traveller cultures in "doorstep fraud"'. *Theoretical Criminology*. 23(3), pp. 333–354.

Phillips, N. and Chagnon, N. (2020). 'Where's the panic, where's the fire? Why claims of moral panic and witch hunts miss the mark when it comes to campus rape and MeToo'. *Feminist Media Studies*. Ahead of print, pp. 1–18.

Pickard, S. (2020). 'Waiting like a girl? The temporal constitution of femininity as a factor in gender inequality'. *British Journal of Sociology*, 71, pp. 314–327.

Plummer, K. (2013). 'A manifesto for a critical humanism in Sociology' in Nehring, D. *Sociology: A Text and Reader*. London: Pearson.

Prins, S.J., Bates, L.M., Keyes, K.M. and Muntaner, C. (2015). 'Anxious? Depressed? You might be suffering from capitalism: contradictory class locations and the prevalence of depression and anxiety in the USA'. *Sociology of Health and Illness*, 37(8), pp. 1352–1372.

Possamai-Inesedy, A. (2002). 'Beck's Risk Society and Giddens' Search for Ontological Security: A Comparative Analysis Between the Anthroposophical Society and the Assemblies of God'. *Australian Religion Studies Review*, 15(1).

Putnis, N. and Burr, J. (2020). 'Evidence or stereotype? Health inequalities and representations of sex workers in health publications in England'. *Health*, 24(6), pp. 665–683.

Rafter, N. (2008). *The Criminal Brain: Understanding Biological Theories of Crime*. New York: NYU Press.

Reay, D., Crozier, G. and Clayton, J. (2010). '"Fitting in" or "standing out": Working-class students in UK higher education'. *British Educational Research Journal*, 36(1), pp. 107–124.

Reeves, A. (2015). '"Music's a family thing": Cultural socialisation and parental transference'. *Cultural Sociology*, 9(4), pp. 493–514.

Reeves, A., Friedman, S., Rahal, C. and Flemmen, M. (2017). 'The decline and persistence of the old boy: Private schools and elite recruitment 1897 to 2016'. *American Sociological Review*, 82(6), pp. 1139–1166.

Refugee Council. (2020). [online] Available at: https://www.refugeecouncil.org.uk/. [Accessed 29/12/20].

Ritzer, G. (2002). 'Enchanting McUniversity: Towards a spectacularly irrational university quotitian' in Hayyes, D. and Wynyard, R. (eds). *The McDonaldization of Higher Education*. Westport and London: Bergin and Garvey, pp. 19–32.

Ritzer, G. (2013). *The McDonaldization of Society*. London: Sage.

Rosenhan, D.L. (1973). 'On being sane in insane places'. *Science*, 179(4070), pp. 250–258.

Rottenberg, C. and Orgad, S. (2020). 'Why the rise of the domestic "Tradwife" tells us more about modern work culture than feminism'. *Prospect Magazine* [online]. Available at: https://www.prospectmagazine.co.uk/philosophy/tradwife-meme-neoliberal-work-traditional-domestic-feminism. [Accessed 5/1/21].

Roulet, T.J., Gill, M.J., Stenger, S. and Gill, D.J. (2017). 'Reconsidering the value of covert research: The role of ambiguous consent in participant observation'. *Organizational Research Methods*, 20(3), pp. 487–517.

Rudolph, M. and Starke, P. (2020). 'How does the welfare state reduce crime? The effect of program characteristics and decommodification across 18 OECD-countries'. *Journal of Criminal Justice*, 68.

Saeed, T. (2016). Islamophobia and Securitization: Religion, *Ethnicity and the Female Voice*. London: Palgrave.

Said, E. (1978). *Orientalism*, New York: Pantheon.

Sangaramoorthy, T., Jamison, A.M., Boyle, M.D., Payne-Sturges, D.C., Sapkota, A., Milton, D.K. and Wilson, S.M. (2016). 'Place-based perceptions of the impacts of fracking along the Marcellus Shale'. *Social Science & Medicine* (151), pp. 27–37.

Savage, M. (2015). *Social Class in the 21st Century*. London: Penguin.

Schuster, L. (2015). 'Unmixing migrants and refugees'. In A. Triandafyllidou, ed., *Routledge Handbook of Immigration and Refugee Studies*. Abingdon: Routledge, pp. 321–327.

Sellers, C. (2019). '"Fitting in" and "standing out": the peer group and young people's development of reader identity'. *British Journal of Sociology of Education*, 40(7), pp. 938–952.

Shah, H. (2020). 'Global Problems need Social Science' [online]. Available at: https://www.nature.com/articles/d41586-020-00064-x [Accessed 23/12/2020].

Shakin, M., Shakin, D. and Sternglanz, S.H. (1985). 'Infant clothing: Sex labeling for strangers'. *Sex Roles*, 12(9–10), pp. 955–964.

Shilling, C. (2005). 'The rise of the body and the development of sociology'. *Sociology*, 39(4), pp. 761–767.

Showalter, E. (1985). *The Female Malady: Women, Madness, and English Culture*, 1830–1980. London: Virago.

Sillard, J. (2020). 'Coronavirus: £1.9 bn grocery stockpiling spree ahead of lockdown'. [online]. Available at: https://news.sky.com/story/coronavirus-1-9bn-grocery-stockpiling-spree-ahead-of-lockdown-11966036 [Accessed 19/11/20].

Skeggs, B. (2008). 'The Dirty History of Feminism and Sociology: Or the War of Conceptual Attrition'. Urban Studies, 56(4). doi: 10.1177/0042098020951438.

Ślęzak, I. (2019). *Social Construction of Sex Work: Ethnography of Escort Agencies in Poland*. Krakow: Jagiellonian University Press.

Smart, C. (1995). *Law, Crime and Sexuality: Essays in Feminism*. London: Sage Publications.

Smart, C. (2007). *Personal Life*. Cambridge: Polity Press.

Smiley, C. and Middlemass, K.M. (2016). 'Clothing makes the man: Impression management and prisoner re-entry'. *Punishment & Society*, 18(2), pp. 220–243.

Smith, L.T. (2013). *Decolonizing Methodologies: Research and Indigenous Peoples*. London: Zed Books Ltd.

Smith, J. (2007). '"Ye've got to 'ave balls to play this game sir!" Boys, peers and fears: the negative influence of school-based "cultural accomplices" in constructing hegemonic masculinities'. *Gender and Education*, 19(2), pp. 179–198.

Smithers, R. (2019). 'UK households waste 4.5 million tones of food each year' [online]. Available at https://www.theguardian.com/environment/2020/jan/24/uk-households-waste-45m-tonnes-of-food-each-year [Accessed 30/3/21].

Social Metric Commission. (2020). *Measuring Poverty 2019*, [online]. Available at: https://socialmetricscommission.org.uk/social-metrics-commission-2020-report/ [Accessed 28/12/20].

Social Mobility Commission. (2020). *State of the Nation 2018-19* [online]. Available at

https://assets.publishing.service.gov.uk/government/uploads/system/uploads/attachment_data/file/798404/SMC_State_of_the_Nation_Report_2018-19.pdf [Accessed 28/12/20].

Sointu, E. (2017). '"Good" patient/"bad" patient: clinical learning and the entrenching of inequality'. *Sociology of Health and Illness*, 39(1), pp. 63–77.

Spicker, P. (2011). 'Ethical covert research'. *Sociology*, 45(1), pp. 118–133.

Stahl, G. (2014) 'White working-class male narratives of "loyalty to self" in discourses of aspiration'. *British Journal of Sociology of Education*, 37(5), pp. 663–683.

Sterling, A.F. (2000). *Sexing the Body: Gender Politics and the Construction of Sexuality*. New York: Basic Books.

Strand, S. (2012). 'The White British–Black Caribbean Achievement Gap: Tests, Tiers and Teacher Expectations'. *British Educational Research Journal*, 38(1), pp. 75–101.

Strand, S. (2014). 'Ethnicity, gender, social class and achievement gaps at age 16: intersectionality and "getting it" for the white working class'. *Research Papers in Education*, 29(2), pp. 131–171.

Strand, S. (2015). 'Ethnicity, deprivation and educational achievement at age 16 in England: trends over time'. Department for Education.

Sumerau, J.E. (2020). 'Expanding Transgender Studies in Sociology'. *Sociological Inquiry*, 90(2), pp. 217–225.

Sutton Trust. (2019). 'Private Tuition 2019' [online]. Available at: https://www.suttontrust.com/our-research/private-tuition-polling-2019/ [Accessed 28/12/20].

Tassinari, A. and Maccarrone, V. (2020). 'Riders on the storm: Workplace solidarity among gig economy couriers in Italy and the UK'. *Work, Employment and Society*, 34(1), pp. 35–54.

Taylor, S. and Workman, L. (2019). 'Why socialisation is key to understanding delinquency'. *Open Access Journal of Behavioural Science and Psychology*, 2(1), 180013

Tiidenberg, K. and Gómez Cruz, E. (2015). 'Selfies, image and the re-making of the body'. *Body and Society*, 21(4), pp. 77–102.

Triventi, M., Skopek, J., Kulic, N., Buchholz, S. and Blossfeld, H.P. (2020). 'Advantage "Finds Its Way": How Privileged Families Exploit Opportunities in Different Systems of Secondary Education'. *Sociology*, 54(2), pp. 237–257.

Tromp, P., Pless, A. and Houtman, D. (2020). 'Believing Without Belonging in Twenty European Countries (1981–2008): De-institutionalization of Christianity or Spiritualization of Religion?'. *Review of Religious Research*. 62(4), pp. 509–531.

Trussell Trust. (2020). '2600 food parcels…' [online]. Available at: https://www.trusselltrust.org/2020/11/12/2600-food-parcels-provided-for-children-every-day-in-first-six-months-of-the-pandemic/ [Accessed 19/11/20].

Trussell Trust. (2020). 'New Report reveals how coronavirus has affected food bank use'. Available at: https://www.trusselltrust.org/2020/09/14/new-report-reveals-how-coronavirus-has-affected-food-bank-use/ Accessed 23/12/2020

Truth, S. (1851/2020). *Ain't I A Woman?*. London: Penguin.

Turner, B.S. (2012). 'Post-secular Society: Consumerism and the Democratization of Religion'. In P.S. Gorski, D.K. Kim, J. Torpey and J. Van Antwerpen (eds). *Post-secular in Question: Religion in Contemporary Society*. New York: New York University Press. pp. 135–58.

unicef.org. (2020). 'Child labour' [online]. Available at: https://www.unicef.org/protection/child-labour [Accessed 23/12/2020]

Ussher, J.M. (1991). *Women's Madness: Misogyny or Mental Illness?* London: Harvester Wheatsheaf.

VanderPyl, T. (2019). '"I Want to Have the American Dream": Messages of Materialism as a Driving Force in Juvenile Recidivism'. *Criminal Justice and Behavior*. 46(5), pp. 718–731.

Venkatesh, S.A. (2008). *Gang Leader for a Day: A Rogue Sociologist Takes to the Streets*. London: Penguin.

Vijayayalakshmi, A. (2020). *Violence No More: India's COVID-19 opportunity for anti-domestic violence campaigns*. [online] Available at: https://www.warc.com/newsandopinion/opinion/violence-no-more-indias-covid-19-opportunity-for-anti-domestic-violence-campaigns/3641 [Accessed 23/12/2020].

Vincent, C., Ball, S., Rollock, N. and Gillborn, D. (2013). 'Three generations of racism: Black middle-class children and schooling'. *British Journal of Sociology of Education*, 34(5–6), pp. 929–946.

Voas, D. (2009). 'The rise and fall of fuzzy fidelity in Europe'. *European Sociological Review*, 25(2), pp. 155–168.

Waddington, P., Stenson, K. and Don, D. (2004). 'In proportion: Race and police stop and search'. *British Journal of Criminology*, 44, pp. 889–914.

Wade, L. (2017). 'Mother, Sex Object, Worker: The Transformation of the Female Flight Attendant'. [online] Huffington Post. Available at https://www.huffpost.com/entry/female-flight-attendants_b_4612229 [Accessed 23/12/2020].

Warde, A. (1994). 'Consumption, identity-formation and uncertainty'. *Sociology*, 28(4), pp. 877–898.

Warde. A. (2020). *What is sociology?* [online] The British Academy. Available at: https://www.thebritishacademy.ac.uk/blog/what-is-sociology/ [Accessed 22/12/2020].

Weare, S. (2013). '"The mad", "the bad", "the victim": Gendered constructions of women who kill within the Criminal Justice System'. *Laws*, 2, pp. 337–361.

Williams, A., Cloke, P., May, J. and Goodwin, M. (2016). 'Contested space: The contradictory political dynamics of food banking in the UK'. *Environment and Planning A: Economy and Space*, 48(11), pp. 2291–2316.

Willis, P. (1977/1981). *Learning to Labour: How working class kids get working class jobs*. Abingdon: Routledge.

Wilkinson, R. and Pickett, K. (2010). *The Spirit Level: Why Equality is Better for Everyone*. London: Penguin.

Wilson, H. (1987). 'Parental supervision re-examined'. *The British Journal of Criminology*, 27(3), pp. 275–301.

Wilson, J.Q. and Herrnstein, R.J. (1998). *Crime and Human Nature: The Definitive Study of the Causes of Crime*. London: Simon and Schuster.

Wilson, J.Q. and Kelling, G.L. (1982). 'Broken windows'. *Atlantic Monthly*, 249(3), pp. 29–38.

Wu, C., Chen, X., Cai, Y., Zhou, X., Xu, S., Huang, H., Zhang, L., Zhou, X., Du, C., Zhang, Y. and Song, J. (2020). 'Risk factors associated with acute respiratory distress syndrome and death in patients with coronavirus disease 2019 pneumonia in Wuhan, China'. *JAMA Internal Medicine*, 180(7), pp. 934–943

Young, T. (2009). 'Girls and gangs: "Shemale" *gangsters in the UK?*'. Youth Justice, 9(3), pp. 224–238.

Young, I.M. (2005). *On Female Body Experience: 'Throwing like a girl' and Other Essays*. Oxford: Oxford University Press.

Zafar, Z., Sarwar, I. and Haider, S. I. (2016). 'Socio-Economic and Political Causes of Child Labor: The Case of Pakistan'. *Global Political Review*, 1(1), pp. 32–43.

GLOSSARY

absolute poverty when a person's household income is not enough to sustain a basic standard of living and meet essential human needs (food, shelter, clothing)

agency the notion that individuals have the capacity to act freely, often contrasted with determinism and social structure

alienation (Marx) a process in which someone becomes disconnected from their work and from other humans

anomie an absence of shared norms or values (integration) and guidance (regulation)

beliefs ideas about the world that people hold to be true, although they may not be based on evidence; beliefs lead us to take on certain values that are deemed socially important (*see also* **values**)

Black feminism feminism that focuses on the way that women's subordination is rooted in racism and classism as well as sexism; it calls for an intersectional understanding of inequality and a recognition that women's experiences are not homogeneous

bourgeoisie (Marx) the social class that owns the means of production and so is made up of more powerful members of society

breaching experiment (Garfinkel) an experiment that intentionally disrupts (breaches) social norms

bureaucracy (Weber) a hierarchical organisation that operates according to rational sets of rules and procedures

capital (Bourdieu) a set of skills and resources that take numerous forms; Bourdieu identifies five types of capital – cultural, economic, physical, symbolic, and social – and it is the accumulation of different types of capital that constitutes someone's social status

> **cultural capital** knowledge, lifestyle choices, values, leisure activities and education
>
> **economic capital** how much income and wealth someone has
>
> **physical capital** bodily dispositions and shape (including how attractive someone is deemed to be)
>
> **social capital** a person's social networks, relationships and who they know
>
> **symbolic capital** a person's status and prestige

capital (Marx) economic relations and wealth

capitalism (Marx) a system defined by its economic relations of production, where goods and services are bought and sold for profit, and in which two distinct 'classes' emerge – those who own the goods and services (the bourgeoisie) and those who have to sell their labour to earn a living (the proletariat)

causation the scientific belief that a variable ('x') directly impacts on, and changes, another variable ('y')

cisnormativity the dominant social belief that a person's gender corresponds with their biological sex at birth

citizen a person who belongs to a community and has equal rights and duties under law

class, social an individual's economic position, and also their social status and political power; can be simply divided into the upper class (historically landed and wealthy) or the elite, the middle class (who work in professional occupations) and the working class (who engage in manual and low skilled work), measured by occupation for research purposes

class for themselves (Marx) a unified working class (proletariat) able to resist the bourgeoisie

collective conscience (Durkheim) a set of shared values, beliefs and moral attitudes

collective effervescence (Durkheim) a communal experience, when a community unites in a shared thought or participates in the same action (e.g. the exchange of gifts at Christmas or attendance at a sporting event)

colonialism the process through which a country or group of countries takes over the land and people of another country or countries

colonial modernity the history of modernity produced within and from the perspective of colonising countries, without consideration of the history of modernity from the perspective of the colonised countries (*see also* **modernity, subjugated knowledges**)

communism (Marx) the final stage of society's development, in which the proletariat has overthrown the bourgeoisie, taken over the means of production and the institutions of power (e.g. police, law) and distributed wealth equally among all people in society

conceptual framework a theoretical guiding principle – the 'glasses' sociologists put on to interpret the social world

conflict theories social theories that emphasise that relations of conflict define and maintain the social order (e.g. Marxism)

consensus theories social theories that support the idea that it is consensus and collective harmony that gives society order and allows it to function (e.g. Durkheimian theory)

constructionism a social scientific perspective that focuses on how the social world/social reality is a product of shared meanings rather than being an objective entity

consumer colonialism the notion that colonial power relations persist through the production and distribution of goods at low cost in some parts of the globe (former colonies) to the benefit of those in the former colonising nations in other parts of the globe

conversational analysis a technique developed from ethnomethodology, which involves analysing people's conversations

correlation the scientific belief that a variable ('x') has a relation to another variable ('y'), but that it cannot be explicitly said that the relationship causes a change to occur

cottage industry a small-scale business, usually based in the home; pre-modernity, families would often work together in cottage industries such as basketweaving or beekeeping, in which each family member would have a role

covert research doing research undercover; concealing one's identity from the research subjects

conviviality in sociology, the connections and independencies that can be forged between diverse groups

crime an act or acts that break criminal law

critical race theory   an academic movement made up of scholars and activists who examine how White privilege, social constructions of race and racism continue to underscore inequity and injustice

culture   the customs, practices, beliefs, ideas, meanings, languages, rituals, symbols shared by particular social groups

cultural appropriation   when one group (usually a dominant one) adopts, borrows or steals a custom, practice or idea from another culture, without acknowledging its origin, and passes it off as its own

cultural assimilation   the expectation that someone from another culture will 'fit in' (bend to the customs, practices, beliefs, languages, etc.) of another culture

cultural capital   knowledge, lifestyle choices, values, leisure activities and education

cultural deprivation   the theory that an entire cultural group can be deprived because of its shared, collective norms, which are deemed to be inferior; often levelled at the working class; many sociologists now regard this theory as problematic

cultural racism   discrimination based on cultural practices and beliefs; some sociological *cultural deprivation* theories have been criticised for reproducing this type of thinking (e.g. deprivation theories tend to blame doing less well at school or having poorer health on the values and lifestyles of some groups) (*see also racism*)

data   bits of information, or empirical material, that are collected to produce research evidence (*see also primary data, secondary data*)

decolonial feminism   a form of feminism that focuses on the extent to which feminism is Eurocentric and tends to universalise the female experience; it challenges the assumption that Western feminism is progressive, showing the importance of feminisms that can appreciate differences

decolonise the curriculum   to subject colonial knowledge to critique for its privileging of White, mainly European and/ or Global Northern ideas, at the expense of other histories and ways of knowing about the social world

deductivism   a scientific research process that begins with a theory (or hypothesis), which the research attempts to prove or disprove (*see also inductivism*)

determinism   the belief that all our actions are pre-determined – that we have no freedom or agency (*see also agency*)

deviance   an action or a behaviour that violates social norms

disciplinary society   (Foucault) a society in which we are under constant surveillance and in which we come to internalise social norms and monitor our own behaviour so that we fit in with those norms

discourses   dominant knowledges that circulate about the social world, e.g., science, medicine, law

discourse analysis   the contextual examination and deconstruction of meanings conveyed in text and verbal exchanges

discursive power   (Foucault) language is not neutral or innocent but is produced in social contexts where some ways of knowing are seen as better than others; these powerful ideas can both constrain and liberate us

distinction (Bourdieu) the process by which one group distinguishes itself from another by putting emphasis on certain forms of capital intimately linked to one's habitus

division of labour where the production of an item (such as a car) is not completed by one person but instead by lots of people who have their own small but specialised role; the term also refers more generally to the specialisation of roles (doctor, car mechanic, hairdresser) and how this means that we are always dependent on others

double consciousness (Du Bois) a critical awareness in oppressed social groups of how they are regarded by the socially dominant

double hermeneutic (Giddens) referring to the crossover between concepts used in our everyday lives and those used in sociology and the influence they have on each other

dramaturgical sociology (Goffman) the idea that life is like a play and that we are all actors in our own lives, performing different roles

dual burden (also double burden or double shift) the burden on women to be mothers and also go to work

ecological fallacy a generalisation made about all members of a particular group based on a statistical pattern that has been observed, even when it only applies to a minority of that group

economic capital how much income or wealth someone has

elaborated code a theory of language use, deriving from the work of Bernstein, which describes a complex and diverse range of language and grammar which is said to be associated with the middle and upper classes (*see also* **restricted code**, **cultural deprivation theory**)

emotional labour the work that is undertaken to manage feelings and support others usually undertaken by women

empirical describing information and data that is gathered through using research methods such as observation, interviews, or surveys

episteme (Foucault) a period of time defined by shared sets of beliefs/ ways of knowing the social world; a shared social order

ethics a set of moral principles that govern the conduct of research, maintaining anonymity, for instance

ethnicity a social group defined by a shared culture (contrast with **race**)

ethnography the study of people and their cultures

ethnomethodology the study of the methods people use to make social order: how it is produced and maintained (generally attributed to the work of Garfinkel)

eugenics practices that attempt to selectively breed and/or remove sections of the human population based on ideas of superiority/inferiority

Eurocentric describing a world view that is centred on a European perspective (*see also* **decolonisation of the curriculum**)

exaggerated (emphasised) femininity the condition brought about by hegemonic masculinity where women overemphasise their 'feminine' characteristics (those traits typically associated with women and girls) in order to conform to the patriarchal social order (see also **hegemonic masculinity**, **patriarchy**)

feminism(s)   various theories that attempt to understand women's place in society (*see also **Black feminism, decolonial feminism, liberal feminism, Marxist feminism, patriarchy, radical feminism***)

feudal(ism)   a social, economic and political structure that characterised the medieval period, where landowners held power over labourers (serfs), who worked for the lords or rented the land

functionalist theory/functionalism   a consensus theory that suggests society requires social norms and customs in order to function; different social institutions (the family, Church, education, etc.) all have different functions in socialising us into the norms and customs of the wider society, and that they are interdependent – a dysfunction in one area of society can impact other areas

gender   the socially produced characteristics associated with the male and female sex; the learned ways of being male or female such as being strong or fragile

gender blindness   when academic research does not take into account the experiences of women

gender identity   a personal experience of gender that may or may not correlate with biological sex assigned at birth

gender order   the system that produces a hierarchy between men and women in society

generalisation/generalisability   the extent to which a research study's findings are said to be applicable to the broader population that it represents

gig economy   a system of organising work where jobs are often temporary and workers have little job security

glass ceiling   an invisible barrier that explains why people who are qualified (e.g. women, minority ethnic groups, disabled people) do not reach their potential level of success due to discrimination

Global North   a way of dividing the globe to acknowledge the social and economic differences that characterise nations; northern countries are more likely to be wealthy and powerful in part due to the legacy of colonial exploitation

Global South   a way of dividing the globe to acknowledge the social and economic differences that characterise nations; southern countries are more likely to be poorer and indebted to northern countries as a result of colonialism

globalisation   the process of increased global interconnectedness – a historical constant but with recent acceleration

going native   a problematic phrase referring to the complete immersion of the researcher in the community they are studying, so that they can no longer view it with objectivity; this may put the researcher in a potentially harmful position

grand theory   an overarching theory that attempts to explain the social world in its entirety (e.g. Marxism)

habitus   (Bourdieu) the deeply ingrained habits, dispositions, norms, skills and other characteristics of a person that are defined by different types of capital (social, economic, cultural, etc.)

hegemony   the dominance of one social group (usually a minority) over another (usually the majority); described from a neo-Marxist perspective as a type of power exercised through ideologies that use language and persuasion to make the masses believe a certain 'truth', established by a ruling class, that conceals reality

hegemonic masculinity   the legitimation of men's dominance over women through the use of gendered ideologies about how men should conform to gendered norms of masculinity and women should conform to gendered norms of femininity

heteronormativity   the normalisation of heterosexuality and its associated character traits for both men and women

heterosexual masculinity   masculinity that is exercised in a way that reflects cultural pressures to conform to masculine gender norms that are also heterosexual (e.g. being muscular and strong)

hidden curriculum   the things that we learn in school that are not part of the formal classroom content

humane sociology   a sociology that follows a humanist doctrine and endeavours to be empathetic, caring and compassionate, focusing on social justice

hyperreality   a state in which we are unable to separate the real world from the simulations of reality that are all around us in postmodern times

hypothesis   in research, a statement about the predicted outcome of an experiment

ideal types   (Weber) the use of abstract concepts to understand society and social relations; ideal types aim to capture the main elements of a social phenomenon, but they are generalised and never exactly as seen in reality, so are best seen as a type of measuring stick, an example would be bureaucracy

identity   who we think we are as a person – our personality, skills, dispositions and

different forms of capital; identity is also socially produced, made possible by the opportunities afforded to us, differentially, along different axes of social stratification (*see also* **social stratification**)

ideology   a set of ideas that presents a particular, distorted view of reality that serves the interests of those in power

ideological state apparatus (ISA)   (Althusser) institutions (e.g. education, the Church) that enable the dominant ruling class ideology to spread and to lead the working classes into a state of false consciousness

immiseration   (Marx) a process in which, as capitalists get richer, workers get poorer – wages stagnate as profits increase

individualisation   the process through which individuals come to take responsibility for their own independent lives, at the expense of wider welfare systems and communal frames of reference; individualisation is said to have intensified in the era of neoliberalism

inductivism   the development of theory from the ground up – the belief that scientific laws can be inferred by looking at observable (empirical) social facts, from which theories can be built about how the social world works (*see also* **deductivism**)

interpretivism   an epistemological perspective that suggests we can only gain knowledge about the social world through our interpretations of observable phenomena

intersectionality   the idea that oppressions are interlocking; we cannot know about oppression only by examining one axis of social stratification (e.g. social class) but instead we must look at how different people experience oppressions through multiple axes (e.g. social class *and* ethnicity *and* gender)

intersex   the general term used to describe people who are born with variations of sex characteristics

institutional racism   a form of racism that is hard to see, but that occurs in the practices, rules and decisions within organisations such as schools, the police, banks and health services (*see also **racism***)

iron cage of bureaucracy   (Weber) the idea that we are trapped in a bureaucratic organisation of social life, whereby everything is increasingly rational (rule-bound and prescribed)

labelling   applying terms to describe or categorise people, which impact behaviour and sense of self (e.g. labelling someone the 'naughty child' will reinforce naughty behaviour)

late modernity   (Giddens) a term used to discuss key changes from modern to 'late' modern societies

liberal feminism   feminism that focuses on bringing about gender equality by removing barriers to full participation in society, e.g. voting rights, educational opportunity, equality legislation to ensure equal pay

liquid modernity   (Bauman) describes how contemporary societies are more in-flux than traditionally modern societies

longitudinal study   research that involves repeating data collection over a period of time

macro   describing things that occur on a large scale, typically referring to sociological theories that look at how large institutions and norms shape human conduct

malestream   sociology that either ignores women or fits them into male rules of thought and male areas of interest

marginalisation   being pushed to the outskirts (margins) of society; social exclusion

Marxist feminism   feminism that focuses on the interplay between capitalism and patriarchy to explain the subordination of women

McDonaldization   (Ritzer) the rationalisation of society, characterised by four features: predictability, calculability, efficiency and control

meaningful social action   (Weber) action in which individual actors take into account the behaviour of others (in contrast to action that is simply reactive or unaware)

means of production   who or what produces goods in society (e.g. families, factories, machines)

mechanical solidarity   (Durkheim) a form of social integration where people share the same values and beliefs – a characteristic of pre-modern society

medicalisation   the process by which human conditions and problems come to be defined as medical conditions

meritocracy   the belief that achievements in life are based on ability and the effort that individuals put into things

metanarrative   (also *grand narrative*) an overarching story about how the world operates; metanarratives are generally presented as truth, but some postmodern sociologists argue that they are a false presentation of reality and that there can be no universal truths about the world

micro   describing sociological studies that zoom in at the level of individual interactions between people

modernity   the 'modern' period, starting in the mid-17th century, characterised by the scientific revolution, industrialisation, urbanisation and secularism; a Eurocentric account (*see also colonial modernity*)

moral panic   widespread anxiety among the general public, usually relating to a certain condition or a group of people seen to threaten social norms; the media plays a significant role in generating moral panics by sensationalising and exaggerating an issue

multiculturalism   a society comprising people from numerous different ethnicities and cultures, freely living alongside and mixing with one another (*contrast with cultural assimilation*)

nature   the idea that we are born with our attributes (e.g. class, gender, race, disability and sexuality)

neoliberalism   a political approach that promotes competition, free trade and a reduction in government spending, and places emphasis on each individual to be responsible for themselves (*see also ideology, individualisation*)

non-binary   describing people who do not identify with either the male or female gender category

normative   shared values and beliefs that have a moral dimension

nuclear family   a small family unit typically comprised of a heterosexual couple and their children in which the man acts as the breadwinner and the woman fulfils the domestic, caring, expressive role

nurture   the idea that we acquire our characteristics (e.g. class, gender, race, disability and sexuality) through a process of *socialisation*

objectivity   the belief that it is possible to study the social world without personal bias and in turn produce statements of fact

ontological insecurity   (Giddens) the state of insecurity and anxiety that arises from having too few social norms and routines, and too much perceived freedom

operationalisation   the process of turning an abstract concept into something measurable

organic solidarity   a form of social integration based on the mutual dependency of members in a society

panopticon   a visual metaphor derived from the work of Jeremy Bentham of a prison where the prisoners were aware that they could always be seen but were not sure when they were actually being watched, and used by Foucault to explain how individuals internalise social norms and adapt and manage individual behaviour in accordance with them

paradigm   meaning 'world view', the view that over time different world views replace one another as one idea becomes more scientifically accepted and dominant; Kuhn referred to this process as that of 'scientific revolutions'

patriarchy   the hierarchical organisation of society in which men are the dominant group and exercise power over women, who are the subordinate group

personal troubles   (truths and triumphs) the experiences that we have as individuals, which must always be understood in relation to the wider social norms and institutions that shape them

physical capital   bodily dispositions and shape (including how attractive someone is deemed to be)

pluralism   the coexistence of ideas and peoples, a recognition and acceptance of diversity

positionality   our social location and identity – who we are, what characteristics and axes of social stratification define us (e.g., social class, gender, race, ethnicity, sexuality, (dis)abilities)

positivism   a world view that assumes sociology can and must emulate the natural sciences (such as physics, chemistry and biology); the notion that we can understand the social world objectively, free from any subjective bias or interpretation of events

poverty   the status of not having enough material possessions or income (*see also absolute poverty, relative poverty*)

power   the ability of a person or an entity to control or direct others' actions; a contested term in sociology, given different meanings by different theorists; Marx regarded power as something that was held by a dominant group and wielded over a subordinate group; Foucault regarded power as more diffuse, not held by any individual, but instead as something that was bound up in what he called dominant knowledges or discourses that circulate in society

primary data   new data that is created by a researcher through the use of research methods, e.g. data produced through an interview or through a survey

primary socialisation   socialisation that takes place within the family (*see socialisation*)

profit   (Marx) the value that is accrued by the capitalist over and above the cost of the labour that goes into the production of goods by the worker

proletariat   (Marx) a social class whose members have to sell their labour for a wage because they do not own the means of production

proxy measure   a way of measuring social phenomena that cannot be directly observed by using a substitute or stand in variable, social class is most commonly measured by occupation

public sociology   a call for sociology to have relevance to, and an impact on, the world it studies (*see also humane sociology*)

qualitative research   research that produces written data

quantitative research   research that produces numerical data

queer theory   a perspective that explores and challenges the way that sex-based binaries between men and women dominate our thinking and social norms and are oppressive for those who cannot, or do not wish to, live according to such norms

race   a social construct that historically emerged to categorise people according to physical features, such as skin colour, but which has no foundation in real biological differences between people

racism   discrimination against people based on the constructed categories of race (*see also cultural racism, institutional racism, scientific racism*)

radical feminism   feminism that focuses on the patriarchal roots of inequality between men and women, and demands radical social and cultural change in both the public and private (home) sphere

realism   a philosophical perspective that focuses on revealing the hidden truths and causes behind social phenomena

reductionist   a critique often levelled at grand sociological theories for attempting to explain a phenomenon in relation to a single point of focus – i.e. reducing an analysis to a particular level of structure (e.g. some people accuse Marxism of being reductive, believing it 'reduces' everything to the issue of social class); biological theories are also often critiqued for being reductionist in that they explain a person's actions purely by recourse to biological factors

reflexive project   (Giddens) the late modern imperative that individuals continually create their own self-identity

reflexivity   a key sociological disposition; reflexivity demands that sociologists continually subject their work (and that of others) to critical reflection

relations of production   (Marx) the social relations people must enter into in order to survive; in capitalism, this refers to the relationship between owners of the production (e.g. factory owners) and the workers (Marx sees these as relations of conflict)

relative poverty   when someone's household income is below the median income (mid-point) of a society

reliability   the repeatability of research, which is considered reliable if different researchers could achieve the same result by using the same method

response rate   the number of people to whom a survey is sent, divided by the number who complete it; the higher the response rate, the more valid the survey

restricted code   a theory of language use, deriving from the work of Bernstein; it is often problematically associated with the working class and is said to account for differential achievement in education, whereby those from lower social class backgrounds tend to use informal language, non-standard grammar and a more limited vocabulary (*see also* **elaborated code, cultural deprivation**)

right realism   a perspective that assumes that individuals make a rational choice to commit crime and therefore emphasises tough measures to combat crime

risk society   (Beck) a society preoccupied with the identification and management of risk, hazards and insecurities; said to be a product of modernity and science

sampling frame   the full list of people that you want to study and from which a sample is drawn

saturation   a term used to describe the point in the research process when no new information is being found and the researcher can assume that data collection is complete

scientific racism   attempts to divide humans into distinct racial groups based on their skin colour, and other physical attributes; these arbitrary categories are used to justify hierarchy and oppression

secondary data   data that already exists, typically in the public domain (e.g. official statistics)

secondary socialisation   socialisation that takes place in institutions outside the family, such as education and religion (*see* **socialisation**)

secular society   a society that is not bound by religious principles, institutions or laws

self-fulfilling prophecy   when expectations about someone impact their behaviour and become true (*see labelling*)

self-surveillance   (Foucault) the process by which we monitor and control our own behaviour in accordance with wider sets of social norms

sex   the biological traits that society associates with being male or female

sexuality   a term comprising sexual identity, interests and behaviours towards others; often categorised as heterosexual (opposite sex attraction); homosexual (same sex attraction); or asexual (does not have sexual feelings); bisexual (attracted to both men and women); pansexual (not limited in sexual choice with regard to biological sex, gender or gender identity); etc.; sexuality (including all these categories) is a social construct

social action   a theoretical position that emphasises the role of the active individual and interactions between people for shaping identity and wider society (*see also agency*)

social capital   a person's social networks, relationships and who they know

social change   changes at the level of social organisation that impact on personal interactions and relationships (e.g. the shift from feudal-based societies to industrial ones)

social class   *see class, social*

social control   the way in which social order is maintained through norms, rules, laws, power and bureaucracy

social construct   a belief, norm or institution that is taken to be fixed, natural or inherent but which is in fact human made

social facts   (Durkheim) the values, norms and social structures that shape people's behaviour and life chances

social institutions   particular institutions (predictable and stable social arrangements bound by norms, values, rules and laws) that meet social needs such as education, the family, religion, healthcare, economy and government

social mobility   the movement of people between social classes, either upwards or downwards (*see also meritocracy, capital*)

social norms   shared values and beliefs that shape our behaviour

social order   the status quo of society, maintained through norms, rules, laws, power and bureaucracy

social roles   the socially defined categories associated with different subject positions (e.g. gender, occupation, age); social roles comprise sets of norms and expectations and we are expected to conform to them, although they are constructs

social structures   institutions and institutional relationships that are often seen as stable and predictable (e.g. education, the family, religion, healthcare, economy and government); sometimes structures are said to constrain individual behaviour; structure is therefore sometimes pitted in contrast to agency (*see also agency, social institutions*)

socialisation   the process through which people learn social norms and customs – acceptable and unacceptable ways of behaving in society (*see also primary socialisation, secondary socialisation*)

sociological imagination   (Mills) the practice whereby individual experiences are understood in relation to the wider influences of history and society

spoiled identity   (Goffman) an identity that results if we act in a way that others perceive to be out of line with social norms, which 'tarnishes' our identity

stigma   (Goffman) a socially discredited attribute, behaviour or reputation that prevents someone from being socially accepted

stratification, social   the different axes of inequality upon which society is divided (e.g. gender, race/ethnicity, sexuality, social class, dis/ability)

structural racism   the exclusion from wider society of people from minority ethnic backgrounds, resulting in a higher likelihood of negative experiences such as living in poverty

subculture   a grouping of people based on shared cultural ideas and identities

subjectivity   a personal position, insight, and experience, sometimes influenced by opinion

surveillance   the process through which public or individual behaviour is monitored and/or recorded

symbolic capital   a person's status and prestige

symbolic interactionism   a micro theoretical perspective that focuses on how individuals make sense of their world, and how an individual's sense of self is produced by interacting with others and understanding how they are perceived by others

transgenderism   when an individual has a different gender identity than the sex they were assigned at birth

triple shift   the three different roles women play: mother, employee and carer; the triple shift suggests that a woman's work is never done: she is responsible for the domestic work, goes to work and comes home to caring responsibilities

validity   the extent to which research measures what it intends to measure

values   personal things – the standards or principles that we hold dear, what we deem as important, worthwhile or credible; sociologists argue that values are societally held but can also be specific to groups, so they are normative

variable   a factor that is measured in sociological research; variables can be dependent (i.e. they change) or independent (seen to have an impact/effect on other variables), for example, the social class (independent) has an impact on educational attainment (dependent)

verstehen   (Weber) an empathetic understanding; being able to put yourself in someone else's shoes while researching them

white-collar crime   non-violent crime, often financial, such as fraud or money laundering, which tends to be committed by members of the middle classes and elite

INDEX

Acknowledgements

We are grateful to the following for permission to reproduce copyright material:

Extracts on pp.7 and 147 from *Sociology: An Introductory Textbook and Reader* by Ken Plummer, ed Daniel Nehring, Routledge, copyright © 2013. Reproduced by arrangement with Taylor & Francis Group; A quote on p.56 from "My life is more valuable than this': Understanding Risk Among On-demand Food Couriers in Edinburgh' by Karen Gregory, 07/12/2020, SAGE, copyright © 2020. Reprinted by Permission of SAGE Publications, Ltd; An extract on p.78 from *State of the Nation 2018–19: Social Mobility in Great Britain, Social Mobility Commission*, April 2019, https://assets.publishing.service.gov.uk/government/uploads/system/uploads/attachment_data/file/798404/SMC_State_of_the_Nation_Report_2018–19.pdf, Open Government Licence v3.0, © Crown copyright 2019; Figure 4.1 on p.83 'Percentage of 16–64-year-olds who were employed, by ethnicity', *Employment*, Office for National Statistics, 29/01/2021, https://www.ethnicity-facts-figures.service.gov.uk/work-pay-and-benefits/employment/employment/latest#by-ethnicity, Open Government Licence v3.0, © Crown copyright 2021; Figure 4.2 on p.109 'Ethnicity proportions throughout the CJS, 2016', *Statistics on Race and the Criminal Justice System 2016*, Ministry of Justice, November 2017, https://assets.publishing.service.gov.uk/government/uploads/system/uploads/attachment_data/file/669094/statistics_on_race_and_the_criminal_justice_system_2016_v2.pdf, p.7, Figure 1.01, © Crown copyright; Figure 4.3 on p.109 'The proportion of adults throughout the criminal justice system in each ethnic group, 2018', *Statistics on Race and the Criminal Justice System 2018*, Ministry of Justice, November 2019, https://assets.publishing.service.gov.uk/government/uploads/system/uploads/attachment_data/file/849200/statistics-on-race-and-the-cjs-2018.pdf, p.2, Figure 1.01, © Crown copyright; Extracts on p.119 from 'First names and social distinction: Middle-class naming practices in Australia' by Jo Lindsay and Deborah Dempsey, *Journal of Sociology*, 53(3), 2017, p.577–591, SAGE; Extract on p.134 from 'The Dirty History of Feminism and Sociology: Or the War of Conceptual Attrition' by Beverley Skeggs, *The Sociological Review*, 56(4), 2008, pp.670–690, SAGE; Extract on p.140 from 'Animals just love you as you are: Experiencing kinship across the species barrier' by Nickie Charles, Sociology, 48(4), pp.715–730, 2014, pp.715–730, SAGE, copyright © 2014, 2017, 2018. Reprinted by Permission of SAGE Publications, Ltd; An extract on p.152 from Sociologist Careers, The British Sociological Association, https://www.britsoc.co.uk/what-is-sociology/sociologist-careers/. Reproduced with permission; An extract on p.152 from Careers in Sociology, American Sociological Association https://www.asanet.org/careers/careers-sociology. Reproduced with permission; and an extract on p.155 from 'Community participation is crucial in a pandemic' by Cicely Marston, Alicia Renedo and Sam Miles, *The Lancet*, 395(10238), 04/05/2020, Elsevier, copyright © 2020. Reproduced with permission from Elsevier.

The publishers would like to thank the following for permission to reproduce images on these pages: p.14 Alpha Historica/Alamy Stock Photo, p.14 FALKENSTEINFOTO/Alamy Stock Photo, p.14 Don Tonge/Alamy Stock Photo, p.15 Lynea/Shutterstock, p.15 B-D-S Piotr Marcinski/Shutterstock, p.16 Granger Historical Picture Archive/Alamy Stock Photo, p.17 Hulton Deutsch/Getty, p.18 Trinity Mirror/Mirrorpix/Alamy Stock Photo, p.18 Everett Collection Inc/Alamy Stock Photo, p.18 Dennis Diatel/Shutterstock, p.22 Leremy/Shutterstock, p.24 Granger Historical Picture Archive/Alamy Stock Photo, p.24 Everett Collection/Shutterstock, p.27 Everett Collection/Shutterstock, p.28 Archivio GBB/Alamy Stock Photo, p.29 Laurent MAOUS/Getty, p.29 Ulf Andersen/Getty, p.30 Pictorial Press Ltd/Alamy Stock Photo, p.32 Granger Historical Picture Archive/Alamy Stock Photo, p.34 Stokkete/Shutterstock, p.35 Kaleo/Shutterstock, p.37 Bettmann/Getty, p.38 Album/Alamy Stock Photo, p.40 WDC Photos/Alamy Stock Photo, p.40 IanDagnall Computing/Alamy Stock Photo, p.41 Everett Collection Historical/Alamy Stock Photo, p.42 CPA Media Pte Ltd/Alamy Stock Photo, p.43 Chronicle/Alamy Stock Photo, p.45 Everett Collection/Shutterstock, p.45 MediaPunch Inc/Alamy Stock Photo, p.46 WENN Rights Ltd/Alamy Stock Photo, p.49 katatonia82/Shutterstock, p.51 Jeff Morgan 12/Alamy Stock Photo, p.51 jackbolla/Shutterstock, p.52 PhotonCatcher/Shutterstock, p.53 GagliardiPhotography/Shutterstock, p.54 andersphoto/Shutterstock, p.56 Claudio Divizia/Shutterstock, p.59 jokter/Shutterstock, p.62 Lost_in_the_Midwest/Shutterstock, p.64 Phrompas/Shutterstock, p.65 Arthimedes/Shutterstock, p.66 Bakhtiar Zein/Shutterstock, p.66 Bakhtiar Zein/Shutterstock, p.66 Bakhtiar Zein/Shutterstock, p.74 Enrique Ramos/Shutterstock, p.75 Hyejin Kang/Shutterstock, p.76 © Andy Watt/The Independent, p.79 Ink Drop/Shutterstock, p.80 jesadaphorn/Shutterstock, p.85 © Hans Traxler, reproduced with permission., p.93 Tupungato/Shutterstock, p.94 Dino Fracchia/Alamy Stock Photo, p.114 len4foto/Shutterstock, p.114 Nestyda/Shutterstock, p.118 Chronicle/Alamy Stock Photo, p.118 Sean Locke Photography/Shutterstock, p.119 Monkey Business Images/Shutterstock, p.120 Rawpixel.com/Shutterstock, p.120 vectorfusionart/Shutterstock, p.122 Anna Kraynova/Shutterstock, p.125 fizkes/Shutterstock, p.128 Fox Photos/Getty, p.130 ZikG/Shutterstock, p.137 GoodIdeas/Shutterstock, p.138 Kolbakova Olga/Shutterstock, p.140 SakSa/Shutterstock, p.140 Mykola Komarovskyy/Shutterstock, p.150 Alexyz3d/Shutterstock,